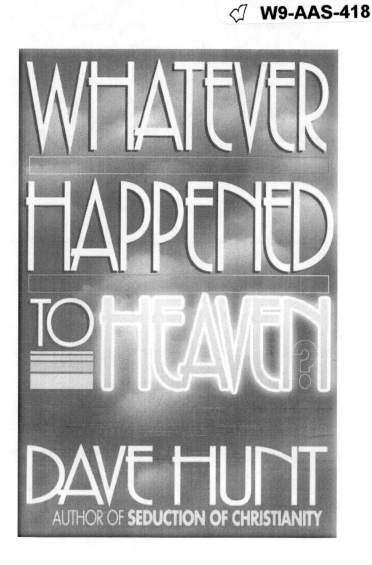

WHATEVER HAPPENED TO HEAVEN?

DAVE HUNT

AUTHOR OF SEDUCTION OF CHRISTIANITY

The Berean Call

BEND • OREGON

Except where otherwise indicated, all Scripture quotations in this book are taken from the King James Version of the Bible.

WHATEVER HAPPENED TO HEAVEN?

Copyright © 2011 by Dave Hunt
Published by The Berean Call
PO Box 7019, Bend, OR 97708

ISBN: 978-1-928660-70-5

Previously published © 1988 by Harvest House under ISBN: 0-89081-698-0

PRINTED IN THE UNITED STATES OF AMERICA

To the many, who must remain anonymous, who have so faithfully and selflessly provided me with valuable research and insights—and to all whose longing for Christ's return has become a passion.

Contents

A Growing Dilemma

As the title so obviously declares, this book is about heaven. Unfortunately, too many persons—even dedicated Christians—find such a topic of only minor interest because they consider it to be largely irrelevant to the challenges of this present life. In the following pages we will attempt to show, on the contrary, that nothing is more important in shaping how life on earth is lived and what is accomplished both for time and eternity than a person's attitude toward the life to come.

As the title also implies, something has happened to adversely affect the way heaven is viewed, with grave consequences for the church and the world. What has happened and why? And what is the growing dilemma that now confronts so many in the church?

In attempting to answer such questions, it will be necessary to begin with a serious consideration of death, a most important but uncomfortable subject. That leads, of course, to the unique claim of Christianity that Christ, through His death for our sins and resurrection, has conquered death and offers eternal life to all who come to Him in repentance and faith. What Jesus had to say about this present life and the life to come, and the peculiar promises He made concerning heaven, gave the early church a hope unknown to the followers of any other religion. That hope, while still retained in theological and theoretical form, is so unreal to the average Christian of today that it has lost its transforming power.

Much of the reason for the present state of affairs lies buried in history and can only be understood by taking a brief excursion into the past. This will include the bitter persecution of Christians under the Roman Empire, the sudden Christianization of the civilized world of the day under Constantine and his successors with the resulting destruction of the empire, along with the subsequent earthly mindedness and corruption of the church that led belatedly to the Reformation. An understanding of the successes and failures of the Reformation and the vital issues separating Protestantism and Catholicism that remain unchanged but largely misunderstood or forgotten today is essential in our pursuit of an answer to the question "Whatever happened to heaven?"

During the Reagan years evangelicals became more enthusiastic about periodic marches upon Washington and getting their candidates voted into key offices than they were about the possibility that Christ might at any moment take them home to heaven. The church succumbed once again to the unbiblical hope that, by exerting godly influence upon government, society could be transformed. It is anathema to suggest a flaw in this dream, even though it so manifestly failed in the post-Constantinian era and was a major impediment preventing the Reformation from accomplishing what the reformers originally intended. Nevertheless, sound doctrine, the voice of reason, and the facts of history—no matter how unpopular—must be faced. In this context we will consider the current perversion of the Great Commission which has resulted from the false dream of Christianizing secular culture—and where it seems to be taking the church.

While our remarks will by no means be limited to a response to their positions, the burgeoning (and, in at least some respects, deceptive and dangerous) influence upon the church by three groups of dedicated Christians will be addressed in the following pages. These relatively new groups whose beliefs and impact will be examined are: the Reconstructionists, Kingdom Now Dominionists, and the Coalition on Revival (COR). Although there are many differences among them, there are also important similarities; and all three groups are beginning to work together for the accomplishment of common goals, which will be thoroughly analyzed. COR is particularly important to understand because its membership includes many of the world's most respected Christian leaders, some of whom may not be fully aware of the true nature of the agenda which their names and reputations are being used to promote.

All three of these groups either reject the belief that Christ will one day take His church out of this world and home to heaven, or relegate it to a position of such minor importance that it has no practical role in today's Christianity. In fact, there is an increasing antagonism against eagerly watching and waiting for Christ's return, which surely was the attitude of the early church. After the overwhelming popularity of Hal Lindsey's *Late Great Planet Earth*, a backlash has developed against the rapture.

Within the evangelical church today the numbers are dwindling of those who retain in meaningful form the hope of the imminent return of Christ to take them to the mansions of His Father's house before the whole world explodes in the Great Tribulation judgment and Armageddon. In contrast, the numbers are growing rapidly of those who view such a hope as the negative product of a defeatist theology—a theology that undermines the "victory" they believe could be won by the church if Christians would only catch the vision of taking over the world for Christ and unite to fulfill it. The tension is building to a climax between those individuals who long to leave this earth for heaven in the rapture, and other equally sincere people who believe it is our duty to Christianize society, and that until this has been accomplished our Lord cannot return. For many others, perhaps the majority, the seeming contradictions present a confusing dilemma.

Heaven remains the place that everyone hopes to reach someday, but which almost no one wants to be taken to right now. What is wrong, if anything, with such an attitude, and what are its consequences? Here we have the crux of an issue that many people are not yet aware has even been raised, but which will be the most important concern confronting the church in the immediate future.

We are now in the beginning stages of a growing controversy. It could ultimately prove to be as divisive and as important as the Reformation itself. Indeed, some of the same issues will have to be faced again. It is within this context that we propose to consider what surely should be to everyone a significant and vital question: "Whatever happened to heaven?"

In the process of answering that question, we may well arrive at a deeper understanding of Christ's love than we thought was possible, and find awakening within us a renewed and richer love for Him. We may even thrill to the discovery that there is a romance between Christ and His bride—and find ourselves caught up in its wonder and joy. To encourage such love is the real purpose of the following pages.

1

Life, Death, and Immortality

The subject of heaven, at least for the vast majority of mankind, is invariably associated with death. After all, how else does one get there? Consequently, few people (including many Christians) think any more fondly of going to heaven than they do of dying. No matter how beautiful, peaceful, and joyful someone believes heaven may be, rare is the person for whom it is *desirable*, until death can no longer be postponed. And of course the unhappy thought of one's own demise is generally avoided as long as possible. Unpleasant though the subject may be, however, we dare not neglect or postpone the sober consideration of death and what it may bring.

It is an inescapable fact that the uncertainty of life and the inevitability of death are two of the most basic elements of human existence. Heaven, therefore, ought to be of far greater importance than any future plans for this world. After all, those who take the subject seriously hope to spend eternity there, while life here is like a vapor in comparison. We dare not forget that for each of us heaven (or hell) is just a breath away.

Yet mankind persists in deluding itself by suppressing, rather than openly facing, the nearness and reality of death. Even most funerals, with their beautiful flowers and flowery sermons, are an attempt to deny the truth of that unspeakable event which has drawn the mourners together. We find it extremely difficult to face the inexorable fact that death will one day put its terminating stamp upon every earthly passion, position, possession, and ambition. Yet he lives as a fool who forgets the solemn reminder of Homer's eighth century B.C. *Iliad* that "Death in ten thousand shapes hangs ever over our heads, and no man can elude him."

Even though death is as much a part of life as life itself (Freud went so far as to foolishly claim that "The *goal* of all life is death"), mankind has never been able to accept it. The universal feeling persists that death, though it comes as regularly as birth, is an alien intruder that ought not to be and which robs us of that to which it has no right. Although we know it is inescapable, nevertheless it seems an unbearable injustice that death should have the last word to say about life.

Something within us rises up in anger and cries out in helpless protest whenever death snatches away what no one can deny it, but which all struggle to retain. Though death has been taking its toll regularly since the beginning of time, something still seems horribly *wrong*—not only that a baby or child, but that the elderly as well, should become, as Milton in *Paradise Lost* expressed it, "Food for so foule a Monster."

Struggling for words to express our grief, we find it inexpressible. Of Juliet, Lady Capulet lamented: "Death lies on her like an untimely frost upon the sweetest flower of the field." Untimely or not, however, the solemn fact remains that our time on this earth, no matter how prolonged, is at most very brief—which is reason enough to give serious thought and careful preparation to that which lies beyond death's door. What then?

The Hope of Immortality

At the same time that death is acknowledged to be inescapable, there is an equally universal and overpowering conviction that death does not end human existence. That man is a *spiritual* being, who survives the death of his physical body, is a basic human instinct which is denied only with the greatest effort. The attempt by skeptics to portray life after death as a nightmare that haunts man with needless fears is betrayed as wishful thinking by ordinary human experience and logic. Since the mind can think of intangibles such as truth or justice or grace, nothing physical, including the

brain, could be responsible for originating such thoughts. Thus there must be a nonphysical component of man, which the Bible calls the soul and spirit, and which uses the body to interface with the world of matter and sensibility.

It makes no more sense to credit the physical matter in man's brain with morals and ethics than it would to speak of an honest liver or an immoral kidney. We all know that references to an "evil eye" or a "wicked heart" have nothing to do with physical organs, but with the spirit within. Clearly the selfless commitment of love, the appreciation of truth and beauty, the loathing of evil, and the longing for ultimate fulfillment do not arise from any quality of the atoms, molecules, or cells that comprise the body. There is therefore good reason to believe, as the Bible so clearly declares, that the spirit to which these undeniably *spiritual* capacities belong will continue to exist even when the body it has inhabited dies.

While the death of the body prevents the spirit which indwelt it from any longer expressing itself in the physical universe of space, matter, and time, there is no reason to believe that the spirit would thereby lose its capacity to function in a nonphysical dimension of existence. That there is a spirit world—which includes both heaven and hell—has always been the conviction of all mankind. The evidence of this belief can be found in abundance in every culture as far back as archaeologists have been able to uncover traces of human life.

Of course, the fact that a belief is universally held by mankind does not mean it is true, nor is the above reasoning offered as *proof* of life after death. Even the Bible does not attempt to prove the existence of God or of the human spirit or immortality. No doubt the reason is because mankind is incapable through either its philosophy or its science to deal with evidential proof in the realm of spirit. For the Christian, however, enough evidence for what he can understand has been given to justify faith in God and His Word for what it declares that he cannot rationally comprehend. How we personally know God, and how faith derives from reason and evidence has been dealt with in other books and is outside the scope of this one.

While there is general agreement that the spirit and soul survive the death of the body, what that continuing existence on the other

side of death may be like remains shrouded in mystery for the non-Christian, in spite of the great advances in knowledge mankind has made in other areas. As Thomas Hobbes declared: "Now I am about to take my last voyage, a great leap in the dark." To Omar Khayyam, death led through "the door of Darkness [to] the road which to discover we must travel too." Had he accepted the testimony of the Bible and of Christ, who resurrected from the dead, he would not have remained in such ignorance.

Not only the world's religions and occultism, but its philosophy, literature, poetry, art, music, and drama throughout human history have given considerable speculative attention to the theme of life after death. In spite of a materialistic binge over the past 200 years, modern thought is returning to a recognition of the importance of this great issue. Addressing a November 1987 conference of scientists in Washington, D.C., Senator Claiborne Pell declared:

> Certainly we need qualified scientists [researching] . . . the full experience of humankind—body, mind, and soul. Any lesser vision of science would be incomplete because it would not open to discovery the full range of humanity's . . . spiritual capacity. . . .
>
> This study may also help us face the greatest question and the greatest adventure of all: What actually happens when physical death occurs?[1]

Surely if nothing occurs, if "death ends it all," as many people want desperately to believe, then Senator Pell's reference to "the greatest question and the greatest adventure of all" should not have been taken seriously by a conference of top scientists. Yet it was. His high evaluation of the question of life after death echoes the universal conviction of mankind to which we have already referred—a conviction that has persisted in spite of public education's attempt (beginning with John Dewey and continuing through his humanist successors) to eliminate this ancient belief as mere superstition unworthy of today's sophistication. Even in the space age, Plato's

Gorgias speaks with compelling power: The soul exposed naked before the divine judge bears no mark from the evil it has suffered in life, but only from the evil it has done—and who is not convicted by his own conscience of wrongdoing?

The Fear of Life After Death

That state to which death escorts us has almost universally been understood to involve either torment or bliss. Man's obsession with avoiding the former and being assured of passage to the latter has provided the major motivation for most involvement in religion. Thus it is death, more than life, which has kept the world's religions in business. Promises of healing to delay one's demise and guarantees of an escape from punishment and a privileged status in the next world are the stock-in-trade of all manner of religious hucksters, providing them not only a steady income but power over the lives of those who believe their promises and subscribe to their rituals.

In spite of religious convictions and priestly promises, however, the predominant attitude toward death and what it may lead to remains what it has always been: *fear*. Belief in life after death seems to be less a comfort than a terror. This is evidenced by the rarity of suicide and the desperate effort to cling to life even by those living in the most pitiable conditions. Most individuals seem very reluctant to exchange this world for whatever heaven they imagine death might bring.

The universal fear of death is evidenced, for example, in the widowed survivor of an enemy raid, who, having lost husband and children to the ravages of war, continues to scrape out a tortured existence in the ruins of her bombed-out village. Clearly she does so more out of fear of what may await her in death than out of hope for what may be offered to her by life. Many a person tempted to commit suicide in order to escape the misfortunes of this present existence has been restrained by the realization that death, rather than being the end, could be the doorway into something far worse. That possibility and the fear it arouses were expressed eloquently by Shakespeare's Hamlet, who at the same time exposes as folly the

apparent bravery of those who attempt to face death calmly while confessing that they know not what it holds:

> To die; to sleep;
> No more; and by a sleep to say we end
> The heart-ache and the thousand natural shocks
> That flesh is heir to, 'tis a consummation
> Devoutly to be wish'd. To die; to sleep;
> To sleep? perchance to dream. Ay, there's the rub;
> For in that sleep of death what dreams may come
> When we have shuffled off this mortal coil,
> Must give us pause. . . .
> For who would bear the whips and scorns of time,
> . . . To grunt and sweat under a weary life,
> But that the dread of something after death,
> The undiscover'd country from whose bourn
> No traveller returns, puzzles the will
> And makes us rather bear those ills we have
> Than fly to others that we know not of?
> Thus conscience does make cowards of us all. . . .

Without that restraint of conscience, however, evil would be even more rampant on this earth. Solomon presented death as a wise tutor: "It is better to go to the house of mourning [i.e. a funeral] than to the house of feasting: for that is the end of all men; and the living will lay it to his heart" (Ecclesiastes 7:2). A confrontation with death has a sobering effect upon attitudes and a way of changing our thinking. We do well, said Solomon, instead of pushing such thoughts away, to take hold of this wisdom while there is still time to change our lives and thus affect for the better what will happen to us when we take leave of this earthly existence.

"On death and judgment, heaven and hell," said Sir Walter Raleigh, "who oft doth think must needs die well." Raleigh's maxim, however, is not necessarily true. To think of heaven and hell will not in itself break man's stubborn will. Such an exercise is of little value unless it brings us to Christ and thereafter causes us to live in willing and holy obedience to the God who made us.

Death, Wisdom, and Ultimate Purpose

If there is no God who created us for His eternal purposes, then human life is not only a meaningless accident but a cruel practical joke perpetrated by an impersonal cosmos that has somehow spawned beings who inexplicably long for meaning and purpose when there can be none. Life has no ultimate meaning unless it continues, not temporarily, but eternally, beyond both the grave and the passing existence of this physical universe. Consequently, life is only lived wisely to the extent that it is spent in preparation for the eternity which follows. Though he did not write from a Christian standpoint by any means, yet life as a preparation for death is the theme of Plato's *Phaedo*, which records Socrates' thoughts on the day he drank the hemlock potion. To barter away eternal happiness for any temporary pleasure or success offered by this fleeting life upon earth is to make a bad bargain indeed.

Both Blaise Pascal and John Locke argued that the man who misses out on what this life offers in order to prepare for the next loses nothing if death ends it all. However, the man who, in living wholly for this brief world's rewards, brings torment upon himself for eternity has gambled against impossible odds and has only himself to blame for the consequences of such stubborn folly. In his unique way, William Law presented 250 years ago some of the biblical wisdom on this subject through a fictitious character called Penitens. This "very prosperous and busy young tradesman," who was "about to die in his thirty-fifth year," had these comments for friends who came to express their sympathy at his fate:

> You look upon me with pity, not that I am going unprepared to meet the Judge of quick and dead, but that I am to leave a prosperous trade in the flower of my life. . . . And yet what folly of the silliest children is so great as this?
>
> Our poor friend Lepidus died, you know, as he was dressing himself for a feast. Do you think it is now part of his trouble that he did not live till that entertainment was over? Feast and business and pleasures and enjoyments

seem great things to us whilst we think of nothing else; but as soon as we add death to them they all sink into an equal littleness. . . .

If I am now going into the joys of God, could there be any reason to grieve that this happened to me before I was forty years of age? Could it be a sad thing to go to heaven before I had made a few more bargains or stood a little longer behind a counter? And if I am to go amongst lost spirits, could there be any reason to be content that this did not happen to me till I was old, and full of riches? . . .

Now that judgment is the next thing that I look for, and everlasting happiness or misery is come so near me, all the enjoyments and prosperities of life seem vain and insignificant. . . . But, my friends, how I am surprised that I have not always had these thoughts. . . .

What a strange thing is it that a little health or the poor business of a shop should keep us so senseless of these great things that are coming so fast upon us![2]

Like Penitens, many discover too late that the only values by which to live are those that retain their appeal in the face of death. Today's sensuously enticing television commercials featuring the "good life" of materialistic success, exotic perfumes, and the latest fashions in clothes modeled by macho men and seductive women present a set of false values—values that become embarrassingly empty when someone lies dying in the wreckage of a flashy sports car or stands in front of a coffin to pay last respects to the remains of a beloved family member or friend.

On the other hand, that which is generally disdained by today's get-all-the-gusto-you-can, high-tech me-generation shines all the brighter in the presence of death: love devoid of lust, fidelity, patience, kindness, meekness, humility, commitment to truth, and selfless service to God and neighbor. Such are the only values we can carry with us into heaven.

The story is told of two men walking through a cemetery who come upon an unusual funeral: a gold-plated Rolls Royce with stereo, television, and built-in bar is being lowered into a grave. "What is happening?" one man asks in astonishment.

"Why, they're burying J.B., the multibillionaire," replies the other.

Stopping to watch this amazing scene, the first man exclaims in reverent wonder as the Rolls Royce disappears into the ground, "Man, that's what I call really livin'!"

Even the transformation of society which Christian political and social activists hope to effect will ultimately be no more "really livin' " than J.B.'s funeral. Moreover, in placing a wrong emphasis upon this world we may rob those whom we hope to help of really living in the world to come.

There's a Whole New Universe Coming!

The best an atheist can hope for is that death ends it all—a hope, which Shakespeare reminds us, flies in the face of conscience and is denied by the universal instinct of mankind. Nor can the man who refuses to believe in God find any purpose or meaning to his own life except in the attempt to make life better for future generations; and their only purpose, in turn, can be to contribute to the happiness of generations yet further in the future, all of whom are heading for atheism's oblivion. Nor does reincarnation offer a better hope: It merely represents a recycling of that which is ultimately doomed. For one day, according to the Second Law of Thermodynamics, the universe will have run down like a clock. Suns and stars will all have been extinguished and the schemes, dreams, and accomplishments of mankind will be like sand castles washed out into a cosmic ocean of nothingness. All existence will be as though it had never been and will thus bear the final stamp of meaninglessness written across the universe itself. This is not the way it will end, however, because God has other plans.

The Bible claims (and there is more than sufficient evidence to support that claim) to have been inspired by the God who created the universe and all in it, including mankind. It tells us that death is indeed, as we all instinctively feel, not a normal part of what life was originally intended to be, but an enemy that gained entrance through the disobedience of Adam and Eve, who joined Satan in his rebellion against God. Thus the universe is subject to disease, decay, and death as a just consequence of the sin which has cut it off from its Creator and source of life. However, because the God of the Bible (in contrast to the inadequate gods of pantheism/polytheism or the Universal Mind of Religious Science) is not part of the universe, He can reach in from outside to bring forgiveness, genuine healing, and new life in place of death.

It is easy enough to believe that the God who created the present universe (it obviously didn't just happen by chance) is able to create a new one to take its place, from which sin, suffering, disease, and death will be excluded forever. Likewise, it would be a small thing for the God who created us in the first place to recreate our bodies, not merely as they once were in our prime, but in a new form immune to fatigue, disease, or death—bodies suited to His new creation. Since by His own immutable law, however, the "wages of sin is death" (Romans 6:23), God could not allow our bodies to be returned from the grave unless that penalty of eternal death required for our sins had been fully paid. Yet there was no way that we, as finite beings, could pay the eternal penalty demanded by our violation of infinite justice. It would require our separation from God forever.

God, being infinite, could have paid that penalty, but that would not have been just because He is not a member of our race. He therefore became a man through the virgin birth in the person of Jesus Christ. Being uniquely both God and man in one person, and thus infinite, Christ was able to accept in our place upon the cross the judgment for our sins and to endure the death that would have separated us from God forever. Therefore, the resurrection of Christ—because He had died *in our place for our sins*—proved that the penalty demanded by God's justice had been paid in full.

The very same dead body that went into the grave came out alive, still bearing the identifying marks of crucifixion, but now completely victorious over death. That unique event—the death, burial, and resurrection of Christ for our sins—in which death was forever conquered, sets Christianity apart from every religion the world has ever known. It is thus the Christian—and only the Christian—who can look forward with confidence to the resurrection and transformation of his body, making it suitable for the universe to come.

God's promise that He will create a new eternal universe for His children to inhabit, into which sin, sickness, and death can never enter,[3] places the fulfillment of life's purpose beyond both our wildest imagination to conceive and our most heroic efforts to achieve. With that understanding, life ceases to be a struggle and becomes a privilege and joy to receive daily in simple faith from the hand of God, our Creator and Redeemer. For those who attempt to carry it themselves, however, life eventually proves to be a burden too great to bear. Nor can there be any real peace in this life for those who are fearful of what death may bring. One must, moreover, question the sincerity of those who claim to trust God for eternity but who betray by their worry and fear that they do not trust Him to care for their needs in this present life.

The Resurrection—Christianity's Distinctive Essential

In contrast to Mohammed or Buddha or the founders of other world religions, whose "final resting places" are holy shrines visited by their followers, there are no decayed remains in the grave of Jesus Christ. His uniqueness is not only in the claim that He died in payment of the penalty God's justice demanded for our sins, but that as death's conqueror He returned victorious from the tomb. Christ is the great exception and the only answer to Omar Khayyam's lament that "of the myriads who before us passed the door of Darkness through, not one returns to tell us" what we all must face. Furthermore, Christ has done more than that. He has not only returned from the grave, but He has delivered His followers from death's power. The eyewitness accounts of those who saw Him after His resurrection are supported by the fact that His tomb, though closely guarded by Roman soldiers to prevent His disciples from stealing His body and falsely claiming a resurrection, was found to be empty (to the consternation of the Roman guard) three days after He was placed there—just as He had promised.

It is of great significance that the resurrection of Buddha or Mohammed or Confucius is not even imagined, for such an event would be irrelevant to the religions such persons have founded. In complete contrast, the resurrection of Jesus Christ is declared to be absolutely essential to Christianity. "If Christ be not risen," wrote Paul, "then is our preaching vain, and your faith is also vain" (1 Corinthians 15:14). Consequently, a person must believe in the resurrection of Jesus Christ in order to be a Christian. And by resurrection the Bible refers not merely to some "spiritual survival" beyond death, but to Christ's literal *bodily* resurrection.

There are a number of reasons for this necessity. First of all, as Thomas Aquinas argued, unless man is erroneously treated as a purely spiritual being such as an angel, the joining of soul and spirit with the body is the necessary condition of man's intended existence. Therefore, there can be no resurrection that leaves the body in the state of separation from soul and spirit that characterizes death. If the body, which has succumbed to death, is not raised to life again, then death has not been conquered and Christ's promise to do so is proven to be false.

Moreover, if the disciples lied in claiming that Christ had risen bodily from the dead, then Christianity is based upon an outright fraud. The disciples did not run off to Siberia or South America to testify of the resurrection, where no one could have disputed their word. No, as Christ had commanded, they immediately and boldly began to proclaim the resurrection right in Jerusalem where, if Christ had still been dead, it would have been a simple matter for the Romans or rabbis to produce His lifeless body and stop this troublesome "new religion" in its tracks. And nothing less than proving Christ was still dead could have refuted Christianity, for the heart of the disciples' message was not some new theology to be argued but the claim of eyewitnesses that Christ had resurrected.

Liberal theologians speak in glowing terms of the marvelous "myth" of the resurrection and the "transcendental truths" which "live on" through such an idealistic concept. Paul bluntly called such sophistry a lie, pointing out that if Christ had not in fact resurrected, then "we are found false witnesses of God; because we have testified of God that he raised up Christ..." (1 Corinthians 15:15). Even such celebrated "Christians" as Malcolm Muggeridge, one of the featured speakers at the 1974 Congress on

World Evangelization in Lausanne, Switzerland, promotes the folly that historical fact is of no consequence; what is important is the enduring spiritual meaning of the "legend."

In a shocking book whose most disturbing feature was the glowing recommendations given to it by leading evangelicals, Muggeridge had made his position clear five years before Lausanne:

> Whether it [the resurrection] happened as described in the Gospel narrative, and endlessly repeated by Christian apologists, is another question. In any case, what does it matter?
>
> I even prefer to suppose that some body snatcher, accustomed to hanging about Golgotha... finds out where the corpse [of Jesus] has been laid, drags the stone away, and then, making sure no one [including the guarding Roman soldiers!] is watching, decamps with the body. . . .
>
> The man [having found nothing of value on the "King of the Jews"] contemptuously abandons the body to the vultures, who in their turn leave the bones to whiten in the sun—those precious, precious bones![4]

Such blasphemy represents not only a cynical disregard of the clear testimony of Scripture but a blatant denial by a professed Christian of the very *sine qua non* of Christianity. It defies logic as well. As we have already noted, death brings about the separation of soul and spirit from the body. Thus to suggest a "spiritual resurrection" which leaves the soul and spirit in disembodied form is to offer meaningless platitudes where substantive hope alone will suffice. Jesus specifically refuted such a belief when He said to His disciples: "Handle me, and see; for a spirit hath not flesh and bones, as ye see me have" (Luke 24:39). Yet Muggeridge writes that it was merely the *spirit* of Jesus that "manifested itself to his disciples" after the crucifixion.[5] This is the unbiblical teaching of numerous cults.

Nor will reincarnation into a new body qualify, for the previous body (or bodies) remains the victim of death. Rather than conquering it as an enemy, reincarnation accepts and perpetuates death as a normal part of an ongoing life cycle. Resurrection and reincarnation are not only incompatible but contradictory. Both cannot be true. Therefore someone cannot be a Christian and at the same time believe in reincarnation. To do so is a denial of the essential and historical once-for-all-time bodily resurrection of Jesus Christ, which is the very heart of Christianity.

Resurrection and the Christian Faith

A person becomes a Christian through believing the gospel: "How that Christ died for our sins according to the scriptures; and that he was buried, and that he rose again the third day according to the scriptures. . . ." The resurrection of Christ is repeatedly presented in the New Testament as an essential part of the "gospel . . . by which . . . ye are saved" (1 Corinthians 15:1-4), the gospel which alone is declared to be "the power of God unto salvation to everyone that believeth" (Romans 1:16). Other Scriptures, such as Romans 10:9 ("That if thou shalt confess with thy mouth the Lord Jesus, and shalt believe in thine heart that God hath raised him from the dead, thou shalt be saved") make it clear that belief not only in Christ's death for our sins but in His bodily resurrection also is essential for salvation. People are free to reject the resurrection, but those who do so have no legitimate basis for calling themselves Christians and certainly have no hope that their sins are forgiven.

Being a Christian does not consist in following a set of rules or principles, or embracing a religious philosophy that "lives on" after the death of its founder. Nor is it appeasing a deity through ritual or tuning into some cosmic power through a patented meditation process. True Christianity is based upon faith in Jesus Christ and in His death, burial, and resurrection as historic events that actually took place upon this planet and were essential for our salvation in satisfying the claims of divine justice on account of our sin. It is Christ's victory over death that alone gives the assurance of eternal life to those who believe in Him. Moreover, the resurrection of Christ is the pledge that those who have received Him as Savior and Lord will have their bodies raised from the dead also.

Herein lies another unique element of Christianity. Its heaven is not a disembodied spiritual existence beyond the grave, but the eternal abode of resurrected, immortal, glorified beings whose bodies have been reunited with soul and spirit to live eternally with God. The bodies of millions upon millions of Christians have been laid in graves all over the world to decay and disintegrate. The very atoms which once made up those bodies have been absorbed into the soil or have become part of earth's flora and fauna in the endless cycle of nature. How could such bodies be resurrected?

Of course, all through life the atoms in a person's body are constantly being replaced through the intake of food and the elimination of waste. There are no oxygen, hydrogen, or carbon atoms with individual names engraved upon them. Nevertheless, God will gather together the elements of each Christian's body as it was at death and bring it back to life. But that is not all. In the process of resurrection there will be a complete transformation to what the Bible calls a "spiritual body" (1 Corinthians 15:44). We will be recognizable for who we are, yet we will be new and glorious creations with bodies like our Lord's.

Heaven is thus not only a *place* but a *state of being* beyond anything earthlings can presently imagine (1 Corinthians 2:9). The resurrected body undoubtedly has a completely different composition of elements and capabilities unknown to modern science, which fit it for the new universe to come. There was, as a Scripture previously quoted tells us ("a spirit hath not flesh and bones [not blood], as ye see me have"), no blood in Christ's resurrected body, for that "life of the flesh" (Leviticus 17:11) had been poured out in death for our sins. No longer the blood flowing through veins and bringing nourishment to cells, but the indwelling Spirit of God will provide the eternal source of life to those who, because of their faith in Christ as Savior and Lord, are resurrected with bodies like His. He promised: "Because I live, ye shall live also" (John 14:19).

Such was the faith of the early Christians. The ancient "Apostles' Creed," which predated the Nicene Creed of A.D. 325, included, "I believe in the resurrection *of the body* and life everlasting."

Absent from the Body, Present with the Lord

Firm in that faith and refusing to deny their testimony of Christ's resurrection, all of the apostles except John were martyred. This is the strongest possible evidence that they were not lying, for who would be willing to die for a lie that gained nothing for its perpetrators except persecution and martyrdom? One source of their courage was the confidence that their souls and spirits, released from their bodies by death, would be instantly with Christ in His Father's house of many mansions.

Here is another distinctive of Christianity—the assurance that though death may claim the body, the souls and spirits of those who belong to Christ escape death's clutches and are immediately transported into the presence of God. Of course, the Moslem who dies in *jihad* (holy war) is promised immediate entrance into the "seventh heaven." For the Christian, however, no matter how he dies, it is to be "absent from the body, and to be present with the Lord" (2 Corinthians 5:8), which Paul assures us is "far better" than to remain here upon earth (Philippians 1:23).

Millions of Christians have been taken to heaven by death, many of them, like the apostles, cruelly killed for believing in their resurrected Savior. And that same faith—that to die is to be instantly with Christ in heaven—has sustained them whether facing lions in Roman arenas, the flames of the Inquisition, torture and starvation in Communist prisons, or the many other ingenious ways the physical lives of the martyrs have been wrenched from them. John Bunyan, who spent years in prison for his faith, wrote:

> Let dissolution come when it will, it can do the Christian no harm, for it will be but a passage out of a prison into a palace; out of a sea of troubles into a haven of rest; out of a crowd of enemies, to an innumerable company of true, loving, and faithful friends; out of shame, reproach, and contempt, into exceeding great and eternal glory.

Only a true Christian has the confidence Bunyan expressed. What of those people who do not know Christ? If the soul and spirit do indeed survive the death of the body and continue to exist eternally, and if all do not go to heaven, where does the rest of mankind spend eternity? The Bible is very clear about this. All who refuse to admit their sin, who are not willing to repent of their rebellion against God and to accept the death of Christ in their place, must endure the penalty they deserve. Having forfeited the right to live in God's presence, they must be separated from Him forever if they refuse the pardon He offers.

What About Hell?

Rare is the criminal who admits the justice of the sentence imposed upon him by an earthly court. It is not surprising, then, that those who reject God's gracious and merciful offer of forgiveness complain against the consequences which they bring upon themselves. Always the complaint puts God on trial, calls into question His character, and blames Him for what is obviously man's guilty doing. Typical is the indignant and self-righteous demand: "How could a loving God sentence someone to eternal torment!"

It may be helpful to consider a simple illustration. Imagine a colorful fish, full of life and a beauty to behold, swimming vigorously in the ocean. On the shore the fish sees a man smoking a cigar, holding a fishing pole, and leaning back comfortably in a lounge chair. Convinced that this would be the "good life," the fish leaps out of the water and manages to wriggle its way onto an empty chair. Instead of the comfort and enjoyment it expected, however, the fish finds itself gasping for oxygen. Falling from the chair, it flops around in the dirt and gravel, gills opening and closing desperately as it slowly and painfully dies.

Pausing to observe the scene, a passerby exclaims angrily, "What kind of a God would create a fish to suffer like that!"

Of course, God did not intend for the fish to suffer in this manner at all. Nor did He ever intend that any man would suffer in hell, which Jesus Himself described as "everlasting fire, prepared for the devil and his angels" (Matthew 25:41). Created to swim in the ocean of God's love, man has been given the power of choice, without which he could neither love nor respond to the love of God or of other people. Those who reject the life and love for which God has created them bring their unhappy fate upon their own heads, as did the fish.

Hell is not a metaphor or a state of mind. It is a real place. But more than that, hell—like heaven—is also a *state of being*. Not only is it punishment meted out by a God who is justly angry with the wicked, but hell is a real, objective fate which sinners bring upon themselves through willful abuse of their spiritual lives. It would be as impossible a contradiction for a Christ-rejecter to dwell in heaven as it would be for a worm to teach calculus or a lion to appreciate great works of art.

God will not force anyone to go to heaven, for that would not be an act of love. Moreover, it would turn heaven into hell, filling it with rebellious monsters for whom not only God but the angels and the redeemed could only feel intense loathing. Christ says that believers will be "as the angels of God in heaven" (Matthew 22:30). One shudders, then, to consider what the lost will be.

If heaven and hell are the only two alternatives, why would anyone choose eternal torment instead of eternal bliss? Of course, no one would be such a fool. The problem is not a choice between heaven and hell. In fact, most of those people who are on their way to hell try to convince themselves that such a place does not even exist. It is too late when they find out otherwise. The choice they have made is not deliberately to go to hell, but to disobey God deliberately, refusing to allow Him to forgive them and to make of them the sanctified and happy persons that He desires. Hell is not God's will for any man. He has provided, through Jesus Christ, a way of escape that is freely available to everyone.

One day every complaint will be silenced as every tongue confesses that Jesus Christ is Lord; but for many people, that confession will be forced from their lips by the awesome sight of Christ as their Judge on the Great White Throne (Revelation 20:11-15). That cry, however, will have come too late. Nor should we assume that the lake of fire to which they will be confined forever will bring a change of heart, for its tortured inhabitants have spurned the grace which alone makes repentance possible. Those who end up in that horrifying place are beyond recovery: "And he which is filthy, let him be filthy still" (Revelation 22:11). As Master's College professor John Pilkey says:

> The list of Revelation 21:8 ["the fearful, and unbeliev-
> ing, and the abominable, and murderers, and whore-
> mongers, and sorcerers, and idolaters, and all liars . . ."]
> should be read as a description of *eternal character*, not
> as a roll of "former sins" which incurred the wrath of
> God for abstract reasons known only to Him.[6]

Hell, and the lake of fire into which its inhabitants are cast after the Judgment, is no doubt even more terrifying and horrible than Dante depicts it in *The Divine Comedy*—but not because it involves "material fire [that] will torment the bodies of the damned," as Augustine imagined. "Everlasting fire" that was specifically de-signed for Satan and his minions, who are spirit beings without bodies, could hardly be physical. The eternal fire which torments the damned will be much worse and far more painful and *real* than physical flames.

The excruciating torment of people in the lake of fire will surely involve remorse ("Son, *remember . . .*" said Abraham to the rich man in hell—Luke 16:25), but it will be painfully unrepentant remorse as they live over and over in vivid memory the sins they have committed and in whose web they are inextricably caught for eternity. That anguish will be all the more unbearable under the horrifying realization that willful folly and stubborn selfishness has sent them there—a place to which they need not have come and from which fate God Himself did all He could to rescue them.

Burning Thirst—or Bliss Indescribable

The rich man's cry of anguish included these words: "I am tormented in this flame!" Inasmuch as his body was not in hell, but only his soul and spirit, we know that the "flame" he spoke of was not physically tormenting his body, which in fact was decaying in its grave. Moreover, Jesus, who said, "If any man thirst, let him come unto me, and drink" (John 7:37), likened the rich man's torment not to that of perpetually burning flesh but to unquenchable thirst. Surely the thirst he felt in hell was the full force of that which he had tried to slake in illegitimate ways while upon earth—a thirst for God which can only ultimately be satisfied in Christ Himself, from whom he was now hopelessly cut off forever.

Thirst for water begins rather mildly but eventually it burns like a flame. So the thirst for God may seem to be filled for a time by drinking at the ultimately disappointing wells of this world. The day comes, however, when death at last puts an end to all of those games—and the real thirst begins to burn like an eternal conflagration out of control. It ever consumes its victims, yet they are never consumed.

Thirst is such torture for the same reason that a drink of water is so satisfying: Water is essential to life. In the same way that our bodies must have water, so our spirits and souls thirst for God's love, which is essential to spiritual life. Hell, then, is an inexpressible torment for the same reason that heaven is bliss beyond description. The flaming thirst that tortures those in the lake of fire is caused by the lack of the very love that fills heaven and makes it a state of bliss.

While heaven and hell are presented at times as reward or punishment, the crux of the matter is really *relationship*. Heaven is the enjoyment of God's presence forever, while hell is eternal separation from Him. Neither Buddha, Mohammed, Confucius, nor any other religious leader even pretended to bridge the chasm between God and man. Christ alone made such a claim, and He fully accomplished it. In their rejection of Jesus Christ, the world's religions offer conflicting diagnoses of mankind's basic problem, and ultimately inadequate solutions. One thing is certain: No one ever regretted being a Christian on his deathbed.

Death, however, is not the only way to heaven. Christ made the astonishing and wonderful promise that He would come back again to take His followers to their eternal home without their dying. This unique hope of Christianity, which powerfully inspired and motivated the early church, is being increasingly minimized or rejected by a growing number of today's Christian leaders who represent what has become known as the Kingdom Now movement.

Promoted in varying forms by both charismatic and noncharismatic groups, pastors and popular teachers (some of whom we will name later), this new kingdom/dominion teaching is literally exploding in the church today. In the following pages we want to examine this dynamic movement and learn why it is so appealing. We also want to discover when and why the hope of being taken to heaven at any moment was lost to the church and how it can be recovered, if indeed it should be.

2

The Hope of the Early Church

Those who complain about the injustice of hell and the incompatibility of such punishment with God's love must face the fact that nowhere in the Bible do we find so many solemn warnings to avoid the flames of hell as we do from the lips of Christ Himself. What He had to say on this important subject is not at all in agreement with the theory that death is just an illusion and that "the only hell is the one we create for ourselves here upon earth." Such a philosophy, offered as positive religion, represents in fact a cynical contempt for the solemn warnings of Jesus.

In attempting to deny the reality of death, the Religious Science cults teach that "God is good and God is All." That sounds so appealing, as does the corollary that logically follows: Therefore "all is good, and thus there can be no evil." Such was the message of the cover story featured in the Summer 1986 issue of Robert Schuller's *Possibilities* magazine: ". . . nothing exists except God. There is no other reality. . . . The Christ spirit dwells in every human being whether the person knows it or not."[1]

If God is indeed the only reality, then sin, sickness, and death must not be real but merely illusions of faulty perception created by a person's negative thinking. The proposed solution to every problem, therefore, is to change an individual's perception by adopting a positive mental attitude. Reporting on three California court cases involving parents who, because they held to this appealing but impractical Christian Science philosophy, allowed their infant children to die, *Newsweek* explained:

> Ill much of her life, church founder Mary Baker Eddy
> concluded that Jesus came not to die for man's sins but to
> demonstrate that disease and even death are errors of the
> "materialistic" human mind.[2]

"She Is Not Dead, but Sleepeth"

A favorite Scripture which is used to support the metaphysical
theory that death is not real is the statement of Christ concerning
Jairus' daughter: "She is not dead but sleepeth" (Luke 8:52). This
expression is used in Scripture, however, not because death is
merely a dream, but because death for the Christian is only temporary due to the promise of the resurrection.

It would be no miracle for Jesus merely to awaken a sleeping girl.
That Jesus was not denying that Jairus' daughter was dead when He
said she was "asleep" is quite clear from numerous Scriptures.
Take, for example, the following exchange between Christ and His
disciples before He went to raise Lazarus from the dead:

> He saith unto them, "Our friend Lazarus sleepeth, but
> I go, that I may awake him out of sleep."
> Then said his disciples, "Lord, if he sleep, he shall do
> well."
> Howbeit Jesus spoke of his death, but they thought that
> he had spoken of taking of rest in sleep.
> Then said Jesus unto them plainly, "Lazarus is dead"
> (John 11:11-14).

The same expression is used in 1 Thessalonians where Paul refers
to the "dead in Christ" as "them also which sleep in Jesus" (1 Thessalonians 4:13-18). We have already seen from Scripture that death
for the Christian means that his soul and spirit are "absent from the
body and present with the Lord." Consequently, even though their
dead bodies are decaying in graves, the souls and spirits of those
Christians are with Christ in heaven. This is why, in speaking of the

rapture, Paul says that Christ will *bring with Him* "those who sleep in Jesus" when He personally descends "from heaven with a shout." He will raise the bodies of dead Christians from their graves and reunite them with their souls and spirits which have been in His presence since their death. At the same time He will transform the bodies of those alive, and catch them all up together to His Father's house in glory.

The Bible only uses the term "sleep" concerning the *bodies* of Christians who have died, but never concerning their souls and spirits, which have not died at all but have been enjoying the bliss of heaven since the moment of separation from their temporarily useless dead bodies. Paul would never have called this disembodied state "far better" than being alive on earth and serving Christ and others, as we have already noted that he did, if it were an unconscious suspension of existence.

Barabbas and Saul Who Became Paul

Far from suggesting that sin and the suffering and death it brings are mere illusions, Christ endured the full force of their terrible reality in our place. He was in agony in the Garden of Gethsemane in contemplation of the terrors of death—not because He wasn't enlightened enough to know that death was an illusion, but because He knew all too well the horror of the penalty required by God's justice that He would have to endure. To claim, as the Mind Science cults do, that death is not real is to accuse our Lord of tilting with windmills.

"O my Father," He cried in Gethsemane as His sweat became like blood, "if it be possible, let this cup pass from me" (Matthew 26:39). The fact that He had to go to the cross in spite of this earnest prayer is evidence that there was no other way that mankind could be forgiven by God. There are those, of course, who object that it does not serve the cause of justice at all but only compounds the crime to punish an innocent person in the place of the guilty. They simply do not understand that Christianity involves much more than mere *substitution*.

The difference between false and true Christianity can be readily seen by comparing Barabbas and Saul of Tarsus. The former could say "Christ died for me" as no one else in history could. In prison for insurrection and murder, Barabbas had literally been set free when Christ was condemned in his place—free to continue a self-centered life in pursuit of his own evil ambitions. In contrast, Saul accepted the death of Christ as his own death. It was the end of Saul of Tarsus and the beginning of a new man, Paul the Apostle.

"I am crucified with Christ!" declared Paul. This is no empty metaphor. Those who receive Christ as Savior and Lord acknowledge their own death in Him. The eternal life He offers is *resurrection* life, which only dead people can receive—those who have died in Him to life as they would have lived it. They are no longer their own but belong to Him who has become life itself to them. "I live," said Paul, "yet not I, but Christ liveth in me" (Galatians 2:20).

The Most Wonderful Promise

True Christianity stands in stark contrast to every other religion ever known. It did not take even the casual listener long to realize that the teaching and conduct of Jesus were poles apart from that of the scribes and Pharisees. They argued complex matters of the law, split religious hairs, and attempted to instruct the people in theological dogma that enslaved them in legalistic observances. In contrast, Jesus spoke with an authority that left no room for debate, even while it set men free. Moreover, the freedom He offered to all men was not based upon their ability to achieve it under His inspiration, but upon who He claimed to be and what He would personally do for them that they could not possibly do for themselves.

Startling promises about an unearthly dimension of existence fell continually from the lips of our Lord. In referring to heaven, Jesus used a term previously unknown: He called it "my Father's house." There He had dwelt in eternity past, there He would return, and there He promised to prepare a place of everlasting habitation for His followers.

In the entire history of Israel not even one of her greatest prophets or kings had ever called God his "Father." How dare this carpenter do so! In response to the rabbis' angry accusations and questions about His "Father," Jesus replied bluntly: "Ye are from beneath, I am from above; ye are of this world, I am not of this world" (John 8:23). Firmly, but with great compassion, He solemnly warned those who rejected Him:

> I go my way, and ye shall seek me, and shall die in your sins; whither I go, ye cannot come . . . for if ye believe not that I am he [Jehovah, the I AM of the burning bush, the Messiah, the Son of God], ye shall die in your sins (John 8:21,24).

Here was a man who authoritatively, yet graciously and humbly, claimed to be different from everyone else—God's one and only Son, who had come from heaven to visit earth on a special mission. He offered to make all men children of God and citizens of heaven. They could be "born again" if they would only believe in Him as the Savior of the world who had come to earth to die for their sins.

Such unorthodox but convicting statements enraged the Jewish religious leaders. Recognizing that Jesus was claiming to be God, the rabbis unsuccessfully attempted several times to stone Him. Eventually, of course, they had Him crucified for this "blasphemy," unaware that they were thereby fulfilling the predictions of their own prophets that Israel would despise and put to death the Messiah the first time He came to His own people (Isaiah 53).

Instead of presenting a religious philosophy, Christ offered *Himself*. Nor did He offer to point out the way to heaven or *guide* men there. He claimed to *be* the one and only way to that place of bliss and joy that all men hoped somehow to reach when they died. And to that audacious claim He added yet another, even more astonishing and wonderful. It was a concept beyond the imagination—something that no religious leader had ever conceived of, much less dared to propose.

The heaven Jesus referred to as His "Father's house of many mansions" was no mere paradise where He would only welcome His followers' disembodied spirits after they died. On the contrary, He assured them that one day very soon He would *take them there alive* and *bodily*. And even if they died before His return, He would resurrect their bodies and completely transform them. As we have already noted, the Christian's heaven is not only a place but a higher state of being in glorified spiritual yet tangible bodies in the very presence of Christ for eternity.

The day before He was crucified, in the process of explaining what was happening and calming their troubled hearts with the assurance that He was not abandoning them, Jesus told His bewildered disciples:

> Let not your heart be troubled; ye believe in God, believe also in me.
> In my Father's house are many mansions; if it were not so, I would have told you. I go to prepare a place for you.
> And if I go and prepare a place for you, I will come again and receive you unto myself, *that where I am, there ye may be also* (John 14:1-3).

What an incredible promise! It filled their hearts with joy and wonder, but it also raised so many new questions that they were afraid to ask. *Where* was His "Father's house," and *how* would He take them there? *How long* would their Lord need to "prepare" those mansions for them in heaven? Knowing His miraculous power, the disciples could not have thought it would take much time.

There can be no doubt that the early church expected Christ to "come again" very soon to take them back to His heavenly home. This was the great hope that sustained them through the persecution and trials that came on the heels of His departure from this earth. And if they should be martyred first, which seemed more than likely in those days, they knew they would be instantly in His presence, though their bodies would temporarily be left behind.

A Little While

After spending 40 days with His disciples following His resurrection, Christ had miraculously ascended into the sky and disappeared in a cloud as they watched in astonishment. Two angels in human form had suddenly appeared to speak these comforting words: "This same Jesus, which is taken up from you into heaven, shall so come in like manner as ye have seen him go into heaven" (Acts 1:11). That didn't sound as though it would be very long until He returned. Had not Christ Himself told them, "Verily I say unto you, 'Ye shall not have gone over the cities of Israel, till the Son of man be come' " (Matthew 10:23)?

At the "last supper," after Judas had slipped out to betray Him, Jesus had explained: "A little while and ye shall not see me; and again, a little while and ye shall see me, because I go to the Father" (John 16:16). That seemed clear enough. He was going away to His Father's house for *a little while* to prepare it for their soon arrival and then He would return from heaven to take them there. As the months after His ascension stretched into years, however, and the years into decades, the early Christians must have pondered with increasing wonder the meaning of *a little while*—a phrase which seems all the more incomprehensible to us nearly 2000 years later.

Why has it taken so long for our Lord to return? Could it be another 2000 years, or even more, before His promise is fulfilled? From the human perspective, such a lengthy delay seems inexplicable. From the perspective of eternity, however, 2000 years is almost nothing. Moreover, since previous "dispensations" in human history—such as the period from Adam to the Flood, from the Flood to the Promised Land, and the Jewish era prior to the birth of the church at Pentecost—have occupied similar lengths of time, it hardly seems unreasonable that the church should be on earth for 2000 years as well.

That Christ has not yet returned does not change the fact that the early church, in obedience to His clear commands, was waiting and watching for Him to come at any moment. Nor should His seeming delay cause us to abandon that hopeful vigil. He would come like a thief, Jesus had warned, "in such an hour as ye think not" (Matthew 24:42-44). Therefore, the first-century Christians were to watch expectantly, and so should we. It was not for them (or for us) to know the time, but to be ready at all times: "But of that day and that hour knoweth no man, no, not the angels which are in heaven, neither the Son, but the Father" (Mark 13:32).

Nevertheless, Christ provided His disciples with numerous "signs"* which would let them know that His coming was near so they would not be taken by surprise. Having apparently already expounded upon those signs to them, Paul reminded the believers at Thessalonica that the Lord's return, though it would come as a shock to the world, need not catch them completely unawares:

> But of the times and seasons, brethren, ye have no need that I write unto you.
>
> For yourselves know perfectly that the day of the Lord so cometh as a thief in the night.
>
> For when they [the non-Christians] shall say, "Peace and safety," then sudden destruction cometh upon them, as travail upon a woman with child, and they shall not escape.
>
> But ye, brethren, are not in darkness, that that day should overtake you as a thief. . . .
>
> Therefore let us not sleep, as do others, but let us watch and be sober (1 Thessalonians 5:1-6).

Lay Not Up for Yourselves Treasures upon Earth

One cannot read the New Testament without seeing its heavenly orientation. Heaven was continually on the heart of our Lord and it was the context for everything that He taught His disciples. He made it clear that He was calling them to turn their attention and affection

---

* For a detailed and different discussion of these signs see Dave Hunt, *Peace, Prosperity and the Coming Holocaust* (Harvest House Publishers, 1983).

and interest from this world to heaven, from what had been their earthly home and hope to His "Father's house" from whence He had come and to which He would soon take them. He tried to wean them away from their natural earthly mindedness to heavenly mindedness by contrasting the superiority and eternality of heaven with the emptiness and temporary nature of all this world has to offer.

Christ had said that His true disciples were "in the world" but "not of the world" because He had chosen them "out of the world" (John 17:6,11,14-18). There can be no doubt that the hope of the early Christians was not in their grim future of certain persecution on this earth, but in leaving it for heaven to be forever with their Lord. They knew that they were "partakers of the heavenly calling" (Hebrews 3:1). Their only reliable and worthwhile hope was "laid up for [them] in heaven" (Colossians 1:5). Typical of the way in which our Lord continually sought to turn His disciples from this earth to heaven is the following exhortation:

> Lay not up for yourselves treasures upon earth, where moth and rust doth corrupt, and where thieves break through and steal, but lay up for yourselves treasures in heaven, where neither moth nor rust doth corrupt, and where thieves do not break through nor steal, for where your treasure is, there will your heart be also (Matthew 6:19,20).

In sharp contrast to such commands from Christ and the heavenly orientation of the early church, there is a large and growing number of Christians today for whom long-range earthly ambitions have all but obscured the traditional hope of heaven—ambitions which they believe to be not carnal but biblical and very spiritual. They have become convinced that the Great Commission calls for a reconstruction of society that will result in a "Christianized" world. Since they believe that this reconstruction could take a long time, even thousands of years, it makes no sense not to lay up treasure upon this earth.

Unfortunately, in order to fulfill their agenda of building a financial and material base for the future establishment and expansion of

an earthly kingdom, the "take-over-the-world-for-Christ" advocates find themselves in direct conflict with the Lord's specific
commands. Of course, they could argue that none of us follows the
above admonition to the letter. Even those who believe in Christ's
imminent return and expect to leave it all behind at any moment
nevertheless have savings accounts, buy homes, and build churches
and Christian schools.

As we will see clearly in the next chapter, however, there is a great
difference in attitude and incentive between those who realize that
statistically—for a very small percentage of the populace—death
could come unexpectedly, and those who sincerely believe that
Christ could take all Christians home at any moment. The latter
hold the things of this earth far more loosely and for good reason.
There are those people, however, who would rob us of hoping for
Christ's imminent return and who actively oppose such a perspective in order to turn the Christian's focus from leaving earth for
heaven to taking over the world in His name.

A Genuine Cause for Concern

The largest and most influential group advocating a Christian
takeover of the world is the Coalition on Revival (COR). The
membership of COR's steering committee reads like a *Who's Who*
of evangelical leadership. As COR founder and director Jay Grimstead explains to audiences as he travels promoting the COR *Manifesto*:

We felt we had to get a whole list of heroes to sign this
[*Manifesto*] to start with so that the average pastor and
the average warmhearted layman would . . . know that
this is coming from a group of major national Christian
leaders. . . .
You can hold your head high with confidence that this
document has been thoroughly looked over and agreed to
by most of the people you would consider your spiritual
intellectual heroes in the Body of Christ.[3]

Unfortunately, in spite of its prestigious leadership, COR's agenda fosters an unbiblical earthly mindedness which is contrary to that which Christ encouraged and which characterized the early church. The Coalition on Revival's *Manifesto*, for example, which Christian leaders, pastors, and churches across America and Canada are endorsing, seems to discourage the expectancy of Christ returning soon to take us to heaven. Of course, the COR attitude makes sense if Christ cannot return until we have Christianized the world. Yet if that is the case, then His command to watch and wait for His return as though He could come at any moment is extremely misleading.

There are other groups, some of them far more extreme than COR, advocating a Christian takeover of the world to the detriment of the heavenly hope that motivated the early church. The growing acceptance of the teaching that a Christian elite has a mandate to set up the kingdom without Christ's personal presence is genuine cause for concern. The kingdom of God is understood to involve absolute power. We would feel comfortable only if such authoritarian absolutism were exercised by Jesus Christ Himself, *in person*. We would be very uncomfortable if any man or group of men, religious or political, and no matter how seemingly trustworthy, claimed to have the right to wield such power in His name. Nothing could be more dangerous. C.S. Lewis writes:

> I am a democrat because I believe that no man or group of men is good enough to be trusted with uncontrolled power over others. And the higher the pretensions of such power, the more dangerous I think it both to the rulers and to the subjects.
>
> Hence Theocracy is the worst of all governments. If we must have a tyrant, a robber baron is far better than an inquisitor. The baron's cruelty may sometimes sleep, his cupidity at some point be sated; and since he dimly knows he is going wrong he may possibly repent.
>
> But the inquisitor who mistakes his own cruelty and lust of power and fear, for the voice of Heaven will

torment us infinitely because he torments us with the
approval of his own conscience and his better impulses
appear to him as temptations.[4]

Strangers and Pilgrims in the Earth

Many of those involved in COR call themselves "PreMillennial
Reconstructionists." Their adoption of the Reconstructionist* agenda
leads to contradictions that can only be resolved by a denial of that
longing for Christ's imminent return that characterized the early
church. That hope is incompatible with the determination to take
dominion over the world in the name of Christ. In *The Reduction of
Christianity*, written as a response to *The Seduction of Christianity*,
Gary DeMar and Peter Leithart quote fellow Reconstructionist
David Chilton:

> God works to overthrow the ungodly, and increasingly
> the world will come under the dominion of Christians—
> not by military aggression, but by godly labor, saving,
> investment, and orientation toward the future.[5]

That Christ's promise to take His own to heaven has no significant
place in their future plans is quite clear. Yet no support for Christians adopting such earthly mindedness can be found in Scripture.
Nor can any consistent historical trend be cited to suggest that
"increasingly the world [has been] com[ing] under the dominion of
Christians" or that it will ever do so in the future. Reconstructionists claim that the hope of an imminent rapture discourages the

---

*Reconstructionism is a militant and growing brand of postmillennialism founded
25 years ago by two prolific and influential authors, Christian economist Gary
North and his father-in-law, Rousas J. Rushdoony. They believe we are now in the
millennium (which could last tens of thousands of years), during which Satan is now
"bound," Christians are in the process of taking over the world, and at the end of
which Christ will finally return to reward the predominant faithful and to punish
the few remaining unsaved.

Christian from being properly concerned with social and political action. They justify their postmillennial view to a large extent on the basis that the rapture hasn't happened in the nearly 2000 years since Christ's ascension.

During the same period of time, however, no evidence has surfaced of any consistent trend that would indicate that Christians are taking over the world for Christ. In fact, all indications are to the contrary. While those who hope for Christ's imminent return have His promise that He will do so, the hope of establishing the kingdom without the king flies not only in the face of logic and evidence but of much Bible prophecy and the words of Christ Himself. Scripture repeatedly predicts apostasy for the last days, an increase in ungodliness, and God's judgment upon the earth rather than a takeover by a triumphant church. Revelation 13, for example, clearly tells us that the Antichrist, not the church, will be in control of the world. And the description of Armageddon in Zechariah 12 and Revelation 19 with Jerusalem surrounded by the world's armies and in the process of being destroyed hardly sounds as though Satan is bound and Christians are in worldwide control. Nor is such a scenario compatible with the heavenly hope of the church.

In Hebrews 11 we read of Abraham and his Old Testament descendants who, by faith, "confessed that they were strangers and pilgrims on the earth." They had left the country of their natural birth and were on a journey "seek[ing] a country" not of this world. They looked for a heavenly country prepared for them by God Himself (Hebrews 11:13-16). Paul explained to the Ephesians that they were once citizens of this world and "strangers from the covenants of promise" that God made with Israel. Yet through the new birth they were "no more strangers and foreigners [to heaven], but fellowcitizens with the saints" (Ephesians 2:12,19). Moreover, that heavenly citizenship and hope had made them (and us as well) like the faithful of Hebrews 11 before them, "strangers and pilgrims on this earth."

Set Your Affection on Things Above

Providing further insight into the proper Christian attitude, both for the early church and for us today, Paul wrote: "If [since] ye then be risen with Christ, seek those things which are above, where Christ sitteth on the right hand of God. Set your affection on things above, not on things on the earth" (Colossians 3:1,2). We find it difficult to turn away from those things in this world upon which we ought not to set our affection. This would not be the case at all if those things which we are to seek "above, where Christ sitteth" were understood and had captured our affection.

How convicting such Scriptures are, and how desperately we need clarification and help to obey them! Yet a person searches the scholarly COR documents and the voluminous writings of the Reconstructionists in vain to find such important teaching expounded. For them to do so would undermine their entire earthly oriented program.

Our hope, our ambition, our desire, our passion and dreams for the future are all to involve our eternal home in heaven and not what we can achieve or accumulate on this earth. To call that impractical is to deny the inspiration of Scripture. We are in this world but not of it, using but not abusing it, holding everything loosely, considering everything in this life of transitory worth. We are to live as strangers and pilgrims on this earth who are already (by faith and interest and affection) "sit[ting] together in heavenly places in Christ Jesus" (Ephesians 2:6). The challenge to every true Christian is clear.

This does not mean that we have no concern for the poor or that we do not actively seek to improve the moral and social climate of our world. Yet everything we do to benefit others on this earth must be done not for its social value alone but for the sake of Christ and for the glory of God. Furthermore, rescuing souls for heaven must always take precedence over providing earthly benefits. The old saying that a person can be "so heavenly minded as to be no earthly good" is popular but false. Clearly no one could be more heavenly minded than Christ, nor could anyone be of more earthly good than He. His life is our model in keeping the proper balance.

Though so highly acclaimed that a person risks universal condemnation for daring to suggest that she might have a flaw, Calcutta's Mother Theresa provides a sad example of what is wrong with so much social action by Christians. While she cannot be faulted for her self-sacrifice and tireless effort to provide a clean bed and loving environment for the last earthly days of the dying, she must be reproved for neglecting their far more important eternal welfare. It is against the policy of the mission she founded to point out that Christ is the only way to heaven. Instead, its aim is to help dying Hindus to become better Hindus, dying Buddhists to become better Buddhists, and those of all religions to draw closer to their gods, no matter how false.

While she does her social work in Christ's name, Mother Theresa disobeys His command by purposely refraining from telling the dying that unless they receive Him as Savior and Lord they will spend eternity in hell. The brief comfort she and her followers diligently and selflessly provide for dying bodies is a poor substitute for the eternal torment to which she allows thousands to go by neglecting their souls.

Perverting Christianity with Worldly Dreams

It is because there is so little appreciation of what the New Testament teaches that heaven (and hell as well) seems so nebulous and of such doubtful importance alongside the great plans we have for "changing the world for Christ." Could this also be why so much that is presented as Christianity today is simply a sanctification of worldly desires in the name of Jesus? The same selfish ambitions and longings which motivate the world, the same fleshly goals, and the same kind of success are offered as enticements to get people to "come to Jesus"—a "Jesus" who never rebukes sin but only heals, prospers, and "positively reinforces" a person's self-esteem.

Many Christians imagine that victory in Christ is to become the epitome of what the world desires in wealth and success and fame and to do it all better than the ungodly because Christians have "Jesus on their side." Such is the misguided promise of Positive Confession, while Reconstructionism and COR teach much the same thing, as we shall see. Though such a false hope may seemingly be supported by an isolated verse here or there taken out of context, it is the very antithesis of the consistent message of the New Testament.

Christ did make promises, of course, for this earthly existence. He told His disciples that those who would leave father or mother or lands or houses for His sake would receive a hundredfold in this life. He was not granting *ownership* of these benefits, however, as is suggested by Positive Confession advocates, who promise that God will return $100,000 for every $1,000 given to their ministries. Christ offered something more wonderful than the hundredfold accumulation of great properties, luxury autos, and abundant goods. He promised that we would be taken into the homes and share the provisions of many others who know and love Him and who would love us, too, as brothers and sisters in the same heavenly and eternal family of God.

At the same time, however, Christ reminds us that inevitably these blessings come wrapped in "persecutions" (Mark 10:30) as part of the package—persecutions that we are to experience as long as we remain upon earth. Unless, of course, we deny our Lord or compromise our faith. Then and only then can we expect to be popular with the world. Far from offering success, popularity, and "dominion" over cultures and worldly institutions, Christ offers the same hatred and rejection He received. As Paul also reminds us: "Yea, and all that will live godly in Christ Jesus shall suffer persecution" (2 Timothy 3:12). Contrary to the attitude being promoted today, the early Christians "rejoic[ed] that they were counted worthy to suffer shame for his name" (Acts 5:41).

One can hardly reconcile the belief that Christians are going to take over the world prior to Christ's return in power and glory with Paul's statement that in Christ's crucifixion we, too, have been crucified to this world and the world unto us (Galatians 6:14). Nor is the popular teaching of earthly Christian triumphalism compatible with Christ's warning, "In the world ye shall have tribulation" (John 16:33), or with the many other similar statements by our Lord and the apostles. It is, instead, in the life to come that the followers of Christ are to receive their recompense.

Moreover, the Bible makes it abundantly clear that those who would be honored in this world rob themselves of heaven's eternal rewards. Insight into what it means to "let this mind be in you, which was also in Christ Jesus" (Philippians 2:5) is found in these words from our Lord:

> I receive not honor from men.
> How can ye believe [be men and women of faith], which receive honor one of another, and seek not the honor that cometh from God only? (John 5:41,44).

Persecution in This Life, Glory in the Coming Kingdom

Along with turning His disciples to heaven, Christ warned them of the hostility of the world which they would encounter because of their relationship to Him. He promised them bliss and joy and life eternal in His Father's house. Just as surely, however, He warned them that in this world they would be hated, maligned, persecuted, imprisoned, and killed for His sake. Far from promising a Christian takeover of the world, as is now increasingly being taught, Christ said to His disciples:

> The servant is not greater than his lord. If they have persecuted me, they will also persecute you. . . . They shall put you out of the synagogues; yea, the time cometh that whosoever killeth you will think that he doeth God service (John 15:20; 16:2).

Will there not be a time before Christ's return, as the Reconstructionists and the Coalition on Revival assure us, when Christians will be in the majority and become highly honored leaders of society? The answer is clearly, "No!" Peter explains that the trial of our faith is precious to God (1 Peter 1:7) and goes on to speak of the suffering that will inevitably befall and pursue the Christian. Like our Lord before us, we can expect to be misunderstood, maligned, hated, and persecuted by the majority of non-Christians, who, Peter says, will look upon us "as evildoers." Yet we are to "take it patiently," following in the footsteps of Christ who, in His patient suffering at the hands of the world, left "an example, that ye should follow in his steps" (1 Peter 2:11-15,21). There is no way to read into Peter's language any suggestion that such trials will end by Christians becoming the honored majority.

Paul made it very clear that this persecution would continue right to the end. He reminded his converts "that we must through much tribulation enter into the kingdom of God" (Acts 14:22). "Tribulation" is clearly one state of affairs and the "kingdom" another. They are chronologically distinct, with persecution preceding the kingdom. Our hope is not in anything this "present evil world" (Galatians 1:4) can offer. Rather, our hope "is laid up in heaven" (Colossians 1:5), it is based upon "the resurrection of Jesus Christ [and is] . . . reserved in heaven for [us]" (1 Peter 1:3,4). In the meanwhile, here on earth, our suffering at the hands of the ungodly will continue. Nor is this "some strange thing" (1 Peter 4:12). It is normal for this life until Christ returns to take us home.

Thus Paul encourages us with the promise that "the sufferings of this present time are not worthy to be compared with the glory which shall be revealed in us" (Romans 8:18). Indeed, he assures us that suffering is the required schooling and stepping-stone to reigning with Christ: "If we suffer, we shall also reign with him; if we deny him, he also will deny us" (2 Timothy 2:12). While these and many other Scriptures do not say that suffering and persecution must be the lot of every Christian at all times, certainly the overall indication is that the church, like Christ, will be hated and rejected by the world.

The suggestion that Christians will become the majority power and take over the world simply has no foundation in Scripture, and certainly not in history. The Christian's hope is the return of Christ to take him to heaven, to be glorified with Christ in His kingdom, and to share His triumphant reign over this earth.

The Attitude of the Early Church

"And when the chief shepherd shall appear," wrote Peter, "ye shall receive a crown of glory that fadeth not away" (1 Peter 5:4). Referring to the same event, Paul wrote: "When Christ, who is our life, shall appear, then shall ye also appear with him in glory" (Colossians 3:4). When would this great event occur?

Paul cultivated among all of the believers in his day the eager expectancy that this appearing would take place very soon. In so doing he attempted, like His Lord, to wean them from this earth to live as those who were already citizens of heaven. To the Philippians he wrote: "For our conversation [citizenship] is in heaven, from whence also we look for the Savior, the Lord Jesus Christ..." (Philippians 3:20). And to Titus: "Looking for that blessed hope, and the glorious appearing of the great God and our Savior Jesus Christ" (Titus 2:13). One does not "look" for someone who cannot possibly appear for many weeks, much less for many years. Such an expression would only be used concerning someone who might appear at any time.

Encouraging that same expectant attitude, the author of the epistle to the Hebrews wrote: "Unto them that look for him shall he appear the second time without sin unto salvation" (Hebrews 9:28). Nowhere does the Bible teach a "partial rapture" of a select few Christians who have attained to an unusual status of spirituality. Therefore, this verse is not stating that only those who "look for him" will be raptured. It is simply declaring that *looking* for Christ's return is the normal attitude expected of every Christian— an attitude that would be ludicrous if Christ could not return until after thousands of years of "millennium" or even until after the Great Tribulation.

There are those who argue that it is foolish to think of Christ returning today, since the apostles vainly expected that great event in their time. On the contrary, they did not—yet they urged the Christians of their day to remain expectant. The apostle Paul unquestionably knew that this longed-for event would not occur during his own lifetime, which would be cut short by Roman execution. Peter also had the same conviction, as his writings prove. The apostles knew that they were "appointed to death . . . a spectacle unto the world" (1 Corinthians 4:9). Only the apostle John, of whom the Lord had said, "If I will that he tarry till I come . . ." (John 21:22), was the lone exception among them. He was spared martyrdom, yet died without seeing that promised coming.

During his final imprisonment, Paul wrote to advise Timothy that he would be martyred before Christ returned: "For I am now ready to be offered, and the time of my departure is at hand" (2 Timothy 4:6). He had known when and how his end would come much earlier. To their shock and deep sorrow, Paul, after urgently calling the Ephesian elders to meet him at Miletus, had informed them:

> And now, behold, I know that ye all, among whom I have gone preaching the kingdom of God, shall see my face no more. . . .
> Take heed therefore. . . . For I know this, that after my departing [martyrdom] shall grievous wolves enter in among you, not sparing the flock (Acts 20:25-30).

Although he knew he would not be alive on earth when Christ returned, Paul repeatedly encouraged those of his generation to expect that great event in their time. The apostles would not have cultivated this attitude in the early church—indeed, such encouragement by them and by Jesus Himself would have been cruel—if Christ could not actually have come until certain events had occurred. For Paul to encourage his contemporaries to expect Christ at any time, if in fact He could not return until after the Great Tribulation or Armageddon or the millennium, would have been inexcusable deception.

There are those who argue that it doesn't matter whether we think Christ might return before, in the middle, or at the end of the Great Tribulation, or even after the millennium. That is another question, which we will address later. At the moment, all we wish to establish is this one fact: For the early church, the imminent return of Christ was their daily expectancy and hope. And it was a hope which they would not and dared not abandon, because Christ had commanded them to watch and wait and to be ready.

Like the Reconstructionists, COR rightly puts much emphasis upon that part of the Great Commission where Christ commanded His followers that in discipling others they were to teach them "to observe [obey] all things whatsoever I have commanded you" (Matthew 28:20). In order to fulfill the Great Commission, however, it is necessary to teach all Christians to watch and wait for Christ's imminent return, for He repeatedly commanded His disciples to do so. Yet COR actively opposes discipling others to obey such commands from Christ. Consider the following:

> Let your loins be girded about and your lights burning, and ye yourselves like unto men that wait for their lord, when he will return from the wedding; that when he cometh and knocketh, they may open unto him immediately.
>
> Blessed are those servants whom the lord when he cometh shall find watching. . . .
>
> And if he shall come in the second watch or come in the third watch and find them so, blessed are those servants. . . .
>
> Be ye therefore ready also, for the Son of man cometh at an hour when ye think not.
>
> Watch therefore, for ye know neither the day nor the hour wherein the Son of man cometh.[6]

An A Priori Case Against a Post-Anything Rapture

Such language, together with the undeniably expectant posture of the early church, cannot be reconciled with the growing attitude toward the Second Coming prevalent among so many Christians today. It seems the height of folly to be looking for Christ when we know, according to Reconstructionist writer David Chilton, for example, that He cannot come for at least 36,600 years, and in fact may not come for several hundred thousand years.[7] Yet the New Testament makes it very clear that the early church was in a continual attitude of loving His appearing and looking and watching for His return. Neither Christ nor the apostles who encouraged this attitude of watchfulness must have understood what some claim to have lately discovered from their study of Scripture.

In urging Timothy to "keep this commandment, without spot, unrebukeable, until the appearing of our Lord Jesus Christ" (1 Timothy 6:13,14), Paul was clearly implying that Christ's "appearing" *could* occur in Timothy's lifetime. And the expectancy of this event undoubtedly contributed to the purifying heavenly orientation of those first-century Christians which is so lacking in the church today. Moreover, it cannot be denied that Paul considered it a mark of genuine Christianity for his readers in the early church to expect the Lord's return in their lifetime. In writing to the Thessalonians, for example, Paul cited as evidence that these former pagans had truly become Christians, not only that they had "turned to God from idols to serve the living and true God," but also that they had begun "to wait for his Son from heaven . . ." (1 Thessalonians 1:9,10). That makes no sense if Scripture had already decreed that our Lord could not possibly return until *after* some predetermined future event.

"O joy, O delight, should we go without dying!" This line from an old hymn expresses a hope unknown outside Christianity. One need not die in order to enter heaven! Cynics, not only outside but now also within the church, remind us that Christians have sung such hymns and clung to this dream in vain century after century. No one disputes the fact that Christ has not yet come nor that the delay has been a great disappointment to waiting millions of Christians down through the centuries. What is disputed is the claim that they waited and watched in vain.

Obedience to Christ's command to "be ready" at any moment for His sudden return cannot be in vain, for it has its own reward. That attitude has helped watchful Christians to faithfully seek their heavenly home and reward rather than the things of this world. Since life at best is very brief, those who steadfastly kept their affection on things above were in heaven very soon even without the rapture and surely had no regrets at having laid up treasure in heaven instead of in this world. Moreover, the very hope of His imminent return had a purifying effect upon their lives. It also gave an urgency to the Great Commission that can hardly be shared by those who believe there are yet centuries or even decades left for its fulfillment.

It is actually those who hoped to take dominion over earth's cultures and institutions, in the process of a gradual takeover of the world by Christians, who hoped in vain. No one in the past 2000 years ever saw that dream come true. And not only did they not achieve what they hoped for, but it caused them to become earthly minded instead of heavenly minded. Quite possibly they also lost at least some of their heavenly reward as a result.

The fact that our Lord commanded and His apostles urged the believers in that day to watch and wait for His imminent return is proof enough that it must have been possible then (and therefore now) without the necessity of any prior event occurring. It is not enough, however, to establish this fact as a matter of logic or doctrine. Loving our Lord and longing for His coming must become the basic motivating factor in our lives if we are to return to New Testament Christianity. John Pilkey has stated it well:

> Waiting for the Rapture is its own reward in the sense that it establishes a concept of the future superior to anything else that can be imagined.
>
> Resurrection manhood is simply superior to mortal manhood; and, to those who know about resurrection, the only way to cope with mortality is to hope for transformation day and night.[8]

3

The Late Great Rapture Theory?

It is an understatement to say that the winds of change are blowing at gale force through the hallowed halls of tradition. Scientific discovery is advancing in quantum leaps, computer technology is literally exploding, and electronic communications networks are bringing this rapidly expanding knowledge to the world with lightning speed. The inevitable result is a revolution in every field from physics to medicine and from economics to politics. That we currently face dramatic and accelerating worldwide change beyond present comprehension is sensed by almost every person who gives any heed to the contemporary scene. Nor is it possible to seriously doubt the connection between the quickening pace of high-tech's sensuous, self-centered living, and plummeting public morals.

Needless to say, the church has not remained untouched by these currents of upheaval and transformation. Influenced by the world as never before through the subtleties and persuasive power of modern media, Christians are being adversely affected in numerous and deceptive ways. The faith of many, particularly the youth, is being devastated by the challenge of "scientific" or "progressive" ideas which also undermine biblical standards of morality. As Christian lives are caught up in the inexorable deterioration, the world's disillusionment with all things "Christian" grows apace, particularly in the wake of the recent well-publicized scandals.

Yet there is reason for hope. The Word of God remains true regardless of the failures of those, great or small, who teach its precepts and attempt to follow them. Moreover, John tells us that if we will but return to that which sustained the early church—the earnest expectation of Christ's imminent appearing, and our deliverance from sin and death by transformation into glorious bodies like His—we will find that such a hope will inevitably have a powerful purifying effect in every area of our lives. John wrote:

> Beloved, now are we the sons of God, and it doth not yet appear what we shall be; but we know that, when he shall appear, we shall be like him, for we shall see him as he is.
> And every man that hath this hope in him purifieth himself, even as he is pure (1 John 3:2,3).

The Purifying Effect of Expecting Christ's Imminent Return

Paul declared that when Christ returned, as He had promised, He would resurrect the dead and catch away all living Christians together with them to meet Him in the air (1 Thessalonians 4:13-18). No adventure could be more rapturous, so the word "rapture"—which in English means a sudden and ecstatic catching away—was adopted to describe this unprecedented event. Moreover, the word "rapture," while not found in English translations of the Bible, is the Latin word for "caught up" (1 Thessalonians 4:17) used in the Latin Vulgate translation, and is therefore quite biblical. With respect to Christ's return, we are repeatedly urged to have toward it an attitude of *watching and waiting*.

We do well to consider why this continual expectancy of His imminent return, which is unquestionably commanded by Christ, should have such a special purifying effect. Oddly enough, it seems quite apparent that its value for us, and the importance the Bible obviously attaches to it, do not depend upon whether the Lord's return is actually imminent or not. It is the eager *expectancy* that counts and which is not only a major purifying factor, as John says, but must, as a consequence, also be a barometer of our spiritual life.

While there are many indications that the Lord's return may very well be imminent for *us*, we now know in retrospect that it was *not* imminent for all those generations of Christians who came before us. If the sole value of their "expectancy" lay in its being satisfied by the Lord's actual return during their lifetime, then the fact that Christ has not yet returned would mean that they waited and watched in vain. Yet the Lord urged this "expectant" attitude knowing full well that millions of Christians would be taken to heaven in death before He returned. Therefore, there must be something important, something integral to a good Christian life, about the mere *attitude* of expecting at any moment Christ's return and our transformation into His likeness. Why?

There can be no doubt that a conviction that we could be caught up into heaven at any moment would impart an added seriousness to our lives. The transient nature of our earthly tenure should cause us to make every moment count for eternity. In this regard, the expectancy of Christ's imminent return should weaken our tendency to identify ourselves too closely with a world which does not hold our ultimate destiny. It should also help to remind us of our true citizenship in a world to come which is based upon eternal rather than earthly values. This attitude certainly ought to characterize a Christian life, and a lively sense of the possibility of Christ's imminent return is more than justified if it has this wholesome effect.

Recognizing that one could momentarily be taken to heaven in the rapture also presents a profoundly sobering challenge to examine the reality of one's faith (2 Corinthians 13:5). But doesn't the possibility of imminent death have the same effect? There are several reasons why it does not. The expectancy of being caught up at any moment into the presence of our Lord in the rapture has some definite advantages over a similar expectancy through the possibility of sudden death.

The Superior Value of the Rapture Hope

First of all, if we are in a right relationship with Christ, we can genuinely look forward to the rapture. Yet no one (not even Christ in the Garden) looks forward to death. The joyful prospect of the rapture will attract our thoughts, while the distasteful prospect of death is something we may try to forget, thus making it less effective in our daily lives.

Moreover, while the rapture is similar to death in that both serve to end our earthly life, the rapture does something else as well: It signals the climax of history and opens the curtain upon earth's final drama. It thus ends, in a way that death does not, all human stake in continuing earthly developments, such as the lives of one's children left behind, the growth or dispersion of one's accumulated fortune, the protection of one's personal reputation, the success of whatever earthly causes one has espoused, and all other seemingly legitimate interests which bind us to this present world. The rapture strips us of earthly hope and purifies our hearts in a way that death does not.

People often cope with the finality of death through such forms of pseudoimmortality as just mentioned. Thus man can, through the things he has done and cared about, "live on" after he is gone. Even Christians, who have genuine immortality to look forward to, may nevertheless be tempted to find consolation in some of these forms of pseudoimmortality. The rapture, however, undercuts all of these; and to whatever extent these pseudoconsolations are weakened, our postmortem hope becomes purified of its earthly elements. Being thus forced to face the fact that our destiny lies in heaven, we will be motivated to live with that goal in mind.

Furthermore, the incentive provided by death is also weakened by the fact that we generally have at least some control over its relative imminence. Certainly we are radically contingent beings, and our lives could be snuffed out at any time. But this is not the way people usually die. The cancer victim might have refrained from smoking, or added more fiber to his diet, or sought treatment earlier. The guilty auto accident victim could have driven within the speed limit or taken a taxi when he had too much to drink.

Though death can come suddenly and without warning (we are not complete masters of our own fate), it is nevertheless true that we make decisions daily that increase or decrease the chances of our dying tomorrow, next month, or in ten years. This not-altogether-illusory sense of control over the time of our demise reduces the incentive for godliness by making us feel that we can afford to postpone a closer relationship with God until next week, next month, or next year.

In contrast, we have absolutely no control over the timing of Christ's return to earth. It will just happen "out of the blue"—and for many of us, as Christ warned, when we least expect Him (Matthew 24:44). Belief in the imminent return of Christ, then, does not allow us to postpone anything or substitute anything for that blessed hope, and thus it has a most powerful purifying effect upon those who truly have their hearts fixed on His return.

Even so, there are many Christians today (and their number is growing rapidly) who view the hope of an imminent rapture as the negative product of a defeatist theology. They sincerely believe that the expectation of being taken home to heaven at any moment undermines the "victory" they are convinced could be won by the church if Christians would only catch the vision of taking over the world and would unite to fulfill it.

On the contrary, there is a much more exciting and worthwhile hope for those who believe in the rapture. We will return with Christ from heaven in transformed bodies to reign over this earth with Him. That hope involves a truly new world order far superior to anything we could establish in these mortal bodies and without His physical presence on earth. Such a vision of the future helps us to realize that we are not part of this old world order and to make a clear break with it even now.

The ground is being laid for a major confrontation between those who long to leave this earth for heaven in the rapture, and others equally sincere who believe it is the Christian's duty to establish the kingdom upon this earth and that only when this has been accomplished by the church in His absence will our Lord at last return. That such an attitude could be prevalent and growing in influence today seems astonishing in view of the widespread expectation of the any-moment rapture that prevailed so recently.

The Late Great Rapture Theory?

With sales of more than 25 million copies, including dozens of foreign editions, Hal Lindsey's *The Late Great Planet Earth* was the biggest-selling nonfiction book of the 1970s, according to the *New York Times Book Review*. Its spiritual impact was incalculable. With its breezy, easy-to-understand style, *Late Great* made the once-dull topic of prophecy intriguing and exciting reading to millions who had never been interested in the subject before. Its message was compelling: All of the "signs" pointed to an apocalyptic windup of history in fulfillment of biblical prophecy.

Lindsey presented the pretribulational view: that the rapture could be expected at any moment, to be followed by the Great Tribulation, then the rise of the Antichrist, and later world war (Armageddon) in the Middle East. With Israel under attack by the surrounding world's armies and about to be destroyed, Christ would visibly and personally intervene from heaven to rescue His people, who would then recognize Him as their Messiah. He would destroy His enemies and establish His literal and personal thousand-year reign from Jerusalem, known as the millennium.

Here was good news for Christians. It offered the assurance that they would be taken out of this world before the horrifying suffering foretold in the Bible for the "last days." At the same time it was frightening for those who would be left behind. As a result of reading *Late Great*, thousands of people from all walks of life became Christians and are following the Lord today. Many of them, however, no longer expect the rapture until after the tribulation, having adopted a posttribulational position. Others do not expect the rapture until after the millennium. Still others have joined a growing movement within the church which denies that there will be a rapture at all.

Of course, there have always been diverse views of the Second Coming. The amillennial position, generally held by Lutherans, Presbyterians, and Catholics (among others), sees history moving on for many thousands of years with Christ finally winding things up at some indefinite time in the future and with prophecy having little if anything to say that would give us any hint of timing or events along the way. Similarly, the postmillennial view suggests that we are already in the millennium (which is not a literal thousand years but could be hundreds of thousands), that the church is gradually taking over the world and will eventually establish the kingdom in Christ's absence, after which He will return for the final judgment. While there is a general belief in the rapture, postmillennialism puts that event so far in the future that it has no practical motivating effect in one's life.

In the early 1970s the rapture was the most-talked-about topic in the church. Lindsey had captured the attention and imagination of his generation. Pastors preached about heaven and Christians eagerly anticipated being caught up at any moment to meet their Lord in the air. Even the secular world became familiar with the concept. There were movies, such as "The Omen," about the end times. Radio and television mentioned the Second Coming frequently, and cartoons and bumper stickers also took up the theme. One of the latter solemnly warned: "I'm leaving in the rapture, ride at your own risk!"

All of that has changed. The bumper stickers have worn off, the movies have lost their appeal, and the sermons have gone on to currently popular themes. The subtitle of a recent article in *Moody* reflects present sentiment: "Hal Lindsey was premature. The earth is great, but it's too early to call it late."[1] Outspoken Christian economist Gary North is not so polite. Referring to the waning hope that Christ could return at any moment and, as a result, the upsurging popularity of Reconstructionism, North writes:

> There has been neither a Rapture nor a Great Tribulation. . . . The events of 1948 become steadily irrelevant for dispensational interpretations of biblical prophecy. So do the events of 1988.
>
> Hal Lindsey's second wave of exegetical bills comes due this year (the first wave appeared in 1981). . . . For the remaining life of the movement dispensationalism's spokesmen will try to explain away 1988.[2]

Writing for North, Michael R. Gilstrap adds:

> Dispensationalism* will soon be just one more junker
> added to the scrap heap of antiquated theological sys-
> tems. It's not on the pile yet, but it will be one day soon—
> say about January 1, 1989?[3]

Israel: Key to Last Days Timetable?

North's reference to specific dates is an attack upon the most
persuasive factor supporting Lindsey's rapture scenario: the rebirth of national Israel. This historic event, which is pivotal to
dispensationalism's timing of the rapture, as John F. Walvoord has
pointed out,[4] was long anticipated and when it at last occurred
seemed to validate that prophetic interpretation. After 2500 years
of exile, scattered to the four winds by God's judgment for their
rebellion, and facing extermination countless times through satan-
ically persistent persecution, the proverbial wandering Jews had
come home at last! No other people had retained their identity after
being separated from their homeland for even a fraction of that time,
much less had been restored to the status of a nation once again.
Here was the most significant occurrence in the prophetic timetable
since the days of Jesus.

On November 29, 1947, the United Nations, in a miraculous vote
that would certainly not be duplicated today, had granted Israel the
right to come into existence as a sovereign nation in a designated
portion of its ancient home in Palestine. On May 14, 1948, in a
proclamation from Tel Aviv, the state of Israel was born. It was
immediately attacked by overwhelming Arab forces, but defeated
them and was admitted to the United Nations on May 12, 1949—
again a vote that would probably not have been possible at any time
thereafter, and certainly not today.

---

* A system of viewing history in distinct "dispensations" of God's progressively
different dealings with mankind, popularized by J. N. Darby and C. I. Scofield,
which helped to make the pretribulation rapture belief dominant for 100 years and
which has been associated with such institutions as Dallas Theological Seminary.

The Soviet Union, which had surprisingly cast the deciding vote in November 1947, has ever since joined the Arabs in their dedication to the destruction of Israel. This was not surprising. For at least 200 years, prophecy students had identified Russia, long before it became a world military power, as the leader of a biblically prophesied confederacy of nations that would attack Israel in the last days. Everything seemed to be coming together with astonishing precision to set the stage for Armageddon.

A Question of Dates and "Generations"

While sitting on the Mount of Olives shortly before His crucifixion, Christ told His disciples that the temple (and, by implication, Jerusalem) would soon be destroyed. Shocked by this statement, the disciples asked three questions: 1) "When shall these things be [i.e. the destruction of Jerusalem]?" 2) "What shall be the sign of thy [second] coming?" and 3) "[What shall be the sign] of the end of the world?" (Matthew 24:3). Christ's response, known as the Olivet Discourse, continues through the end of Matthew 25. Its incisive prophecies and related parables answer all three questions, but not in the order in which they were asked. Moreover, there are some statements of Christ that apply to more than one of the questions, and Christ deliberately made no clear distinction. This was in keeping with His manner of teaching only those who had ears to hear and eyes to see. For this reason there have been numerous and contradictory interpretations of what He meant. Each of us must decide for himself under the Holy Spirit's leading.

One of the major causes of confusion has been Christ's cryptic statement: "This generation* shall not pass, till all these things be

---

* The view I have always held associates this statement by Christ with His repeated references to a "wicked and adulterous generation" (Matthew 12:39; 16:4; etc.), a "faithless and perverse generation" (Matthew 17:17; Luke 9:41; etc.), a "generation of vipers" (Matthew 23:33; etc.) and other similar phrases. It is clear that He included in such terms not only the generation to which He spoke, but all of unbelieving Israel of all time, because He also made such statements as: "That the blood of all the prophets, which was shed from the foundation of the world, may be

fulfilled" (Matthew 24:34). The majority view among evangelicals at the time Hal Lindsey presented it was that "this generation" referred to the future generation that would see "all these things come to pass." Another interpretation, however, and one that has been growing in popularity, considers "this generation" to mean the generation that was alive when Jesus spoke those words. The latter view is clearly accurate as to the destruction of Jerusalem, which indeed did occur within the lifetime of most of the disciples. It is equally clear, however, that neither the Second Coming nor the "end of the world" has yet occurred. Therefore, another interpretation of "this generation" is needed in connection with the prophecies pertaining to those two events.

In spite of what seems so obvious, however, many amillennialists, postmillennialists and especially Reconstructionists insist that Christ's Olivet Discourse prophecies and the entire Book of Revelation (with the exception of approximately the last three chapters) were *all fulfilled* with the destruction of Jerusalem in A.D. 70. Even the marriage of the Lamb to His bride in heaven and Christ's return to earth to conquer His enemies depicted in chapter 19, and the binding of Satan and inauguration of Christ's millennial reign described in chapter 20 are also viewed as having been fulfilled within the normal lifespan of the generation alive when Christ spoke these words.

Such an interpretation would seem on the very face of it to be preposterous not only as to the "end of the world" but also as to many other prophecies contained in Matthew 24. The "coming of

---

required of this generation" (Matthew 23:36; Luke 11:50; etc.). Surely such a judgment would not be pronounced only against the generation of His own day. Thus His statement "this generation shall not pass away" should be taken to mean that Israel would still be predominantly in sin and unbelief until all of the Olivet Discourse prophecies were fulfilled. This agrees with Zechariah 12:10, which indicates that Israel will only recognize her Messiah and repent when Jesus suddenly intervenes from heaven in the middle of Armageddon to rescue her miraculously from destruction. Of course such an interpretation does not require fulfillment within any certain period of time after Israel's return to her land and thus leaves the rapture date open.

the Son of man" as visible as lightning shining across the entire sky (verse 27), and the gathering of His elect by angels "from one end of heaven to the other" (verse 31) obviously did not occur in A.D. 70 and has not to this day. Nor could the period involving the destruction of Jerusalem by the armies of Titus be described as "great tribulation, such as was not since the beginning of the world to this time, no, nor ever shall be" (verse 21) for either Christians or Jews. There is no question that far greater tribulation than occurred in A.D. 70 came to the Jews in Hitler's holocaust, and for the Christians in the great persecution that began in A.D. 303 under Diocletian and Galerius—to say nothing of the imprisonment, torture, and extermination of many millions of believers and destruction of tens of thousands of churches under Stalin and Mao. We would have to conclude, then, that most of the events of Matthew 24 and of Revelation (including far greater tribulation than anything the world has known to the present) are yet future and could occur in our time.

For a great many Christians who assumed that Christ was referring to a future generation that would see "all these things come to pass," the sprouting of the fig tree (verse 32) was interpreted to mean the establishment of Israel as a nation. Therefore, 1948 marked the beginning of an exciting countdown from this first of the "last days" events to the pretribulation rapture. If a biblical generation were considered to be 40 years (so argued because that was the length of time Israel wandered in the wilderness to wipe out the generation of those who refused to go into the Promised Land), then by 1988 (1948 plus 40) everything Jesus spoke of in His Olivet Discourse, including the takeover of the world by the Antichrist, the battle of Armageddon, and the Second Coming would have had to take place. If one deducted from 1988 the seven years generally understood to be the length of the Great Tribulation, then a pretribulation rapture would have had to occur in 1981.

The Late Great Planet Earth had only suggested that Christ's statement concerning "this generation" might possibly indicate a fulfillment within 40 years from Israel's rebirth. Yet that possibility had metamorphosed (though not so intended by Hal Lindsey) into *necessity* in the thinking of so many Christians that when 1981 came and went without the rapture there was considerable disillusionment with the pretribulation position. Doubts had already been mounting as that key date had approached. In fact, by the late 1970s the posttribulation view had gained a substantial following even in denominations and institutions that had long been bastions of the (until then) dominant pretribulation position.

The New Issue: Rapture or No Rapture

Needless to say, January 1, 1982, saw the defection of large numbers from the pretrib position. At that point, however, the posttrib theory looked no better, because the Great Tribulation obviously had not arrived on schedule. To many it seemed that the only option remaining was the postmillennial view, a minority belief that had all but died out among evangelicals. After being generally written off, however, as Gary North admits, and in spite of the apparent unreasonableness of the A.D. 70 scenario, the postmillennial view is once again staging a dramatic comeback.

Now that 1988 has become history without the appearance of the Great Tribulation or the Antichrist—and with the prospects of Armageddon fading into the future with the warming of Soviet-American relations and brightening prospects for nuclear disarmament—the controversy is no longer between a pre-, mid-, or posttrib rapture as it has been for so long. The issue has become "rapture or no rapture." And the latter view is gaining strength so rapidly that it promises to become the predominant belief in the near future. While most postmillennialists believe in a rapture, as we have already noted, it is so far in the future as to have little practical effect upon an individual's life and offers none of the purifying and motivating hope normally associated with the expectancy of the imminent return of Christ.

Most Christians no longer know what they believe about prophecy and now realize that their previously held opinions must be given an honest and careful review. Many who were once excited about the prospects of being caught up to heaven at any moment have become confused and disillusioned by the apparent failure of a generally accepted biblical interpretation they once relied upon.

Those who believed in the rapture because it was popular are, of course, abandoning it now that it has become unpopular. They never had a good reason for what they believed based upon their own carefully weighed convictions. It is sad that so few Christians know the Bible for themselves.

The warming debate over the significance of that large part of the Bible which is devoted to prophecy must be carried to a conclusion at this critical juncture in world and church history. The purpose is not necessarily to gain a consensus of agreement, but so that the issues will be made clear enough for each person to make an intelligent decision for himself. In the process, we could see the most dramatic shift in biblical interpretation among evangelicals in more than 150 years, with extremely serious consequences.

Unfortunately, right at this time there is developing a dangerous elitist attitude toward members of the body of Christ who dare to question the teachings of prominent leaders. Those who sincerely desire to exercise their God-given "Berean" privilege and duty to test all things against the Word of God are often told that their lack of a theological degree disqualifies them from questioning what is being popularly taught. The church is in grave danger when her leaders, like the hierarchy of the Roman Catholic Church that rejected the Reformation in the 1500s, refuse to be either questioned or corrected.

Exchanging Heavenly Hope for Earthly Ambition

The church is now ripe for the developing views of history and prophecy that either downplay or eliminate the rapture and put the emphasis upon "Christianizing" (in contrast to "converting") the world. A new genre of books espousing the idea that "victory in Christ" means a Christian takeover of this world is coming off the presses and selling well. Such ideas are being successfully taken into mainstream evangelical churches by the broadly based Coalition on Revival. The very existence of this organization, with its denigrating view of the rapture and promotion of Reconstructionism, represents a major theological shift in the church because of the eminence among evangelicals of its membership and leaders.

With the waning of the rapture hope, the relatively new theology of Reconstructionism is experiencing astonishing growth. The issues raised by this movement are important. Having launched an energetic campaign to convert the majority of Christians to their way of thinking, the Reconstructionists have issued the following challenge—a serious challenge that cannot go unanswered:

> We are calling the whole Christian community to debate us, just as Luther called them to debate him when he nailed the 95 theses to the church door, over four and a half centuries ago.
>
> If we're correct about the God-required nature of our agenda, it will attract a dedicated following. It could produce a social transformation that will dwarf the Reformation.[5]

With 1988 now history, the Reconstructionists are confident that the pretrib rapture must logically be rejected—and they are aggressively working to that end. To a leading spokesman for the pretrib rapture, Gary North recently wrote:

> As you might suspect, we are preparing to give Mr. [Dave] Hunt a run for his theological money. We regard him as the Hal Lindsey of the late 1980's—and with the same future: "Oh, yes, I remember you. You were that fellow who said Jesus was just around the corner because Israel was founded in 1948, and one generation later. . . ."
>
> It didn't happen. It isn't going to happen. And in the year 2002, we pick up the pieces. When Israel gets pushed into the sea, or converted to Christ, Scofieldism dies a fast death. Rest assured, I have a manuscript ready to go when either of these events happens.[6]

We have God's frequent promise that Israel will *never* be "pushed into the sea," so North is wasting his time writing that manuscript. As for Israel being "converted to Christ," Zechariah 12 tells us it will happen only when Christ rescues Israel at Armageddon—an event which North denies.

Today, the once-bright hope of the church being taken home to heaven by Christ at any moment has become the butt of crude jokes and a common subject of ridicule or scorn even among many Christians. The initial ad for the Reconstructionist *Biblical Blueprints* book series derisively called the rapture "God's helicopter escape." Earl Paulk, founding pastor of the 10,000-member Chapel Hill Harvester Church near Atlanta, and a popular Christian television teacher, calls the rapture "The Great Escape Theory." In his March 11, 1988 letter, COR founder and director Jay Grimstead bemoaned the many "good, scholarly pastors" who were still naively saying, "Our solution to the problems of this age is the coming of Christ."

Being taken to heaven in the rapture has been to a large extent replaced by the rapidly growing new hope that the church is destined to take over the world and establish the kingdom of God. The focus has turned from winning souls for citizenship in heaven to political and social action aimed at cleaning up society. Scarcely a sermon is being preached about the world to come. Attention is focused instead upon achieving success in this one. If we have a big enough march on Washington and vote in enough of our candidates, then we can make this world a beautiful, safe, moral, and satisfying "Christian" place for our grandchildren. This is a very enticing scenario. George Grant's appeal sounds logical and extremely persuasive:

> I became very disenchanted over time with the pessimistic mentality that the purpose of world history is to back the Church into the corner and finally at the last second, right before the moment of absolute destruction, God snatches us into the heavenly realms and says: "Well, you lost the world, you lost your culture, you lost your children, you lost the schools, you lost all the unborn babies, you lost South Africa, you lost everything. Well done, my good and faithful servants."
>
> I just couldn't buy that. Reconstructionists say that's not the only view on how the Church is to operate in the world.[7]

Whatever Happened to Heaven?

The expectancy of the Lord's soon return which was so evident in the 1970s at the peak of the popularity of Hal Lindsey's *The Late Great Planet Earth* has all but vanished from the church. Today there is scarcely a favorable reference to the rapture from most pulpits. And the hymns that once expressed the church's longing for heaven are now heard only at funerals.

There has developed a surprising and growing antagonism against eagerly watching and waiting for Christ's return, which surely was the attitude of the early church. The pendulum is swinging to an outright rejection of not only the pretrib but also the premillennium rapture. Reconstructionists are growing increasingly confident of the eventual triumph of their position. Presenting convincing evidence of this trend, Gary North writes:

> Indeed, the National Affairs Briefing Conference, held in Dallas in September of 1980, brought out at least 15,000 fundamentalists, including several thousand pastors, to a revival meeting encouraging Christians to get involved in political affairs. I spoke at the conference, and I was enthusiastically received. Rev. Rushdoony [Co-founder with North of Reconstructionism] was invited to speak, but his schedule prohibited his appearance.
>
> The word "rapture" was not used once, and only one speaker—Bailey Smith, the newly elected head of the Southern Baptist Convention—reminded men of Christ's imminent appearance, and he really did not agree with the emphasis of the conference. . . .
>
> Pat Robertson, head of the Christian Broadcasting Network, reminded the audience of the words of Genesis 1:26-28, calling Christians to exercise dominion, subdue the earth. . . . He even used the phrase, "Christian reconstruction."
>
> In short, a major shift in applied theology, though not of premillennial eschatology, has become apparent among

American fundamentalism's vocal leaders. It represents a kind of theological schizophrenia, but a welcome affliction. . . .[8]

The trend North recognized and identified in its early stages has accelerated. We could cite the current struggle going on in the Southern Baptist Church as one example. It is the largest Protestant denomination, but is presently losing members at a surprising and growing rate to independent churches that deny the rapture, deny any place for national Israel in prophecy, and believe that an elite group of "overcomers" will soon manifest immortality in their bodies without the resurrection or the Second Coming, and take over the world for Christ. Only then will Christ return. Not to take His bride home to heaven as the Bible clearly teaches, however, but to reign over the kingdom that has been established by her for Him here on this earth. One of the leaders in this movement writes:

> You can study books about going to heaven in a so-called "rapture" if that turns you on. We want to study the Bible to learn to live and to love and to bring heaven to earth.[9]

Is this issue even worth discussing? After all, what does it matter when Christ comes or when or how the kingdom is established? Is eschatological debate of any significance? A partial answer would lie in the fact that "last days" prophecy is a subject that takes up about one-fourth of the Bible. How could we dare to suggest that the Holy Spirit would give such importance to something which, in the final analysis, really doesn't matter? Based only upon the amount of attention given to it in the Bible, when and how and why Christ returns must be of great importance both to God and to us. We need to seek to understand why.

One reason for the significance of this issue should be quite obvious. Paul tells us that Christ is going to catch His bride away from this earth to meet Him in the air—"and so shall we ever be with the Lord" (1 Thessalonians 4:17). Consequently, those who expect to meet Christ with their feet still planted on earth—a "Christ" who has arrived to take over the kingdom they have established in His name—will have been badly deceived. In fact, they could have been working to build the earthly kingdom for the Antichrist. Yet this teaching that we must take over the world and set up the kingdom for Christ has become the fastest-growing movement within the church today.

A Changing Attitude Toward Israel

One of the key doctrines of this movement is the claim that the church is now Israel, heir to all of her promises, and that national Israel has been cut off from God and has no further place in the prophetic scheme. This new focus on an earthly inheritance for the church has further turned the hope of being taken to heaven in the rapture into an object of ridicule. It has also produced a drastic change in attitude and a serious reduction in the evangelical church's traditional support of Israel, an about-face which is being viewed with alarm by that tiny nation. Bill Hamon's *The Eternal Church* is one of the popular books promoting the theory that the church is Israel and that Christians are now establishing the kingdom of God. Hamon reports that Kenneth Hagin's Rhema Bible Training Center uses his book as a textbook and that it has been found to be a "valuable and indispensable tool" by: "Kenneth Copeland, Earl Paulk, Jerry Savelle, Gary Greenwald, John Gimenez, Ken Sumrall . . . and many other classical Pentecostal and Charismatic leaders." [10]

Speaking at Edmond near Oklahoma City on April 11, 1988, Rick Godwin, a long-time associate of James Robison and popular speaker on Christian media, delivered the type of anti-Israel rhetoric that is becoming so typical in charismatic circles: "They [national Israel] are not chosen, they are cursed! They are not blessed, they are cursed! . . . Yes, and you hear Jerry Falwell and everybody else say the reason America's great is because America's blessed Israel. They sure have. Which Israel? *The* Israel—the church. . . . That's the Israel of God, not that garlic one over on the Mediterranean Sea!" [11] Earl Paulk's criticism of national Israel and those who look favorably upon her includes the ultimate accusation:

> The hour has come for us to know . . . that the spirit of
> the antichrist is now at work in the world . . . [through]
> so-called Holy Spirit-filled teachers who say, "If you
> bless national Israel, God will bless you."
> Not only is this blatantly deceptive, it is not part of the
> new covenant at all![12]

Currents of change are sweeping through the world and the church. In the crucial days ahead, the evangelical church could well suffer a division over the rapture and the related issue of Israel comparable to that experienced by the Catholic Church as a result of the Reformation in the 1500s. Nor would it be surprising if, in the cause of "unity," the larger faction in Protestantism moved much closer to ecumenical union with Catholicism, which has been traditionally antisemitic and discarded the rapture about 1600 years ago. Some of the reasons why this could happen, and the likely consequences, should become clear in the following pages.

Would Christ's Return Be Inconvenient Now?

We must beware that in our zeal to "change the world for Christ" we do not become so wedded to an ongoing earthly process stretching into the indeterminate future that we lose our vision of heaven. We cannot be truly faithful to the totality of what Scripture says unless we are sufficiently disengaged from this world to be ready to leave it behind at a moment's notice.

There is cause to be concerned that the Reconstructionists and the Coalition on Revival as well as other kingdom/dominion advocates could be fostering a false conception of our earthly ministry—a conception which we must guard against lest we subtly fall into an attitude like that of Dostoevsky's Grand Inquisitor. For him, Christ's return to earth represented an interference with the mission of the church. He has Christ thrown into prison, where he visits him to complain:

> There is no need for Thee to come now at all. Thou must not meddle for the time, at least. . . . fortunately, departing Thou didst hand on the work to us.
>
> Thou has promised, Thou hast established by Thy word, Thou has given to us the right to bind and to unbind, and now, of course, Thou canst not think of taking it away. Why, then, hast Thou come to hinder us?[13]

All human beings are tempted to be more at home in this world than they should be. Christians are not exempt from this temptation, and when they succumb it often leads to an effort to reinterpret Scripture accordingly. Reconstructionists exemplify this temptation. Christ's return before they have taken over the world would be as inconvenient to the Reconstructionists and others in the kingdom/dominion movement as it was to the Grand Inquisitor, and for the same reasons.

Our hope is not in taking over this world but in being taken to heaven by our Lord, to be married to Him in glory and then to return with Him as part of the armies of heaven to rescue Israel, destroy His enemies, and participate in His millennial reign. Yet those of us who claim to believe this too often hold the belief in theory only, while denying it with our lives. Our hearts should be in perpetual wonder and joy at the prospect of being suddenly caught up to be with Christ, with our bodies transformed to be like His body of glory, and our marriage bond to our Lord sealed for eternity.

Heaven is not so much a location *somewhere* as it is being with Christ *wherever* He may be in the universe at the time, for we will be perpetually in His presence. It is not so much a *place* as it is a *state of being*, enjoying a heavenly existence that is beyond our present understanding. In our transformed bodies, made like His body of glory, in which we will share His resurrection life, we will reign with Him over this earth for 1000 years. Then we will spend an eternity during which He will be perpetually revealing to and in us more and more of Himself, His love and grace and kindness. Once this vision has captured us, how could anything else steal our heart's affection?

Part of the problem with the kingdom/dominion/reconstruction movement is its mistaken notion that mortal man can accomplish what only immortal Man, our risen Lord, and we as immortal resurrected beings with Him, can perform. We dare not settle for anything less than the fullness of what Christ has promised! The glory that He offers is light-years beyond the COR agenda of Christianizing and taking over this present world in these bodies of weakness and corruption.

We can miss His best by refusing to take seriously what the Bible clearly teaches and by not standing firm for sound doctrine. And we can also miss out on our true reward by attempting to live in our own strength the Christian life which only Christ can live through us. The joy and glory He has planned and in which He desires that we participate—and the prospect of being caught up at any moment to see this hope realized—are more than enough to excite and inspire and motivate us to victorious living and witnessing.

It seems ironic that the possibility of the rapture, which ought to bring great comfort, has caused great controversy as well. We dare not, however, in the name of unity and the avoidance of controversy, abandon the hope given to us in such Scriptures as the following:

> Behold, I show you a mystery: We shall not all sleep [die], but we shall all be changed, in a moment, in the twinkling of an eye, at the last trump; for the trumpet shall sound, and the dead shall be raised incorruptible, and we shall be changed [all, dead and living, in one instant].
>
> For this corruptible must put on incorruption, and this mortal must put on immortality (1 Corinthians 15:51-53).

> For the Lord himself shall descend from heaven with a shout, with the voice of the archangel, and with the trump of God; and the dead in Christ shall rise first; then we which are alive and remain shall be caught up together with them in the clouds, to meet the Lord in the air, and so shall we ever be with the Lord. Wherefore comfort one another with these words (1 Thessalonians 4:16-18).

trump of God; and the dead in Christ shall rise first; then we which are alive and remain shall be caught up together with them in the clouds, to meet the Lord in the air, and so shall we ever be with the Lord. Wherefore comfort one another with these words (1 Thessalonians 4:16-18).

4

What Holds Christ in the Heavens?

In spite of its prominence in the life and doctrine of the early church, the Second Coming of Christ is becoming an increasingly remote future event of negligible interest to today's average Christian. Furthermore, many sincere Christians for whom the rapture was once a "blessed hope," now argue that to give it any prominence would needlessly divert our attention from the social and political action we ought to be involved in here and now. Their hope of heaven has taken second place to a new conviction that the Christian's primary responsibility is to improve this present world, even to joining with the ungodly in good causes for the mutual benefit of all mankind. Certainly the Christian's sense of duty is rightly stirred by such appeals to conscience as the following from Robert G. Grant, a leading Washington, D.C.-based Christian political/social activist:

> The ultimate responsibility for the destruction of America's moral values during recent generations, in my judgment, will be laid by God at the front steps of America's churches.
> Biblical Christians clearly abandoned the battlefield and allowed evil to occupy it by default. . . . Evangelicals have often had to play "catch up" to Roman Catholics, Mormons, and other value-oriented activists.[1]

Such a statement, while it may contain some truth, nevertheless raises a number of legitimate questions. When did the early church ever enter the social/political activist "battlefield" that he says the modern church "abandoned"? In fact it never did. Was the early church, therefore, to blame for the widespread immorality and idolatry that persisted in spite of valiant efforts to evangelize the Roman world? Was it because the church failed in its mission that Christians by the thousands were thrown to the lions and impaled upon crosses?

Is the Church to Blame for Worldwide Evil?

How much blame for what clearly proceeds from the evil hearts of the ungodly can rightly be placed upon Christians, even when they have failed to be "salt and light" in the world (whatever that might mean)? Exactly what is the duty of the church and of individual Christians beyond living Christlike lives and faithfully proclaiming the gospel to the world? Doesn't it seem odd that Christians can be blamed for the sad state of the world—but the non-Christian is depicted as eager to obey God if only the message were presented to him in the right way? The COR literature declares:

> The world is in desperate trouble and western civilization hangs in the balance because the Church has not fulfilled its God-ordained leadership role on earth of demonstrating how God wants His world to be run according to His biblical principles and laws.[2]

In fact, signing the COR *Manifesto* and acting upon it is presented as urgent because "Millions of souls and the survival of western civilization hang in the balance."[3] It is the church's fault that immorality is rampant in American society, that the dollar is weak, and that war threatens in the Middle East. We can presumably even prevent the Great Tribulation, the rise of the Antichrist, and Armageddon. And if those things do occur, it will be the fault of the church. Reconstructionist author George Grant writes:

> The state-sanctioned despotism that is now rapidly

consuming all our hard-won freedoms in America would not have even been *possible* if Christians had not abandoned the doctrine of Christ's Lordship.

If we had not shied away from His theocracy, the horrors of modern America would never have occurred.[4]

Grant is not referring only to Christ's lordship over His church and individual Christians, but to the church somehow enforcing His lordship on society as a whole, including non-Christians. Such a view has a certain appeal to our pride. Although it blames us, it also credits us with being able to solve the world's problems. There is not one syllable of biblical support, however, to suggest that "Western civilization hangs in the balance" because the church has failed to rescue the world from ruin by showing the ungodly how to be blessed and prospered by God through obedience to biblical principles. The world is in trouble because the human heart, which is in rebellion against its Creator, is "deceitful above all things and desperately wicked" (Jeremiah 17:9) and the vast majority of men refuse to repent. As H. Wayne House and Thomas Ice remind us:

> Romans 1 teaches that the reason society goes downhill is because men are sinners and they manifest their rebellion against God by producing an ungodly culture and society. It is not because believers did not become active in politics.[5]

To the Greeks on Mars Hill, the center of human genius of its day, Paul declared that God "commandeth all men everywhere to repent." That same command holds today. Why must we repent? In order to salvage the world economy and bring financial stability and peace among nations? No! But because God "hath appointed a day, in the which he will judge the world in righteousness by that man whom he hath ordained, whereof he hath given assurance unto all men, in that he hath raised him from the dead" (Acts 17:30,31). To suggest that the Great Commission calls upon the church to lead the world out of its social, economic, and political problems perverts the gospel, gives the world an excuse for its rebellion, provides a false diagnosis, and proposes a wrong solution.

God is disciplining His own people (both Israel and the church) in this present age, but He is not straightening out the world. The time for that will come during the Great Tribulation when the church is in heaven. It is therefore a great error to imagine that the function of the church is to correct and improve secular society. No support for that idea can be found in Scripture at all.

Old Testament prophets boldly rebuked kings for their sin—but their rebukes were directed almost exclusively at the kings of Israel. When the heads of other nations were rebuked, it was generally in relation to their public defiance of God and their treatment of God's chosen people. John the Baptist rebuked Herod Antipas for taking his half-brother Philip's wife. While the Herods were in a sense monarchs directly over the Jews, they were not Jewish themselves (Josephus says they were Edomites). Could it be that John, who was imprisoned and later beheaded by Herod because of this reproof, may have needlessly cut his ministry to Israel short by aiming his remarks at the wrong target?

The Example of Christ

Christ never directed His corrective ministry at government figures, either Herodian or Roman. When told by the Pharisees that Herod sought to kill Him, our Lord did not take the occasion to inveigh against Herod's great wickedness. He simply showed His contempt for Herod and the fact that He had no fear of his power: "Go ye, and tell that fox, 'Behold, I cast out devils, and I do cures today and tomorrow, and the third day I shall be perfected' " (Luke 13:31-33). So far as we know, this was the only public recognition that Jesus ever gave of Herod's existence until He stood silent before him in judgment.

On the other hand, Christ sharply and frequently reproved Israel's religious leaders. Of course, He indicted the common people as well with their sin, but more compassionately. From a survey of Scripture, it would seem that today's Christian leaders ought to publicly rebuke those government leaders who profess to be

Christians. President Reagan, for example, who had declared himself to be a born-again Christian, should be called upon to renounce publicly his involvement in astrology and occultism, and to lead the nation in repentance for its widespread practice of sorcery.* The personal godliness of individual believers and Christian leaders ought to stand as an example to the world—not a model that they can follow, but one that convicts them of their sin and drives them to the cross of Christ in repentance.

The increasing political and social activism of today's church seems paradoxical, if not hypocritical, alongside its careless disregard of doctrinal purity. The unwillingness of its leaders to involve themselves in the necessary process of correcting one another can only encourage the growing contempt for truth. The resultant blindness is evident in the fact that at the same time they are waging an important battle against pornography, abortion, and homosexuality, many Christian leaders are giving their blessing to the equally evil and more seductive elements of humanistic psychology that are infecting the church. In its zeal to selectively impose biblical standards upon the world, the church is neglecting the only sure foundation for morality—its commitment to sound theology—and thereby assuring its own moral corruption.

We have departed from Christ's example and, in fact, exactly reversed the course He followed. His total silence toward an evil Caesar and the corrupt and oppressive Roman presence in Palestine contrasted sharply with His continual and stinging reproof of Israel's religious leaders. Both Paul, who testified under oath of his obedience to Roman law ("nor yet against Caesar, have I offended any thing at all"—Acts 25:8), and Peter urged Christians as "strangers and pilgrims" in this world to "be subject unto" and "submit to" and pray for earthly governments and to set an example of "good works" (Romans 13:1-10; 1 Peter 2:11-20). Obedience, holy and exemplary living, self-sacrifice, loving one's neighbor as

---

* For substantiation of this charge, see Dave Hunt and T.A. McMahon, *America: The Sorcerer's New Apprentice* (Harvest House Publishers, 1988).

oneself, preaching the gospel of Jesus Christ, using the sword of God's Word, and praying seem to be the weapons of transformation which the Christian is to aim at this world.

Render to Caesar ... and to God

While it may disappoint some readers, it is beyond the scope of this book to deal in depth with questions of Christian social/political involvement. In fact, while such concerns are currently given great importance, the Bible itself scarcely addresses such issues directly. This in itself would indicate that the present importance being given to Christian involvement in protests and politics is far out-of-balance scripturally and may thus be leading the church into dangerous waters.

"Render to Caesar the things which are Caesar's, and to God the things which are God's," is as close as our Lord comes to addressing the currently stimulating topic of the Christian's social/political duties in this present evil world. He indicates that these two spheres, Caesar's and God's, both exist, but are separate and thus involve separate duties. Nor does He give a detailed explanation, much less provide even a general plan for Christian social and political action. It is tempting, but certainly not prudent, to go beyond Scripture in discussing such issues.

One reason why our Lord gave no specifics could well be because of the diversity of political systems and regimes which He knew would be faced by His followers down through the centuries. Obviously this bears upon the questions raised above concerning the Christian's obligations for social and political involvement. While it is possible, for example, to protest publicly against immorality or bad government in the United States, it is not possible to do so in many other countries. Of course anything is *possible*. Believers in Albania *could* stage a protest march. It would be very brief and would surely mean the summary execution, probably on the spot, of all participants.

Before getting involved, the Albanian believers would have to ask themselves whether the likely results of their efforts would warrant the great cost in lives for a church that has such a tiny membership.

Perhaps this hypothetical example could cause us to ponder the temporal and eternal results of protests and political activism here in the United States, especially those orchestrated during the past eight years with such high hopes. Have the results been worth it all, or have we lost our balance and perspective?

In His "render unto Caesar" statement, Christ is apparently leaving social and political involvement both to individual conscience and to practical considerations. In whatever is done, however, the eternal destiny of souls must, of course, be given priority over the temporal state of their bodies. Eternity must always have top priority in the allocation of time and resources.

Our natural compassion and the urge to do something concrete to improve this fallen world can lead us into attitudes and actions that may seem to be helpful at the moment but in fact may not be wise for the long term, especially for eternity. It is essential not to go beyond Scripture, and in particular to note some important distinctions. Each individual believer is to manifest Christian charity at all times toward every person whose life and circumstances he is able to affect. There is no teaching in Scripture, however—explicit or implied—concerning organized efforts to influence government policy and practice. The fact that Jesus both commanded and exemplified the former, but neither recommended nor involved Himself or His followers in the latter, ought to weigh heavily as we consider our options.

It is not our intention to attempt to draw from Scripture what only a microscope might find there, but to deal with what is plain on its pages. Surely it cannot be denied that the overwhelming emphasis in the New Testament is upon heaven. Neither can it be denied that this vision has been largely lost in the evangelical church today. The purpose of this book is to restore that vision and passion. If it fails to deal in depth with social and political concerns that are dear to the hearts of readers, then at least the same complaint will have to be made against Christ Himself and those who wrote the New Testament, as well as against the Holy Spirit who inspired them.

For those who wish to probe what we cannot deal with here, there are many good books, such as Charles Colson's *Kingdoms in Conflict.* When all is said and done, however, even Colson—in spite of an excellent discussion of the issues—is short on real answers. And so he should be if he is to be true to the Word of God in dealing with difficult issues upon which it makes no definitive pronouncements. He does point out clearly what we are attempting to emphasize: that "when Christ commanded His followers to 'seek first the kingdom of God,' He was exhorting them to seek to be ruled by God . . . the Christian's goal is not to strive to rule, but *to be ruled* [by God]."[6]

Arguments Against the Imminent-Rapture Hope

Colson goes on to warn of "the ever-present temptation to usher in the kingdom of God by political means," and adds: "Yet this is the temptation to which the church . . . has most commonly succumbed, and certainly this is its greatest temptation today."[7] As we have already noted, increasing numbers of Christians are sincerely involved in attempting to usher in the kingdom of God in the absence of the King because they are convinced that Christ cannot return until the church has accomplished this goal. It is in large part a concern for the very real danger which this delusion poses that has motivated the writing of the present volume.

Of course such teaching represents an assault upon the belief in an imminent rapture. Setting a condition for Christ's return (and a condition that is very unlikely to be fulfilled) removes any possibility of its imminence and thus robs the church of the purification and other benefits we have discussed which result from such a hope. And if Colson is right, then those who have embraced the kingdom/dominion teaching have been seduced by the *greatest temptation* of the present hour—a temptation that carries added danger if we are indeed in the last days just prior to Christ's rapture of the church and the revealing of the Antichrist.

There are those who do not go so far as to imagine they can set up the kingdom of God prior to Christ's return, but they have been seduced by appealing slogans such as: "Help us change the world for Christ!" Most Christians never stop to ask what is really meant by such a phrase, but have a vague idea that somehow through their godly influence Christians will make the world a better place in which to live. Such a goal, in fact, is often presented as though it were part of the Great Commission that tells us to preach the gospel and make disciples.

Some may presume that the world will be "changed" through worldwide revival. Concerning this "revival," we are repeatedly told by charismatic leaders that we are either on the brink or already in the middle of it. We would all like to believe that we are going to "convert the world for Christ," yet Christ Himself told His disciples, in response to their direct question, that only a few would ever respond to His message (Matthew 7:13,14; Luke 13:23-28). That statement can hardly be dismissed as "negative" or "pessimistic" since it came from the lips of our Lord Himself. Such emotionally charged terms carry great weight in some circles, but they cannot nullify the fact that our Lord knew whereof He spoke.

While we may not like the social and political implications, we cannot escape the fact that the first-century Christians never entertained the vain and unbiblical hope of "changing the world for Christ"—nor even of "winning the world for Christ," inspiring as such ambitions may seem today. Instead, they were determined to win a multitude of individuals *out of the world* to citizenship in heaven, and they succeeded in converting about ten percent of the Roman Empire (far from the whole world) in the process. *Heaven* was both the great hope that Christ left with His disciples and an integral part of the gospel preached by the early church. In fact, the very heart of the gospel—Christ's call to "follow me"—requires a choice between this earth and the heaven to which He has gone and to which He leads.

Another common objection is the idea that if we are expecting Christ to return at any moment to take us home to heaven, we will not be prepared for the persecutions of the Great Tribulation, should the church be required to endure them. That argument is proven invalid, of course, by the very fact that the early church, which undoubtedly lived with such an expectancy, nevertheless stood up to terrible persecution. In fact, the early Christians avoided social/political activism yet were at the same time prepared for their trials because they believed what Christ had declared: that they were not of this world just as He was not, and that because they belonged to Him the world would treat them as it had treated Him. It would seem that no one would be less prepared for the Great Tribulation than those who entertain the vain hope that Christians are going to become popular leaders whom the world will enthusiastically follow in building a new society.

Others suggest that the expectation of Christ's soon return would hinder evangelism and the fulfillment of the Great Commission. In fact, the church of the first century, for whom the hope of Christ's soon return was most real, is still the greatest example in history of effective evangelistic zeal. Quickly and fearlessly, in the face of paganism and fanatical opposition, the early church spread Christianity throughout the known world of its day. Surely there is no greater incentive for aggressively preaching the gospel than to believe that our opportunity to evangelize the world and the possibility for the lost to respond and be saved could end at any moment with the Lord's sudden return.

Can Christ Come Only for a Unified and Mature Church?

The current swing of the pendulum away from a belief in the imminent return of Christ has been accompanied by the growing conviction that this event is dependent upon the accomplishment by the church of some great task or the attainment by God's people to some higher state of spiritual perfection. One of the most dangerous errors arising out of this view is the increasingly accepted belief that the church must attain a high degree of worldwide unity before Christ can return. Earl Paulk, a prolific author, is one of the foremost proponents of this theory. He writes:

> Christians must know the reality of Jesus' prayer recorded in John 17. Where is the unity in the body of Christ today? . . . We must come to some recognition of oneness in Christ so that His return will be for a unified body.[8]
> I am certain that Christ cannot return to earth until His Church is joined in spiritual unity of faith (1 Thessalonians 5:4). Who would He come back to receive as

His bride? The Baptists? The Methodists? The Pentecostals?[9]

One looks in vain for logic in such an argument. Obviously denominational labels are nonexistent in heaven. Surely the fact that they have been called Baptists, Methodists, Presbyterians, or Catholics or any other of a hundred names has not barred true Christians from being taken to heaven when they died during the past 1900 years. The promise, "Absent from the body, present with the Lord," has not been suspended because Christians have belonged to different denominations. Neither would varying denominational affiliations bar true Christians from that glorious meeting in the air.

Nevertheless, it is very appealing to imagine that we are destined to accomplish *something special* to bring Christ back, especially if that something is to "restore" the apostles and prophets and the miracles and power known to the church in the Book of Acts. Such was the enticing teaching which came out of the 1948-50 Pentecostal "Latter Rain" revival that began in Canada and spread throughout the United States. This "restoration" hope heavily influenced today's charismatic renewal that has spilled over denominational boundaries and even into the Catholic Church.

Arguing in favor of Latter Rain teaching, Paulk tells us: "Until the Elijah spirit returns to the Church, Jesus Christ cannot come again. . . . Jesus cannot come until the apostolic ministry is re-established. We are now in the period of the prophets. . . . but the period of the apostolic ministry will soon return also. . . . God must have a Church that is mature. . . ."[10] His younger brother and associate, Don, writes:

> We take an orthodox view of Christ's Return. We do believe He *will* return. But He has stated He will return to a mature Bride, His Church that is prepared to receive Him.[11]

Far from setting such a condition for His return, Christ seemed to indicate that He would come for a sleeping church. In the parable of the ten virgins, the five wise as well as the five foolish "slumbered and slept" as the bridegroom delayed his coming (Matthew 25:5). Rather than stating that He would wait until His bride was prepared to receive Him before returning, Christ warned His disciples that He would come when they did not expect Him (Matthew 24:44; Luke 12:40). While every Christian should pursue personal holiness and work for church renewal, it is a serious error to imagine that Christ is held hostage in heaven by our failure.

The Manifestation of the Sons of God

Out of the Latter Rain teaching came the "Manifested Sons of God" movement. Though criticized severely from the very beginning for its extremes by such established Pentecostal groups as the Assemblies of God,[12] and largely confined to Pentecostalism's fanatical fringe, Manifested Sons teaching had an important formative influence upon the charismatic movement. That influence, after a period of relative dormancy, is rapidly growing stronger once again and even spreading into mainstream denominations.

As with most heresies, this movement's foundation is an extreme interpretation of an isolated Scripture taken out of context: "For the earnest expectation of the creature waiteth for the manifestation of the sons of God" (Romans 8:19). According to "visions" and "prophecies" during the 1948-50 revival, this "manifestation of the sons of God" is to be fulfilled in an elite group of "overcomers." Without the resurrection and prior to Christ's return, they will, so it is taught, manifest immortality in their physical bodies because of their great faith and holiness.[13] Impervious to death or disease, these super-Christians will conquer the world and establish the kingdom of God. Only then will Christ return—not to catch away the church to heaven, but to reign over the earthly kingdom that the "overcomers" have prepared for Him.

There are some obvious and extremely serious consequences of such teaching. The true Christ, as the Bible so clearly states, is going to rapture Christians away from earth "to meet the Lord in the air" (1 Thessalonians 4:17) on their way to heaven. The above teaching, however, as already noted, is preparing a badly deceived people to meet a "Christ" with their feet planted on earth—a "Christ" who does not catch them away to heaven but who comes to reign over the kingdom they have established in his name. He can only be the Antichrist. Nor can we avoid the conclusion that the kingdom he takes over will have been produced by the cooperative effort of Christians and non-Christians who joined in social and political action to better this world.

In spite of their rejection of the major Pentecostal-oriented Manifested Sons of God teachings, the Reconstructionists nevertheless adopt a similar interpretation of Romans 8:19. Writing in *The Journal of Christian Reconstruction*, Presbyterian pastor Kenneth J. Gentry, Jr. declares: "The whole creation awaits the godly dominion of the New Creation saints of God (Rom. 8:19-23)."[14] Gentry goes on to argue that this manifestation must occur before Christ returns. This teaching of "dominion theology," which will be explained later, is foundational to the Coalition on Revival's *Manifesto for the Christian Church* and reflects the considerable influence upon COR of certain appealing Reconstructionist and Manifested Sons of God teachings. Apparently unaware of this influence, an august body of evangelical leaders, as we have already noted, has joined the Coalition on Revival. This surprising development has provided questionable Reconstructionist/Manifested Sons related views with a new credibility and far wider dissemination throughout the church than would otherwise have been possible.

Although they are not Pentecostal or charismatic, Reconstructionists are working with such groups because charismatic television and radio networks provide an effective means of propagating related Reconstructionist beliefs. Gary North has openly acknowledged using the charismatics to this end.[15] On their part the charismatics are apparently happy with their new partners because the Reconstructionists provide the intellectual and academic credibility that has been in such short supply within the charismatic movement since its inception.

Reconstructionist scholarship has contributed the missing apologetics and theological base to help support today's revival of certain Manifested Sons of God teachings. And that peculiar doctrine can hardly be taken lightly because it has influenced in varying degree those charismatic leaders who control most Christian television in North America today. Gary North is convinced that a Reconstructionist partnership with "the charismatic telecommunications system" will transform "the whole shape of American religious life. . . ." He goes on to say:

> The holy rollers are rolling less and broadcasting more than anyone could have guessed a decade ago. A technological miracle is with us, and the Pentecostals are alone making good use of it.[16]

> The growing alliance between charismatics and Reconstructionists has [caused] . . . critics [to] worry about the fact that Pentecostalism's infantry is at last being armed with Reconstructionism's field artillery. They *should* be worried. This represents one of the most fundamental realignments in U.S. Protestant church history.[17]

What About the "Restoration of All Things"?

The charismatic/Reconstructionist new alliance is gaining increasing acceptance for two beliefs: one, that the church must itself be "restored" to a state of super-spirituality, and two, that it must effect a "restoration" to both God and man of everything that was lost through Adam's fall. "God waits for us to complete His plan," declares Earl Paulk. "God cannot move again until we fulfill our mission on earth."[18] God's hands are thus literally tied by our failure to perform. Referring to a critic's argument against his teaching that such a "restoration" must take place before Christ can return, Paulk writes:

> I would like to hear his explanation of what Scripture says holds Christ in the heavens (Acts 3:20,21). Certain events must take place on earth before Christ returns. . . .
> I personally believe that though many signs point to the soon coming of Christ, other things yet need to take place before the actual event.[19]

How an obviously faulty interpretation of a single Scripture can be so widely accepted that it becomes the basis for an entire movement is amazing indeed. The favorite proof text to which Paulk refers is a classic example: "Whom the heaven must receive until the times of restitution [Gr. *apokatastaseos*, meaning restoration] of all things, which God hath spoken by the mouth of all his holy prophets since the world began" (Acts 3:20,21). Typical of the misinterpretation of this Scripture was a recent *Christian Life* article titled "Search for the New Testament Church." Prefacing the article was a comment on Acts 3:20 inserted by the magazine editors which ended with this sentence: "The Messiah, Jesus Christ, he [Peter] said, could not return until this restoration took place."[20]

On the contrary, Peter presents three factors which counter today's "restoration" doctrine. It is quite obvious, first of all, that the phrase "the times of restitution of all things" does not indicate that the "restitution" has already occurred, but that the "times" in which the prophesied restoration will take place have finally come. Peter did not declare that the "heaven must receive" Jesus, until the restoration of all things has been accomplished, but until the *time for that to happen* has arrived. As the Revised Standard Version puts it, "until the time for establishing all that God spoke," or as the New English Bible says, "until the time of universal restoration comes."

Secondly, the fact that Christ remains in heaven until the time for the restoration indicates that He leaves heaven specifically to accomplish this restoration in its appointed time. Thus it is clear that Christ returns *not* because all things have already been restored *by the church*, but in order to effect this restoration *Himself*. It is "the *presence of the Lord*" (Acts 3:19) which brings about the restoration—not the "restoration of all things" already accomplished by the church which then brings the Lord's bodily return. Thus, Christ does not return to earth *as a result* of the restoration, but *to accomplish it*.

Peter is clearly referring to the numerous Scriptures (such as Zechariah chapters 12–14) that prophesy a sudden and powerful intervention of the Lord personally upon this earth in order to restore "all things." This is not a task that the church can perform, but something which only the Lord Himself can accomplish. Yet Paulk writes enthusiastically of "the challenge to us . . . the greatest task ever given to mankind—the establishment of the Kingdom of God on earth!"[21] While the idea that *man* can establish the kingdom of *God* is enticing, it is neither logical nor biblical.

The Restoration Is to Israel, Not to the Church

Thirdly, it is equally clear that Peter, under the inspiration of the Holy Spirit, was not addressing the church, but Israel. His audience was a throng of religious Jews; and the restoration to which he referred was specifically that which God had *already promised to Israel by His prophets.* Peter addressed the excited Jewish multitude that day concerning the question he knew was uppermost in their minds. It was the very same question the disciples had asked Jesus after His resurrection: "Lord, wilt thou at this time restore again the kingdom *to Israel?*" (Acts 1:6). Here was the great hope of God's chosen people—the restoration of the Davidic kingdom, with the Messiah reigning over the whole earth from David's throne, a consummation which had been repeatedly foretold by the Hebrew prophets. The angel Gabriel, too, upon announcing the coming virgin birth of Jesus to Mary, had confirmed these Old Testament prophecies with these words:

> He [Jesus] shall be great, and shall be called the Son of the Highest; and the Lord God shall give unto him the throne of his father David; and he shall reign over the house of Jacob forever, and of his kingdom there shall be no end (Luke 1:32,33).

This restoration of the kingdom *to Israel,* which Peter reminded them, "God hath spoken by the mouth of all his holy prophets since the world began" (Acts 3:21), was the subject most dear to the hearts of those religious Jews gathered at the temple for worship.

Peter's sermon had nothing to do with a restoration of the twentieth-century church to first-century power, or with the Bride of Christ becoming pure and spotless, as today's restoration teachers claim. Such a topic is completely foreign to the context and would have been meaningless to the audience Peter addressed in Jerusalem that day.

Peter's inspired sermon is also proof that Israel was not to be cast off at A.D. 70 or any other time. Yet Earl Paulk criticizes those who "continue to be sympathetic toward national Israel as God's chosen people."[22] As we have already noted, the teaching is gaining increasing acceptability today that the church is now Israel, having replaced that nation because of its rejection of Christ.

On the contrary, the specific promises made by the Hebrew prophets to national Israel must and will be fulfilled. The "restitution of all things" relates specifically to Abraham's descendants after they have returned to their land in the last days. Moreover, Christ Himself will intervene from heaven in order to accomplish this. At that time, recognizing the crucified and resurrected One as the Messiah they have so long rejected, "all Israel shall be saved" (Zechariah 12:10–13:1; Romans 11:26; etc.).

Must the Church Be Purged for Christ to Return?

The further unbiblical idea is spreading that the church must not only be united and mature, and victorious over death and disease, but it must also be purged and without blemish before Christ can return. In a classic "Manifested Sons" misapplication of Scripture, Maxwell Whyte writes:

> The restored Church, the Bride of Christ, will be presented to Him a glorious Church, not having spot or wrinkle or any such thing, but holy and without blemish (Ephesians 5:27). . . .
> The Bride must be perfected with no spiritual, mental or physical sickness when the Bridegroom comes for her.[23]

Why must the church on earth at the time Christ returns have attained to spiritual perfection in order to join at the marriage supper of the Lamb millions of Christians who, down through the centuries, died and were taken to heaven without attaining such a state? Yet this erroneous teaching is spreading rapidly and thereby robbing multitudes of Christians of the hope of Christ's imminent return. Some teach a partial rapture that will involve only a "purified remnant." Again this is unreasonable as well as unscriptural since all Christians who die are taken immediately to heaven ("absent from the body, present with the Lord"), so long as they truly are born again. Why should those alive at the rapture be denied entrance to heaven for a lack of perfection that did not prevent millions of other Christians from entering it at death?

To support such a view, reference is generally made (in addition to Ephesians 5:27 quoted by Whyte) to the Scripture, "His wife hath made herself ready. And to her was granted that she should be arrayed in fine linen, clean and white; for the fine linen is the righteousness of saints" (Revelation 19:7,8). It is the entire church, however, which is referred to—a church which is complete in heaven and is presented to Christ "not having spot, or wrinkle." John is certainly not speaking of that small fraction of the church of all ages that would happen to be alive on earth at the time of the rapture. Therefore, in whatever manner this final purification and readiness of "his wife" is accomplished, it must be the common experience of all Christians of all ages and something which is obviously not fully accomplished individually on earth.

Although every true Christian would surely desire always to be in such a state, it is no more required of those alive when Christ returns to have purified themselves on earth and to have dressed themselves in robes white and clean in order to be raptured than it was required of those who lived before in order to be taken to heaven when they died. Consequently, this robing in pure garments must take place in heaven. "We must all appear before the judgment seat of Christ" (2 Corinthians 5:10), where He will deal individually with each of us. The fire of God's purification will test "every man's work . . ." (1 Corinthians 3:13), the dross will be burned up, and He will clothe us in pure righteousness for the wedding supper.

The false teaching that the church must be purified here upon earth in order to fit her for heaven, while by no means as heretical, contains some obvious and significant similarities to Catholicism's doctrine of purgatory. The latter requires each individual to be purged through suffering for his sins here upon earth. Whatever purification of sins is still lacking at the time of death must be accomplished thereafter in a place called "purgatory" in order for the soul to gain entrance into heaven. Both teachings make heaven so elusive a hope that it ceases to be the motivating power it once was for the early church.

The Fading Hope of Heaven

While a discussion of other facets of the doctrine of purgatory must be deferred to a later chapter, it is appropriate at this point to understand that the development of this teaching dimmed the hope of heaven. While Catholics, of course, believe in heaven, few if any expect to go there when they die. Instead, purgatory is their grim hope. Almost any Catholic will testify to the fact that his great hope is to awaken in purgatory after he dies. He will at least have escaped hell, and eventually he will be released to heaven.

Not only does purgatory loom so large that any hope of heaven must be long deferred, but it also destroys the biblical teaching of the rapture. If we cannot be taken directly to heaven when we die because of the need to spend time in purgatory, then of course neither can we be taken directly to heaven without dying, in the manner Christ promised and Paul further explained. The hope that we will "be caught up . . . to meet the Lord in the air" and the Scriptures which promised it had to be suppressed. Consequently, the rapture is still unknown in the Catholic Church today—and the growing denial of its importance (or even of the rapture itself) among Protestants is a big step along the seductive ecumenical path toward reunion with Rome.

The simultaneous reuniting of all the dead in Christ with their transformed bodies in one glorious resurrection fell by the wayside as well. Those in purgatory, having varying degrees of guilt and thus varying lengths of time required for their "purging," could not all be transformed and taken to heaven at once. They would have to be resurrected individually over many thousands of years as each attained the necessary degree of purification for entrance into heaven.

Of course the Scriptures contain no such teaching. God's Word declares on the contrary that the resurrection and the rapture will take place simultaneously for all Christians, "in a moment, in the twinkling of an eye." Yet this once-vibrant hope began to fade when Christ did not return in the "little while" that the early church had expected He would. By the end of the fourth century the doctrine of the rapture was generally unknown.

Nor did it serve the selfish interests of a church that was living in lavish luxury and was preoccupied with building its own earthly kingdom and increasing its power over mankind to encourage a recovery of that expectancy.

For centuries the rapture remained a forgotten doctrine as Roman Catholicism dominated the church—a doctrine which even the Reformation leaders such as Calvin and Luther failed to recover. This hope was not revived on any significant scale until the early 1800s. Why this was the case is extremely important for us to understand if we are to confront intelligently and scripturally the related issues facing us today.

We have a rich heritage in the past, of which most Christians are not aware. Ignorance of church history leaves us vulnerable to current errors, which almost always have their roots in previous important events. Therefore, in order better to understand how the hope of heaven was lost and recovered and to clarify growing controversy surrounding the rapture and related issues, we must take a brief excursion into the past. It will, even for those who imagine that church history must be dull, prove to be surprisingly informative, fascinating, and inspiring.

5

Bringing Heaven Down to Earth

As far as conscience before God will allow, Christians are obliged to cooperate with the lawfully instituted civil authority. They are to submit to its judgment, support it by their taxes, and give it respect and honor in its sphere (Romans 13), and pray "for kings, and for all that are in authority; that we may lead a quiet and peaceable life in all godliness and honesty" (1 Timothy 2:2). This the early Christians did, and the furthest thought from their hearts and minds was today's ambition to take over the reins of government and to Christianize the world. Their consuming desire was to win as many individuals as possible out of the world to faith in Christ. At the same time, they prayed for God's blessing upon the civil authorities and were rightfully submissive so long as government did not interfere with their worship and the preaching of the gospel. In spite of their civil obedience, however, they were regarded with suspicion and hatred and were imprisoned and killed.

It is helpful to understand that the early Christians were persecuted under the Roman Empire not so much because they believed in Jesus Christ, but because they were too "narrow-minded and dogmatic" to include the pagan deities in their faith as well. In that respect the pluralistic society of that day had much in common with our own, for which the saying "We're all taking different roads to get to the same place" pretty much sums up the popular religious sentiment. The exclusivity of Christianity with its claim that Jesus was the only Savior and way to heaven, and that all other gods were false, was extremely frustrating for the broadminded Romans. They were ready to extend worship to any bona fide deity and could not understand the refusal of the followers of this "new religion" to do likewise.

It was not surprising, then, that the idolatrous and superstitious Romans began to attribute calamities of all kinds to the growing sect of Christians. It was assumed that the anger of the gods was aroused by the blasphemous "atheism" of Christianity's refusal to acknowledge or honor the popular deities. Writing early in the third century, Tertullian complained of the tendency to blame and persecute Christians for allegedly causing every natural disaster:

> If the Tiber reaches the walls, if the Nile does not rise to the fields, if the sky doesn't move or the earth does, if there is famine, if there is plague, the cry is at once: "The Christians to the lions!"[1]

Son of a centurion, a successful Roman lawyer and convert to Christianity from stoicism, Tertullian was one of the church's first and most prominent theologians and apologists. He openly attacked every facet of pagan culture and religion. Pointing out the vast contrast between the Christian way of life and that which was fostered by the state, he argued the superiority of the former. In those early days there was no question in anyone's mind that Christians represented a worldview and way of life completely at odds with all other religions and philosophies. The followers of Christ were therefore treated as aliens in a foreign and hostile society.

Systematic Persecution Begins Under Nero

The wrath of the State was first directed against the Christians in a systematic way because Nero needed a scapegoat for the Great Fire of Rome in A.D. 64. Rumor had it (perhaps erroneously) that the fire had been ordered by the emperor himself. One of the few eyewitness historians of that day was Tacitus. Of the beginning of deliberately planned official persecution against the Christians under the Roman emperors, Tacitus made these interesting comments in his *Annals and Histories*:

> Consequently, to get rid of the report [that he had ordered the fire], Nero fastened the guilt and inflicted the most exquisite tortures on a class hated for their abominations, called Christians by the populace.
>
> Christus, from whom the name had its origin, suffered the extreme penalty during the reign of Tiberius at the hands of one of our procurators, Pontius Pilatus, and a deadly superstition, thus checked for the moment, again broke out not only in Judaea, the first source of the evil, but also in the City [Rome], where all things hideous and shameful from every part of the world meet and become popular.
>
> Accordingly, an arrest was first made of all who confessed [Christ]; then, upon their information, an immense multitude was convicted, not so much of the crime of arson, as of hatred of the human race. Mockery of every sort was added to their deaths. Covered with the skins of beasts, they were torn by dogs and perished, or were nailed to crosses, or were doomed to the flames.[2]

Though the immediate persecution spawned by Nero's false charge against the Christians affected only Rome and eventually subsided, the fact that the precedent had once been set made it easier to repeat.[3] The false charges that arose under persecution served to further arouse widespread suspicions. It was therefore not surprising that by the time vague reports of Christian belief in "universal love" and the celebration of the eucharistic meal had been filtered through the popular imagination, they had been transmogrified into tales of incest and cannibalism. This ready reserve of ill will toward the Christians was then available to be tapped as the occasion warranted, whether to advance some pet policy of an emperor or simply to satisfy the desire of a private party to inflict harm on an individual Christian.

A more persistent, carefully calculated, and seemingly logical and lawful basis for persecution arose during the reign of Domitian (81-96), a persecution which is described in the writings of Tacitus. Political orator and later Proconsul of Asia, Tacitus preserved his own life and office by holding his tongue during Domitian's reign of terror, except when the emperor demanded flattery. While the Christians were the direct target of special persecution, everyone lived in fear of the emperor's whims and wrath. In language reminiscent of Communist regimes in our own day, Tacitus tells how friendship and trust were destroyed by the presence of unknown informers everywhere. "We should have lost memory as well as voice, had it been as easy to forget as to keep silence," he wrote after Domitian's welcome assassination in 96 provided the opportunity to keep what had apparently been a determined inner vow to tell at last what he remembered.

Far more enthusiastic than his predecessors in accepting the flattering ascription of divine status that had become the traditional homage due to the emperor, Domitian referred to himself as "Master and God." The traditional oath "by the genius [guardian spirit] of the emperor," together with the worship of the emperor's image, became a strict requirement in an official test of loyalty, which conscientious Christians regarded as blasphemous and therefore refused to profess. Some even felt that Domitian was the prophesied Antichrist. A letter of Pliny the Younger, governor of Bithynia, to the Emperor Trajan reveals the test he imposed to determine whether those accused were Christians or not:

> Those who denied they were, or had ever been, Christians, who repeated after me an invocation to the Gods, and offered adoration, with wine and frankincense, to your image, which I had ordered to be brought for that purpose, together with those of the Gods, and who finally cursed Christ—none of which acts, it is said, those who are really Christians can be forced into performing—these I thought it proper to discharge.[4]

During the second century local outbreaks of violence against Christians led to the martyrdoms of such church leaders as Ignatius of Antioch, Polycarp of Smyrna, and Justin Martyr. The mounting persecution served to reinforce the Christians' sense of being strangers and pilgrims who, though temporarily in the world, were really citizens of heaven. The hatred vented against Christians also intensified their sense of identification with their Savior in His rejection and suffering. Moreover, persecution helped to purify the church, ensuring that it was composed only of those who genuinely knew and loved the Lord. There was everything to lose and nothing to gain in this life by joining the early church. Those to whom love of God and truth, and life everlasting in the world to come, were not worth the attendant shame and scorn, imprisonment, torture, and death in this world were hardly likely to call themselves Christians.

Foreigners on Earth—Citizens of Heaven

The example of holy living and unflinching loyalty to Christ in the face of torture and death, however, proved in the end to be an inspiration that drew earnest seekers after truth into the fold. As Tertullian put it near the end of that century, "The blood of the martyrs is the seed of the church." He reminded his pagan opponents: "Day by day you groan over the ever-increasing number of Christians. Your constant cry is that your state is beset by us, that Christians are [everywhere]. . . ."[5]

The following from a church leader of the time reveals how the Christians in the second century, though they were multiplying in numbers, saw themselves in relation to secular society. It is hardly the perspective of those who believe their purpose is to take over this present world:

> But while they dwell in Greek or barbarian cities according as each man's lot has been cast, and follow the customs of the land in clothing and food, and other matters of daily life, yet the condition of citizenship which they exhibit is wonderful, and admittedly strange.

> They live in countries of their own, but simply as
> sojourners . . . endur[ing] the lot of foreigners. . . .
> They exist in the flesh, but they live not after the flesh.
> They spend their existence upon earth, but their citizen-
> ship is in heaven. They obey the established laws, and in
> their own lives they surpass the laws. They love all men,
> and are persecuted by all.[6]

Even apart from persecution, the Christians' sense of separation was insured by the biblical standard of holy living which they followed in the midst of rank paganism. As one historian explains: "Tertullian demanded that Christians should keep themselves wholly unspotted from the world's idolatrous corruption. They must keep away from the cruel public shows . . . [not] serve in the army, or in the civil service, or even in schools. A Christian may not even earn his living in an occupation producing anything that might indirectly minister to idolatry."[7] The early Christians (who would clearly find today's generally accepted worldly standards of Christianity scandalous) were very conscious of being exactly what Christ had said: in the world, but not of it, having been chosen out of it.

Persecution served to maintain a clear distinction between Christians, who cared not for this world, and all the rest of mankind, for whom this present world was everything. It was not feasible to call oneself a Christian and live like a worldling. Only those who had truly forsaken this world would be willing to accept torture and death rather than to deny their Savior and Lord. On the other hand, "Christians" who lived like the world around them had already denied Christ and would not likely find the courage, when faced by the executioner, which they had lacked when faced with the temptations of popularity and wealth.

In spite of their law-abiding obedience to civil authority, the Christians' conception of themselves as strangers and pilgrims on the earth only added to the suspicion that they were not fully committed to the well-being of Rome. That strong sense of alienation from the rest of society was subversive in a way that the apolitical Christians themselves little understood and surely never intended. As Chadwick points out:

The paradox of the church was that it was a religious revolutionary movement, yet without a conscious political ideology; it aimed at the capture of society throughout all its strata, but was at the same time characteristic for its indifference to the possession of power in this world.
. . . this non-political, quietist, and pacifist community had it in its power to transform the social and political order of the empire.[8]

Pessimism and Hope

What some now perceive as the revolutionary nature of the gospel that might be used to take over society for Christ had no appeal at all for the early Christians. Their hearts were set upon their Lord's promised imminent return. "Changing the world," much less taking it over, had little if any meaning in that context.

Premillennialism was the predominant view in the church for at least the first three centuries: the belief that just as Christ must establish His "kingdom within" by reigning in the hearts of Christians, so He must also personally reign over the millennial kingdom. He was expected to return at any moment to establish righteousness and peace and to rule this earth visibly from Jerusalem for 1000 years as stated in Revelation 20. Such early church fathers as Irenaeus, Tertullian, Justin Martyr, Hippolytus, and others were premillennialists; and it was clearly the theology of the Council of Nicaea (A.D. 325).[9]

In the second century, Justin Martyr, for example, argues from Scripture that "the Messiah must have a twofold coming." He came once in weakness, humiliation, rejection, and crucifixion, as some Scriptures prophesied. He must come again in "majesty and power" and judgment, as other Scriptures just as clearly state. Justin believed that the Second Coming, far from having taken place at A.D. 70 was a future event that would involve a literal millennial reign of Christ from Jerusalem. As J.N.D. Kelly, one of the most widely recognized authorities on the beliefs of the early church fathers, reminds us: "this millenarian, or 'chiliastic', doctrine was widely popular at this time."[10]

Leading Reconstructionists assert, however, in spite of the clear evidence to the contrary, that "orthodox Christianity has always been postmillennialist...[and] amillennialist...[they] are the same thing...[except] 'postmils' believe the world will be converted, and 'amils' don't."[11] They go so far as to call premillennialism a "heresy" that developed later in church history.[12] Such assertions are made with scholarly arrogance but without biblical or historical support.

In actual fact, no genuine scholars of early church history agree with such postmillennialist claims—except for a few Catholics, who do so for obvious reasons. Even Daniel Whitby, recognized as the father of postmillennialism (around 1700) admitted that the early church, up to and including the Council of Nicaea in A.D. 325, held to premillennialism.[13] In *Dominion Theology: Blessing or Curse?*, H. Wayne House and Thomas Ice devote an entire chapter to millennialism. Their book is recommended for those wishing to study this important topic in more depth.

During the first three centuries there was widespread belief that the end was near because of the "signs" that were increasing everywhere. The anticipation of Christ's imminent return seemed to be justified not only by the commands of Scripture but by the intensifying persecutions and blasphemies directed against Christ by the Roman State. What clearer "signs of the last days" could there be?

Probably somewhere between A.D. 70 and 130 *The Epistle of Barnabas* announced: "The day is at hand, in which everything shall be destroyed together with the Evil One...that His beloved might hasten and come to His inheritance....Wherefore let us take heed in these last days."[14] "These are the last times," wrote St. Ignatius in the first part of the second century.[15] In the first half of the fourth century, St. Anthony declared that Arianism "was the last heresy and the forerunner of Antichrist."[16] Down through history Christians have made similar pronouncements, which have only served to increase skepticism about the rapture.

As this book goes to press there is a growing chorus of those who are declaring—some with dogmatic certainty—that Christ will return for His bride during 1988 (1948 plus 40 again!), and most probably on the last day of the Jewish Feast of Trumpets sometime in September. More than likely this latest prediction will provide yet another disappointment for the rapture watchers and further justification for their critics to say once again, "We told you so!" Nevertheless, it is not out of place to attempt to determine when the rapture might occur. How else can we take seriously the "signs" of His return given to us by Christ and the apostles?

From the middle of the third century onward, disappointment that Christ had not yet returned seemed to require a reinterpretation of the Scriptures dealing with this subject. There was also the need to correct the confusion caused by extremists such as the growing sect of the Montanists. Heeding their prophecies, "people abandoned homes, families, and work, and streamed out" to the "desert place" to which Christ would allegedly return.[17]

As a result of widespread disillusionment, amillennialism, which denied the return of Christ to reign over an earthly kingdom, gradually developed from around the middle of the third century onward. Heaven was still the ultimate hope, but now a more distant one. Amillennialism justified the earthly empire that church leaders found themselves engaged in building and governing in conjunction with imperial power from the heady days of Constantine onward. Such is the dream which is now being revived in the Protestant world, as Gary North expresses it, to "rebuild our apostate civilization into the kingdom of God. . . ."[18] Its presence among Protestants represents one more carryover from Catholicism that the Reformation failed to purge.

The "Great Persecution"—And Growing Apostasy

The persecutions of the third century were far more severe than those that had come earlier. Clement reported "roastings, impalings and beheadings" of Christians in Alexandria just before he fled that city around 203.[19] The persecutions came in waves, between which there were often periods of relative tolerance. The savagery was not only turned upon Christians. The entire empire, which was ruled by violence, was being consumed by it. Philip Hughes reminds us:

> Between Marcus Aurelius and Decius (180-250) history counts the names of sixteen emperors, and of them all, one only escaped a violent death. In the thirty years between Decius and Diocletian (251-284) there are eleven emperors more, and of these not one died in his bed.
> The battlefield claimed of the whole perhaps half a dozen. The rest were murdered, either by the troops who had elected them or by the troops of their rivals; and if Gallienus continued to rule for eight whole years, there is record during that time, in one province or another, of nineteen rival emperors set up by the different armies.[20]

Increasingly, in times of grave crisis when the survival of the empire itself appeared to be at stake, it seemed appropriate for the government to assume more and more control over its citizens' lives. This developing totalitarian system made the pagan view of the emperor as deity seem all the more credible. Loyalty to the traditional pagan cults, including the cult of the emperors, became a form of patriotism. As Hughes points out, in the midst of the turmoil of repeated civil war and the strain on the empire caused by political and social upheaval, "the old native religions" had been for centuries "the one means left for the corporate expression of 'national' feeling."[21] The Christians' rejection of these cults became grounds for charges of treason and fueled popular hatred against this "unpatriotic" minority.

The growth of Christianity, which had penetrated to every corner of the empire and probably comprised some ten percent of the population, made it appear more of a genuine threat than it had seemed previously. Aroused by the fact that "the heathen temples began to be forsaken and the Christian churches thronged,"[22] the new emperor, Decius, around A.D. 250 devised a more effective system for identifying all Christians. Among those martyred in this round of persecutions were the bishops of Rome, Antioch, and Jerusalem along with thousands of others, including seven of the emperor's own soldiers who refused to sacrifice to idols.[23]

The hope of heaven sustained the martyrs. They believed that to live was Christ and to die gain, because they were confident that to be absent from the body was to be present with the One who had given them eternal life and whom they longed to see. Nor was the rapture viewed as an escape from trials they were willing to bear, but the joyful prospect of being caught up at any moment into the presence of the Savior and Lord whom they loved unto death.

"Not a town, not a village of the Empire escaped," Hughes informs us, then adds significantly, "but the emperor's intention was not so much the massacre of Christians as their conversion to the old religion... [through] long drawn-out trials... repeated interrogations and the extensive use of torture in the hope of gradually breaking down the resistance."[24] Chadwick further explains:

> [Decius required] that everyone should possess a certificate (*libellus*) that he had sacrificed to the gods before special commissioners.... They [the certificates] were a deliberate attempt to catch people, and were the gravest attack hitherto suffered by the Church.
>
> Especially among property-owners the number of apostates [those denying their faith to save their lives] was immense....[25]

Following a brief respite, the persecution directed by Emperor Valerian (253-60) went beyond the requirement of a loyalty oath to the traditional gods. It forbade all Christian worship and specifically focused on the execution of church leaders. Among ordinary Christians as well, the martyrs were innumerable. The worst, however, was yet to come.

The Great Persecution, as it came to be called, began in 303 under the Emperor Diocletian and his co-emperor, Galerius. It was much like the suffering of Christians under numerous Communist regimes of this century. All Bibles were to be surrendered to the authorities, all churches were to be destroyed, all Christian worship was to be forbidden, all clergy were to be imprisoned, and all citizens of the empire were to sacrifice to the pagan gods on pain of death. The ferocity of this persecution varied according to the zeal of the local authorities, but in many provinces it resulted in a bloodbath. "In one case at least, in Phrygia, where the whole population was Christian, a whole town was wiped out."[26]

In numerous regions, faced with only two choices—apostasy or death—the majority of professing Christians denied their faith. Many excused themselves, however, with the explanation that the "technicality" of simply accepting a certificate from the local magistrate, who knew they had never sacrificed to the pagan gods as it stated, was a prudent expediency.[27] The trauma suffered by believers during these various persecutions led to severe disagreement over how to treat those who had "technically" or actually denied their faith or cooperated in some fashion with the authorities and later wished to reunite with the church. This issue was so divisive that rival parties in Rome each elected their own bishop in 251.

Constantine and the Church Triumphant

At the height of the most devastating persecution, deliverance came from an astonishing direction in the form of a new emperor. Constantine, a brilliant military commander, took control of the empire in the west, while his pagan ally, Licinius, conquered the east. A worshiper of the sun god like his father before him, Constantine's "conversion" to Christianity followed a miraculous vision. Prior to the crucial battle at the Milvian Bridge in 312, a cross reportedly appeared in the sky with these words, "in this sign conquer." A subsequent dream was sufficient to seal Constantine's resolve. By his order, his soldiers' shields were "marked with the sign of God."[28] Victorious against the numerically superior forces of Maxentius, Constantine entered Rome a hero, convinced that his victory had been won under the protection and favor of Jesus Christ, whom he now accepted as his new deity.

Some historians have suggested that Constantine's "conversion" may have had some political motivation as well, since he and Licinius both agreed that the long-standing vendetta against the followers of Christ "menaced the future of the State," and together they signed the Edict of Milan in 313, restoring to Christians full rights.[29] There must be some significance to the fact that he delayed his baptism until just before his death and "kept the position of *pontifex maximus*, chief priest of the pagan state religion." As Frend points out:

> Moreover, his execution of the young men who might have had a claim to his throne was not in keeping with the conduct of a sincere Christian.[30]

Christianity eventually became the official state religion of the Roman Empire with the edicts of Theodisius I in 380 and 381. All other forms of religion were forbidden and as severely punished as Christianity had once been. Paganism was formally prohibited by the Edict of Constantinople in 392, and in 529 Justinian seemed to strike paganism's death blow by ordering the closing of the school of philosophy in Athens. As Frend points out again, however, the partnership "between the church and state brought more drawbacks than blessing to the Christian church."[31] Moreover, it was only after it became "Christian" that the empire fell.

Certainly the Christianization of the world that is being pursued with such high hopes by COR did not produce the benefits for the Roman world that we are being led to believe it would in our day. The empire and the church soon formed a new alliance to persecute pagans and apostates with the same vigor with which Christians had once been made to suffer. Such disappointing and surprising results would have been foreseen by few observers at the time Constantine embraced the religion his predecessors had sought to eliminate. Nor is it likely that any Christians would have wanted to believe the harm that was destined to result. After all, who would have been courageous enough to exchange their favored status under Constantine for the "good old days" of the Great Persecution that had just passed!

With such an astonishing turn of events early in the fourth century, Eusebius, bishop of his native Caesarea, eventual mentor to Constantine and the first historian of the church, seemed only too eager to believe that the gospel of Christ, as Origen had hoped, was gradually triumphing over the world. Like many today, Eusebius believed that Christianity's conquest of the world was inevitable because of the definite social and political advantages accruing from Christian practices. Such benefits must, of course, become apparent and appealing to all. The Roman Empire, he believed, was ordained of God to play a key role in this Christianization of the world. Unity of all men through the joining of empire and church would be the secret.

The temptation for all of Christendom to accept this appealing scenario of the Church Triumphant was especially great when Constantine, upon the defeat and death of his one-time friend and later enemy, Licinius, became sole ruler of the entire Roman Empire. With Christianity elevated to a preferred status, a large percentage of the populace "converted." Many were no doubt drawn to Christ by the emptiness of paganism and a genuine thirst for a personal relationship with God. Many others, however, became "Christians" in name only because it was now the pagans who were suffering discrimination and even persecution. The Christianization of the world in our day, if such occurred, would no doubt produce its crop of opportunists as well.

Unfortunately, the new and exciting possibility that the whole world would become "Christian" began to be viewed as a spiritual Second Coming of Christ. As such it soon took the place of the rapture, which had remained the longing of the church during the years of severe persecution, and justified the growing amillennialism. The hope of heaven had been robbed of its Christian distinctive: the possibility of being taken there *alive at any moment*. As for the Christianized Roman Empire, it became increasingly apparent that a considerable amount of paganism had merely taken on a thin "Christian" veneer and was surviving in an even more dangerous form. Will Durant observes:

Paganism survived . . . in the form of ancient rites and customs condoned, or accepted and transformed, by an often indulgent Church. An intimate and trustful worship of saints replaced the cult of pagan gods. . . . Statues of Isis and Horus were renamed Mary and Jesus; the Roman Lupercalia and the feast of purification of Isis became the Feast of the Nativity; the Saturnalia were replaced by Christmas celebration . . . an ancient festival of the dead by All Souls Day, rededicated to Christian heroes; incense, lights, flowers, processions, vestments, hymns which had pleased the people in older cults were domesticated and cleansed in the ritual of the Church . . . soon people and priests would use the sign of the cross as a magic incantation to expel or drive away demons.[32]

One can hardly blame the Christians of that day for their exuberant optimism. Indeed, it seemed as though the church was well on the way to establishing the kingdom of God without Christ having to return. As support for their position, Reconstructionists quote the following declaration of Athanasius, bishop of Alexandria, around the middle of the fourth century:

Since the Saviour came to dwell in our midst, not only does idolatry no longer increase, but it is getting less and gradually ceasing to be. . . .

And daemons, so far from continuing to impose on people by their deceits and oracle-givings and sorceries, are routed by the sign of the cross if they so much as try.

On the other hand, while idolatry and everything else that opposes the faith of Christ is daily dwindling and weakening and falling, the Saviour's teaching is increasing everywhere![33]

Of course, this enthusiastic appraisal by Athanasius, great man that he was, turned out to be dead wrong. Demons are successfully deceiving millions today, idolatry is more rampant than ever, even in the "scientific" West, and Christianity has lost ground worldwide. The glowing predictions of "dominion" presently being made will prove to be equally wide of the mark.

The "Christian Emperor"—Forerunner of Today's Popes

Constantine set unfortunate precedents that his "Christian Emperor" successors followed, and which were later carried on by the popes. His wrongful assumption of leadership in theological disputes (at Arles in 314 and Nicaea in 325), for example, laid the foundation for the unbiblical infallibility and authoritarianism that would later be ascribed to the popes. In fact, during the Middle Ages the popes themselves would circulate what is generally believed to be a forged document called *The Donation of Constantine* in order to give legitimacy to papal powers they were asserting and which had presumably been given to them by the emperor.

In the *Donation*, Constantine, allegedly cured of leprosy by Sylvester I, decreed that the bishop of Rome was to be the head of the church worldwide. He deeded to Sylvester and his successor popes his palace and other properties in Rome and his imperial powers, including the near-divine status (carried over from pagan times) with which the "Christian Emperor" was regarded as the guardian of theological truth. Eusebius, who used his influence to obtain the emperor's support for his ecclesiastical aberrations and pet projects, wrote in shamelessly flattering terms of Constantine's near-divinity:

> Our Emperor, His [Christ's] friend, acting as interpreter to the Word of God, aims at recalling the whole human race to the knowledge of God; proclaiming clearly in the ears of all, and declaring with powerful voice the laws of truth and godliness to all who dwell on the earth. . . . invested as he [the Emperor] is with a semblance of heavenly sovereignty, he . . . frames his earthly government according to the pattern of that Divine original . . . the monarchy of God.

> Let then our emperor . . . be declared alone worthy
> . . . who alone is free . . . above the thirst of wealth, supe-
> rior to sexual desire . . . who has gained the victory over
> those passions which overmaster the rest of men: whose
> character is formed after the Divine original of the
> Supreme Sovereign, and whose mind reflects, as in a
> mirror, the radiance of His virtues. Hence is our emperor
> perfect in prudence, in goodness, in justice, in courage,
> in piety, in devotion to God. . . .[34]

These are the words of a courtier praising his lord to further his
own personal interests. As historian Hughes, who is a Catholic
priest, reminds us, "The truth [about Constantine] is very different.
In his manners he remained, to the end, very much the Pagan of his
early life. His furious tempers, the cruelty which, once aroused,
spared not the lives even of his wife and son, are . . . an unpleasing
witness to the imperfection of his conversion."[35] Following in their
father's footsteps, the three "Christian" sons of Constantine (Constantine II, Constantius II, and Constans) secured, after their
father's death, their separate regions of the empire by a merciless
family massacre—then took the "Christianization" of the empire
to new heights.

Shameless as Eusebius's flattery was, it articulated the way in
which the church, upon its merger with the state, came to understand the role of the emperor. In its new "Christian" mode, that
supreme office came to embody (for Constantine, his sons, and
those who followed them) a spiritual and sacerdotal aspect not
unlike the veneration it had always enjoyed under paganism. Indeed,
the Emperor Constantine's pagan title of *pontifex maximus* became
even more vital in relation to Christianity and was later taken by the
popes. They, in a sense, stepped into the emperor's shoes when 100
years later "the papacy was able to fill the vacuum left in the West by
the progressive weakness of the imperial power."[36] Eusebius reports that Constantine even considered himself to be a kind of
bishop, once addressing a group of bishops as follows:

> You are bishops whose jurisdiction is within the
> Church: I also am a bishop, ordained by God to overlook
> those outside the Church.[37]

Thus it was Constantine who convened, gave the opening address, and played a dominant part in the first ecumenical council of the church, the Council of Nicaea in 325—and in a number of councils which followed. A dangerous pattern was thereby established of "imperially organised councils under the Caesaro-papist emperors."[38] The bewildering change to being feted by the same ruthless imperial authority which had so recently tortured and killed them was at first accepted by church leaders as a blessing from God. There were those, however, who were from the very beginning uncomfortable with this new alliance. Hughes suggests something of that uneasiness in his description of the Council of Nicaea:

> To the [318] bishops [from all over the empire] who
> assisted at the magnificent festivities with which the
> council opened, the whole affair must have seemed incredible. Most of them had suffered for their faith, some
> very recently indeed, in the persecution of Licinius.
> They had seen their colleagues die atrociously in its
> defence. Many of them, blind and lamed, still bore in
> their bodies eloquent testimony of their own fidelity in
> trial.
> Now all was changed, and the honoured guests of the
> power which so recently had worked to destroy them,
> escorted by that soldiery the sight of whose arms must
> still provoke memories at which they shuddered, the
> Catholic bishops were come together with all possible
> pomp to regulate their differences before the face of the
> world.[39]

"Christianization" of the Civilized World

Unfortunately, it did not take long for the church to adjust to and enjoy its favored status. Eventually it was to be corrupted by it. Because of the support Constantine and his successors were able to give to the furtherance of Christianity, he is even today considered in the Greek Orthodox Church as the thirteenth apostle, "the equal of the apostles," with all the reverence granted to a Peter or Paul. He even had himself buried in the Church of the Apostles at Constantinople, the empire's new capital. The half-Christianized paganism latent in such acts, which remains to this day within both the Roman Catholic and Eastern Orthodox churches, is apparent from the account of Eusebius, who explains that the emperor:

> . . . anticipat[ed] with extraordinary fervour of faith that his body would share their title with the apostles themselves, and that he should thus even after death become the subject, with them, of the devotions which should be performed to their honour in this place, and for this reason he bade men assemble for worship there at the altar which he placed in the midst.[40]

To Constantine's credit, his conversion led to at least some imparting of Christian values to the Roman legal system. He showed his sincerity in "endeavour[ing] to express Christian ideals in some of his laws, protecting children, slaves, peasants and prisoners. An edict of 316 directs that criminals may not be branded on the face 'because man is made in God's image'."[41] Such were the benefits pursuant to the "Christianization" of the institutions of Roman civil government. They are similar to those which certain elements in the church today also hope to accomplish, and which surely would seem to be desirable. Nevertheless, such accomplishments have not in the past succeeded in establishing true godliness on a national, much less international, scale. In fact, the world has rather grown worse.

In order to maintain "the unity of the faith," those who did not agree with the particular orthodoxy backed by the emperor were now persecuted in the name of Christ. The fact that this new state religion was at times enforced upon pain of death, just as it had once been suppressed with the same penalty, ought to have been sufficient evidence that something had gone terribly wrong. Apparently blind to the separation Christ had intended, those who viewed the Christianization of the empire with optimism saw the end result of this metamorphosis as an even grander and more glorious empire—and one which continued without interruption an imperial legacy.

The church "had become the most powerful single factor in the lives of the peoples of the empire. The Virgin and the saints had replaced the [pagan] gods as patrons of cities."[42] With the emperor installed in Constantinople in the east, the pope wielded near-absolute power, not only as the head of the church but as the emperor of the west. "St. Peter and St. Paul, [Pope Leo I] explained in a sermon . . . had replaced Romulus and Remus as the city's protecting patrons."[43] The vision of heaven and especially of the rapture had been largely lost in the more appealing dream of a Christianized world. In this new view, as Frend suggests:

> Christian Rome was the legitimate successor of pagan Rome. [Many Christians] saw the victory of Christianity, the religion of the future, as a sign of progress. . . .
>
> God had made Rome for his own ends to unify the race of humankind and so prepare the way for Christ. Now Christ had triumphed. . . . Rome was ready to extend its sway to the heavens themselves.[44]

That ambition was not to be fulfilled. The Christianity which the empire had patronized would be its Achilles heel when, toward the end of the fourth century and on into the early fifth century, many of its new Christian leaders would abandon public office for a life of asceticism. The "Christianized Empire," which had been so compelling a dream, proved to be unsatisfying once it was realized. Ease and comfort encouraged the corruption in the church from which persecution had cleansed it. Disillusioned with the hypocrisy, many sought for holiness in an unnatural retreat from real life.

Even the remaining pagans were affected. The great families withdrew to their country estates and the emperors could no longer conscript Roman citizens for their armies, having to rely for the defense of the empire on barbarian mercenaries. Tens of thousands entered the monastic life, and thousands more embraced the ideal of celibacy. As Frend again points out:

> As the barbarian armies gathered on the frontiers, a new climate of opinion was establishing itself in which the ascetic virtues were associated not only with personal devotion but hostility toward public service. This was indeed a tragedy . . . [because] members of the senatorial aristocracy had been increasingly entrusted with the task of ruling the empire.
>
> At a crucial moment in the last quarter of the fourth century, too many members of the lettered classes forsook their traditional role as leaders in favor of an uninterrupted quest for personal salvation. *Roma aeterna* could not survive *alienatio* (alienation—the rejection of the world). . . .
>
> [Rome fell due to] the flight of the Western elite from the world they might have helped to govern.[45]

Bringing Heaven to Earth—Two Sides of the Coin

Today's Christian activists may argue that it was the very otherworldliness and pietism which they are attempting with their social and political activism to combat that caused the collapse of the Roman Empire. They are overlooking the corruption which, as we shall see, the "Christianization" of the empire brought into the church—and the fact that the empire itself was weakened by its alliance with Christianity. Genuine New Testament Christianity is not designed for the rule of secular society, and the church was never intended to enter into a partnership with the world to this end. Nothing even remotely approaching such an agenda can be found in the conduct of Christ, who is our perfect example.

In some respects, of course, the church of the fourth century was undoubtedly better off than under the previous persecutions. Christians could now meet freely to worship together and to edify and encourage one another, whereas before they had often had to do so in secret and under very difficult circumstances. It was now also possible to preach the gospel freely. While many no doubt "converted" for social advantage, many others were probably genuinely saved who might not otherwise have even heard the gospel. Moreover, now that Christians could openly declare themselves, it was also possible to clear up some of the falsehoods about Christianity that had circulated before.

In spite of such advantages, however, the partnership between the church and the Roman world was, in the long run, not good either for Christianity or for the empire. What had at first seemed to many to be a blessing granted from God to the church, actually turned out to be an unprecedented opportunity for Satan to pervert the truth. With politics and religion closely linked, what was good for one was good for the other. Consequently, political considerations began subtly to influence Christian life and doctrine, because what was best for the state loomed so large in ecclesiastical affairs. The church would reap the bitter fruit of neglecting James's solemn warning: "Whosoever therefore will be a friend of the world is the enemy of God" (James 4:4).

Under the severe persecution of the first few centuries, doctrinal purity was in general vigorously defended by church leaders, even though individuals succumbed not only to compromise but to outright denial of the faith in order to save their own lives. It was the later popularity of Christianity that accelerated and solidified the perversion of doctrine that had already begun in the days of the apostles. Compromise, when it came, was justified as necessary to preserve the new position and power enjoyed by the church.

We face the same danger today with the rising activist zeal that reinterprets the Great Commission to include social and political action and confuses "saving the world" with saving souls. We would do well to learn from the past in order not to repeat the mistakes the church has so often made. Chadwick reminds us:

Detachment from vanity fair was easier to those who expected the end of the world in the immediate future than to those who expected the historical process to roll on and who possessed some modest property to pass on to their children. . . .

When it became apparent that the time would not be as short as . . . supposed, the precariousness of life under the persecutions kept vividly alive the martyr's sense that true values did not consist in this world's goods.[46]

The unholy alliance between church and state which began under Constantine is still bearing its debilitating fruit today. Even the Reformation, instead of correcting that error, tended to perpetuate it. Witness, for example, the state churches throughout Europe. With the rare exception of a congregation here or there, these spiritually dead institutions have probably done more to destroy the faith of generations than the arguments of all of the critics and atheists combined.

Most insidious is the worldly mindedness that came to be accepted as "Christian" because of the merger of church and state. With the end of persecution, the rewards of this present life loomed larger than those of a distant and increasingly unreal heaven which one would attain only by death. Heaven became, if not unreal, then second in importance to building a "Christian" society.

6

Power Corrupts

The Christianization of the Roman Empire lifted the dread pale of persecution which had periodically imprisoned and slaughtered large numbers of the believers. Joining the church was now an imperative for those who wanted to gain social and political recognition. Inevitably "members of the Roman aristocracy were to become the founders and benefactors of churches . . . and as devoted to the cause of papacy as their forebears had been to the pagan empire."[1] The seeds of the destruction both of the empire and the church were being sown.

The prominent status with which the church was now favored by the imperial power that had once sought its destruction produced a new kind of persecution. The austere John Chrysostom, for example, during his short term as patriarch of Constantinople, preached a sermon about Jezebel unmistakably directed against the Empress Eudoxia, who had recently appropriated some property from its rightful owner. As a result, the emperor had Chrysostom removed from his post on a technicality and exiled to Armenia. Such manipulation of Christian leadership and theology had been unheard of in the days of the persecuted church.

Thus robbed of the independence necessary for the integrity of faith which persecution had been unable to destroy, Christianity, in its new role as the favored (and eventually official) religion of the empire, became polluted by its avid pursuit of position and power. Such carnal quests, formerly unthinkable, now seemed essential in

123

the new scheme of things and were excused on that basis.

Corruption Encouraged by Organizational Structure

The growing compromise with worldly values was accelerated by the increasing centralization of the church, which had actually begun for seemingly legitimate reasons under the fierce persecution. Bishops who were overseeing districts gradually gained disproportionate authority, while local elders steadily lost their original prominence. With leadership thus firmly established in the hands of a central hierarchy, corruption's rewards became greater and the consequences of misconduct to the church became far more serious.

Of course, corruption can spread not only from the top down, but from the bottom up as well. The special status of the Virgin Mary in Catholicism and Orthodoxy, a status that has been retained to this day, resulted in large part from pressure exerted by the common people. It was popular piety that insisted on the veneration of Mary as the Mother of God, while theologians and church leaders tended to resist this idea. In the fourth century the term *Theotokos* (or God-bearer) had already become the popular designation for Mary among the common people. Against this near-deification, the Patriarch of Constantinople, Nestorius, argued that Mary was only *anthropotokos*: the bearer or mother of the man Jesus and of His human nature, not His divine nature. However, in the interests of peace and in recognition of the high feelings aroused on both sides, he suggested that the neutral term *Christotokos* be used instead. It was a designation unacceptable to the masses, and popular riots drove Nestorius out of office.

Such a perversion of Scripture was not, of course, entirely the fault of the people, but of the organizational structure of the church as well. Centralization encourages corruption from both the top and bottom. The mob of Paul's day would have been powerless to sway the great apostle or to divert him from the truth. First of all, neither he nor any of the other apostles, Peter included, had ever taken the position of authority that the bishops of Rome, Constantinople, Alexandria, Antioch, and Jerusalem later assumed and which was eventually consolidated in the two popes, one over Catholicism in Rome and the other over Eastern Orthodoxy in Constantinople.

In the days of the apostles there was no central authority that held sway over the church and upon which rioters could exert pressure. Nor can any support for such a hierarchy with absolute power to dictate to the church be found in the New Testament. Yet this structure, which Catholicism fostered, was not purged at the Reformation. Instead it was retained in new forms and has been the cause of doctrinal corruption in nearly every denomination.

None of the New Testament epistles is written as though it came from a bishop or pope who had to be obeyed under threat of excommunication. On the contrary, like James and John, Peter exhorts equals, he does not command inferiors: "The elders which are among you I exhort, who am also an elder" (1 Peter 5:1). He offers as the basis for his writing not any official ecclesiastical position or power, but the fact that he has been "a witness of the sufferings of Christ . . . [an eyewitness] of his majesty" (1 Peter 5:1; 2 Peter 1:16).

Paul also addresses his readers as equals (calling them *brethren*, *yokefellows*, and *fellowlaborers*) and appeals not to any obligation church organizational structure imposes upon them to obey him, but to their consciences before God and to their individual inspiration by and submission to the Holy Spirit. Thus Paul writes in his first letter to the Corinthians (14:37): "If any man think himself to be a prophet, or spiritual, let him acknowledge that the things that I write unto you are the commandments of the Lord." Avoiding any idea of hierarchical authority, all of the apostles except James use the word "beseech," and Paul does so repeatedly. The following are but a few typical examples:

I beseech you therefore, brethren, by the mercies of God, that ye present your bodies a living sacrifice, holy, acceptable unto God (Romans 12:1); Now I beseech you, brethren, by the name of our Lord Jesus Christ, that ye all speak the same thing, and that there be no divisions among you (1 Corinthians 1:10); Brethren, I beseech you, be as I am (Galatians 4:12); I beseech Euodias, and beseech Syntyche, that they be of the same mind in the Lord. And I intreat thee also, true yokefellow (Philippians 4:2,3); And I beseech you, brethren, suffer the word of exhortation (Hebrews 13:22); Dearly beloved, I beseech you as strangers and pilgrims [on this earth], abstain from fleshly lusts, which war against the soul (1 Peter 2:11).

Unity for Unity's Sake

It was the Roman emperors who eventually put the final touch upon the organizational structure by establishing the bishop of Rome as the pope. Following the precedent already set by Constantine it became, under his successors, fully established "for the final decisions about church policy to be taken by the emperor."[2] Emperors justified their exercise of control not only in the area of church policy but with regard to its theology as well because doctrinal controversy could so easily lead to political crises. Those jockeying for key positions in the church hierarchy found it not only advantageous but necessary to cater to the imperial power. To that end Pope Leo I—ascribing to the secular authority an "infallibility" that would later be claimed for the pope—flattered a new emperor with the heretical and obsequious declaration:

> By the Holy Spirit's inspiration the emperor needs no human instruction and is incapable of doctrinal error.[3]

The emperors considered political unity to be a concomitant of religious unity, and their interest in the former led them to take an active part in the latter as well. "The dissensions of the Christians [for which there had been little time under severe persecution] were not a matter to be regarded with amused indifference or sad resignation," writes Chadwick. "They were a political and social problem which the government had the strongest interest in settling."[4] Politics had entered the church. Thereafter expediency and compromise overruled truth and sound doctrine. The prevailing policy and, even worse, theology at any given time within the church depended upon which rival faction had the imperial ear.[5]

In honor of his patronage, the emperor became recognized as the "vicar of Christ"—a title which the pope would inherit when the Roman Empire disintegrated. Since the emperor, as *pontifex maximus* (another title the pope would also take), acted as chief priest of the pagan cult, it was only natural for him to function as the *de facto* head of the Roman Catholic Church as well. On all matters, including doctrine, the emperor, of course, had the final word. Constantine himself explained his role thus:

> What more can be done, more in accord with my constant practice and the very office of a prince, than after expelling error and destroying rash opinions to cause all men to agree together to follow true religion and simplicity of life and to render to Almighty God the worship that is His due.[6]

It sounded so commendable. However, unity for its own sake in order to produce theological harmony, political peace, and social tranquillity meant that truth must take a secondary place. Indeed, the love of truth became a hindrance to advancement in the church, as it always had been in the world of politics. Integrity and truth were trampled beneath the boots of an army waving the banner of its own compromised version of the gospel of Christ—an army that marched in utopian unity toward the seemingly admirable goal of a world religion acceptable to everyone. The Roman Catholic Church has claimed to be the sole representative and guardian of that universal religion for many centuries; and with the energetic worldwide diplomacy of its present pope, John Paul II, it is making a powerful bid to draw not only Protestants but all other religions into its ecumenical fold.

Not all were immediately pleased with the new developments. There were factions that split with Rome—but eventually they, too, succumbed to the seduction of power. The majority of the North African church, for example, did not look kindly upon Christendom's partnership with civil authority. As Frend points out, they perceived that the emperor's interest in ecclesiastical matters was just another form of suppression of true Christianity. "In their view, the fundamental hostility of the state toward the church had not been altered." He goes on to explain:

> They neither understood nor cared about Constantine's conversion. For them it was a case of the Devil insisting that "Christ was a lover of unity," of inspiring the use of money and gifts to undermine the faithful, and having failed in open persecution [of] now falling back on guile.[7]

Unity for unity's sake has become a major focus in the church today, particularly among charismatics. Correction of serious doctrinal error is often rejected under the claim that being united in love is more important than being biblically sound. Yet a major theme of all the epistles is correction of error and the teaching of sound doctrine. The battle is for truth and it cannot be fought without a clear identification and firm rejection of that which is false. Causing division is condemned in Scripture; but it is not attributed to standing firm for sound doctrine, but to introducing false teaching: "Mark them which cause divisions and offenses *contrary to the doctrine which ye have learned*, and avoid them" (Romans 16:17). Significantly, Paul identifies the whole purpose of Scripture thus:

> All Scripture is given by inspiration of God, and is profitable for doctrine, for reproof, for correction, for instruction in righteousness, that the man of God may be perfect, thoroughly furnished unto all good works (2 Timothy 3:16,17).

Admission Requirement: Blind Submission

The unprecedented partnership between church and state that began with Constantine—and which we will later see violated the clear teaching of Scripture—established destructive patterns that continue to plague the church, both Protestant and Catholic, to the present time. The linkage of imperial authority with the church, and the meddling of the emperors even in theology, made conditions more conducive to the practice that had already begun of imposing upon the laity dogmatic biblical interpretations dictated by a controlling hierarchy of professional clergy.

In exchange for their blind submission to its dogmas the church offered the common people the assurance of heaven—provided that due honor was given to the priesthood and its performance of the sacraments was supported financially and with at least token attendance. Thus, the church became the vehicle of salvation in the place of Christ; and belonging to and obeying the precepts of the church took the place of a personal relationship with the Savior. Roman Catholic catechisms continue to this day to declare:

> This is the only church instituted by Christ for the salvation of mankind. . . . All are bound to belong to the Church, which Christ established, to share in His merits and thus attain life everlasting. . . .
>
> Those who know the Church of Christ cannot be saved outside her fold.
>
> The only Church of the present day which can prove her claim to be the divine Church established by Jesus Christ is the Catholic Church.[8]

As a corollary, the catechisms also continue to teach that the individual cannot understand the Scriptures for himself. Hence there is no point in reading the Bible, since the church is its sole interpreter. For example, *The Convert's Catechism of Catholic Doctrine* declares:

> [The Roman Catholic Church is] the only true Church . . . the custodian and interpreter of Revelation. . . .
>
> Man can obtain a knowledge of God's word [only] from the [Roman] Catholic Church and through its duly constituted channels.[9]

The individual church member was no longer encouraged to know Christ for himself and to look to the indwelling presence and guidance of the Holy Spirit, but to the "one true Church" and its leaders. While many Catholics today claim a measure of independence in their thinking, it is, in the final analysis, the church to which the vast majority look for salvation. Moreover, the actual teaching of the church (of which many Catholics may be ignorant) makes the same demands as a typical mind-control cult that requires its members to check their minds at the door and let the "guru" or "prophet" do their thinking for them. Following its acquisition of imperial power, the Roman Catholic Church has been attempting to wield that kind of control without apology for centuries. For example, the *Convert's Catechism* bluntly declares:

> When he has once mastered this principle of Divine Authority [residing in the Church], the Inquirer is prepared to accept whatever the Divine Church teaches on Faith, Morals and the Means of Grace.[10]

When an elitist inner circle claims to speak for God and all others must obey without the right to test the scripturalness of such teachings for themselves, then God's voice in the individual conscience has been effectively silenced. In such a climate heresy thrives and proliferates. Such is the situation today not only among Catholics but also among many Protestants as well. It can be traced back to the Christianization of the Roman Empire and the expedient submission to hierarchical authority that seemed to make so much sense in keeping the peace at that time.

The Berean spirit, commended as noble for its testing of the apostles' teachings against Scripture in the days of Paul, died in the days of Constantine and his successors of deliberate suffocation at the hands of a church which in a few centuries would hold all of Europe in its grip. Once it had convinced the world that salvation depended upon joining its ranks and participating in its sacraments, the threat of excommunication could be invoked to intimidate the unorthodox and the unruly, both small and great.

The Question of Authority and Faith

Such absolute authority is contrary to Scripture, yet it is still maintained by the Catholic Church to this day. Catholic apologist Karl Keating, for example, argues that we can only know that the Bible is inspired because the infallible Roman Catholic Church that Christ founded says so.[11] Keating writes:

> The Catholic believes in inspiration because the Church tells him so—that is putting it bluntly—and that same Church has the authority to interpret the inspired text.
> Fundamentalists . . . have no interpreting authority other than themselves.[12]

Even Augustine, great thinker that he was, appears to have succumbed to this deadly delusion that does away with individual conscience and the moral responsibility to know God's Word by the leading of the Holy Spirit. Although Augustine testified to the struggles of conscience and reason that led him initially to Christ, Keating quotes him as later saying, "I would not believe in the Gospel if the authority of the Catholic Church did not move me to do so." The lie is so obvious that no one has any excuse for being deceived by it.

First of all, Romans chapters 1, 2, and 3 tell us clearly that all mankind, through the witness of creation and conscience, recognize that God exists, that we are morally accountable to Him, have broken His laws, and cannot be justified by our own efforts or apart from His grace. Quite clearly keeping the law perfectly in the future cannot make up for having broken it in the past. John tells us that Jesus Christ is "the true Light, which lighteth every man that cometh into the world" (John 1:9). Thus all men know in their hearts, when they hear it, that the gospel of Christ is true. There is no other way to be forgiven by God, no other way of salvation. Rejection of the gospel is not for legitimate intellectual reasons but arises out of an unwillingness to submit to the moral consequences of what all men know to be true. Whether a true church exists or not is entirely irrelevant.

Is it not true, however, that the church gave us the Bible? No, it is not. Most Christians seem to assume that the bishops of the Catholic Church meeting at the Council of Nicaea decided upon the composition of the New Testament (the Old Testament had already been compiled and Christ had given it His approval by quoting from it) and that even Protestants recognize Scripture on that basis today. This is a common misunderstanding that is still promoted by Catholic apologists as well as by skeptics who attempt to undermine the authority of Scripture on that basis. Actually, a consensus had already been reached among the believers recognizing the very same 27 books which the New Testament contains today long before the Council of Nicaea (325). In fact, that council had nothing to say about the canon of Scripture, although participants quoted frequently from most of the New Testament.

The fifty-ninth canon of the Council of Laodicea (363) requested that only "canonized" books of both Old and New Testament be read in the churches, but did not list them, showing how firmly the New Testament canon had already been established. Far from deciding upon the canon, the councils merely recognized and quoted from the books that had already been accepted by the church generally and had long been appealed to in the various theological disputes since the days of Clement of Alexandria (155-215). The Third Council of Carthage (397) gives us the first official pronouncement on the New Testament canon, listing the same 27 books we have today, as did the Council of Hippo (419). As church historian Henry C. Thiessen has pointed out:

> It is a remarkable fact that no early Church Council selected the books that should constitute the New Testament Canon. The books that we now have crushed out all rivals, not by any adventitious authority, but by their own weight and worth.
>
> This is in itself a strong proof of the genuineness and authenticity of the books that have survived. It is not until the close of the fourth century that any Council even discussed the subject.[13]

The Gospel and Church Authority

The same leading of the Holy Spirit that causes Christians of all ages to recognize the authority of Scripture begins in the unbeliever with conviction of sin and the recognition, as we have already noted, that the gospel is true. On the day of Pentecost 3000 Jews became Christians through Peter's preaching, without any mention of a "true church." He only preached Christ crucified for our sins and raised from the dead.

In the great outpouring of the Spirit in Samaria where thousands more became Christians, Philip the evangelist simply "preached Christ unto them" (Acts 8:5). There is not a hint that he first of all proved that a true church existed and on the basis of its testimony they then believed the gospel. And to the Ethiopian official who was reading Isaiah 53, Philip "began at the same Scripture and preached unto him Jesus" (Acts 8:35). The Ethiopian believed, not because he was convinced of the existence of an infallible Catholic Church which alone could interpret the Bible for him, but because of the convicting power of God's Word through the Holy Spirit. It is to the sad discredit of the great Augustine if he in fact denied this essential truth.

The apostles and first-century Christians "went everywhere preaching the word" (Acts 8:4) to those who had never heard of the church. Nor did they ever suggest that the gospel should be believed because the "true church" had endorsed it. Paul and his colleagues preached not a church but Christ crucified (1 Corinthians 2:2). In fact the true gospel "by which also ye are saved" (1 Corinthians 15:1-4), which is "the power of God unto salvation to everyone that believeth" (Romans 1:16), doesn't even contain the word "church," much less anything about joining it and blindly following whatever its leaders teach.

The infallibility claimed for the pope and the unbiblical authoritarianism exerted by the Catholic Church deny man's God-given moral conscience and personal accountability whereby every person knows that the gospel is true and is required to believe it. Demanding blind submission to an elitist hierarchy destroys both the gospel and the souls for whom Christ died. Nevertheless, the "confession of faith" to which a convert to Catholicism must subscribe includes the following:

> I admit and embrace most firmly the apostolic and ecclesiastical traditions and all the other constitutions and prescriptions of the Church.
>
> I admit the sacred Scriptures according to the sense which has been held and which is still held by Holy Mother Church, whose duty it is to judge the true sense and interpretation of the Sacred Scriptures, and I shall never accept or interpret them except according to the unanimous consent of the Fathers. [Of course the "Fathers" have not been unanimous.]
>
> I recognize the Holy Roman, Catholic and Apostolic Church as the mother and teacher of all . . . and I promise and swear true obedience to the Roman Pontiff, successor of St. Peter, Prince of the Apostles, and Vicar of Jesus Christ.
>
> Besides I accept, without hesitation, and profess all that has been handed down, defined and declared by the Sacred Canons and by the general Councils, especially by the Sacred Council of Trent and by the Vatican General Council, and in a special manner concerning the primacy and infallibility of the Roman Pontiff. . . .
>
> This same Catholic Faith, outside of which nobody can be saved, which I now freely profess and to which I truly adhere, the same I promise and swear to maintain and profess . . . until the last breath of life. . . .[14]

Today's modern catechism has its roots in the authoritarianism that came into the church through its unholy partnership with Roman imperialism. By the end of the fourth century, the individual Christian was left without the right to follow the leading of the Holy Spirit in arriving at his own understanding of Scripture. To dare to question official dogma meant excommunication from the church, which, with the close link between church and state, meant that one was also an outcast from society. No wonder historians have remarked that the popes "held all Europe in their net."

Of course, Scripture does not justify anarchy—political or spiritual. The New Testament church, of which Christ was the Head, had leaders: apostles, prophets, elders, and deacons, who were to be obeyed by those under them. All, however, were brethren, and none was to lord it over others. Each was to consider others better than himself and to seek to be the servant of all. Under the guidance of the Holy Spirit, submission was "one to another in the fear of God" (Ephesians 5:21). All could prophesy, and whatever one said was subject to challenge and, if need be, correction by the listeners. Belief was not dictated by hierarchical authority but was achieved by the leading of the Holy Spirit in individual minds. Paul's manner of appeal reveals how far from the truth of Scripture all claims to papal or church authoritarianism really are:

> I therefore, the prisoner of the Lord, beseech you that ye walk worthy of the vocation wherewith ye are called, with all lowliness and meekness, with longsuffering, forbearing one another in love, endeavoring to keep the unity of the Spirit in the bond of peace. . . . And grieve not the Holy Spirit of God, whereby ye are sealed unto the day of redemption.
>
> Let all bitterness and wrath and anger and clamor and evil speaking be put away from you, with all malice, and be ye kind one to another, tenderhearted, forgiving one another, even as God for Christ's sake hath forgiven you (Ephesians 4:1-3, 30-32).

The Church Triumphant?

In its new favored role, "Christianity" had amazingly become the requirement for politicians of all ranks and even for army officers who wished to advance in the now Christianized empire. The most desirable profession was in church leadership—and good church connections were virtually essential for any secular career of substance or of merit.[15] Of course, "conversion" motivated by such considerations had little to do with genuine "repentance toward God and faith toward our Lord Jesus Christ" (Acts 20:21).

Having survived the persecution of its enemies, the church was now being paganized by its new friends. The Catholic Church would never recover from the half-converted paganism it absorbed in the process of becoming the partner of the Roman Empire. What appeared at first, to those weary of suppression and the constant threat of martyrdom, to be a great victory for Christianity was in fact a stunning defeat. Chadwick writes:

> By the end of the fourth century the Church had virtually captured society. In worldly terms of status and social influence, the episcopate of even moderately important cities had become an established career to which a man might aspire for reasons not exclusively religious.
>
> Many local churches had become substantial landowners, supporting numerous poor folk. A bishop was expected by his people to be the advocate of their secular interests as well as their spiritual pastor.[16]

Accommodation with the world was justified on the basis that it gave the church the prestige and influence necessary for spreading the gospel. In actuality, however, the church had been in a surprisingly short time so corrupted by its lust for power that it had ceased to present an example of true Christianity to the world. Under the papacy of Damascus (366-84), for example, "the opulence of papal entertainments was said to surpass imperial hospitality."[17] The social status of important clergymen rose tremendously until it became the envy of the established families of wealth. Who could blame them for sending their young men into this new prestige profession?

The blood of the martyrs had indeed been the seed of the true church. Where persecution had purified, power now corrupted. That sad fact had already been demonstrated long before Constantine's "conversion." Even during brief periods of respite from persecution, incidents of moral laxness had increased substantially. As early as the first half of the third century Origen had pointed to the false motivation of many "converts" as a source of corruption within the church:

> I admit that at the present time perhaps, when on account of the multitude of people coming to the faith even rich men and persons in positions of honour, and ladies of refinement and high birth, favourably regard adherents of the faith, one might venture to say that some become leaders of the Christian teaching for the sake of a little prestige.
> Yet at the beginning when there was great risk attached particularly to teachers, no such suspicion could be reasonably entertained.[18]

Early Corruption and Claims to Infallibility

Roman Catholicism's boast that it is the "oldest church" and therefore the *right* church, and its claim to infallibility, are both discredited by the fact that perversions of all kinds plagued the church from its very beginning. There was no guarantee that the early church would be kept from error, and it is clearly false to make such a claim for any church today. To be kept pure the church must have leaders who admit their fallibility and can be corrected. The pronouncement of dogmas, granting tradition equal authority with Scripture, and pretended infallibility, could not protect from error. On the contrary, they only assured that the error which inevitably came would become entrenched and grow.

Such gross and fundamental error had already come into the church during Paul's lifetime as the teaching that "the resurrection is past already" (2 Timothy 2:18). Before his death Paul informed Timothy with sadness, "This thou knowest, that all they which are in Asia be turned away from me" (2 Timothy 1:15). The Apostle John wrote, "Even now are there many antichrists" (1 John 2:18,19)—false teachers in the early church who had departed so far from the faith that they even denied that Jesus is the Christ (1 John 2:22,23; 4:1-3).

Such errors were not only held by insignificant members but were promoted by influential leaders. Peter warned the Christians of his day about false prophets and false teachers who would deceptively bring into the church "damnable heresies" and lead many astray (2 Peter 2:1,2). Jude also wrote of false teachers already within the church who had "crept in unawares" and who had to be resisted by "earnestly contend[ing] for the faith which was once [for all] delivered unto the saints" (Jude 3,4). And the apostles in their epistles warned that worse errors would come into the church after they were gone, and would especially proliferate and deceive many during the last days.

It is not surprising, then, that doctrinal corruption was already gaining ground inside the church well before Constantine. The list of popular false teachings included the cult of the saints, apostolic succession, infant baptism, quasi-magical views on the efficacy of the physical acts of baptism and communion, and the glorification of celibacy. Frend perceptively refers to the latter as "the ultimate barrier between clergy and laity."[19]

The Rock of Ages—And the Rock of the Church

Thus it is folly to claim that the Roman Catholic Church is the one true and infallible church on the basis of its early origins, when there was already in the days of the apostles so much heresy and corruption. Nor can papal infallibility be substantiated by claiming a chain of succession back to Peter. Jesus had no sooner said to him, "Upon this rock [Himself] I will build my church . . . and I will give unto thee the keys of the kingdom of heaven" (Matthew 16:18,19) than He had to rebuke Peter with these harsh words: "Get thee behind me, Satan; thou art an offense unto me; for thou savorest [understandest] not the things that be of God, but those that be of men" (verse 23). Paul, who had more converts, more churches, and far more Scripture to his credit, found it necessary to severely correct Peter (Galatians 2:11-21).

It is a gross error to believe that Peter, who was in fact a very weak reed for a church or series of popes to lean upon in claiming infallibility, was the Rock upon which the true church is built. That position is Christ's alone. In the Old Testament God Himself is called the Rock of Israel and the Rock of our salvation a number of times: "Ascribe ye greatness unto our God; he is the Rock" (Deuteronomy 32:3,4); "The Lord liveth, and blessed be my rock . . . the God of the rock of my salvation" (2 Samuel 22:47); "The God of Israel said, 'The Rock of Israel spoke to me' " (2 Samuel 23:3); "Truly my soul waiteth upon God. . . . He only is my rock and my salvation" (Psalm 62:1,2); and many more. Quite clearly, then, only Christ, who is God as well as man, could be the rock of the church in the New Testament. Paul declares that the church is:

> built upon the foundation of the apostles and prophets, Jesus Christ himself being the chief cornerstone . . . (Ephesians 2:20).

Far from designating Peter as the rock upon which the church would be built, Christ was pointing out the distinction between Himself and Peter, who had just spoken such error and would fail so miserably. In the Greek there is a play on words between "thou art Peter [*petros*—a piece of rock]" and "upon this rock [*petra*—a mass of rock such as Gibraltar] I will build my church" (Matthew 16:18). Even without an understanding of the Greek, however, the meaning is clear both from many Old Testament Scriptures such as the few examples quoted above and from the New Testament. In the parable, for example, the rock upon which the wise man built his house was not Peter but Christ and His teachings (Matthew 7:24-29). Clearly referring to Christ rather than to himself, Peter wrote:

> Wherefore also it is contained in the Scripture, "Behold, I lay in Zion a chief cornerstone [Christ], elect, precious; and he that believeth on him shall not be confounded."
> Unto you therefore which believe he is precious; but unto them which be disobedient, the stone which the

builders disallowed, the same is made the head of the
corner, and a stone of stumbling, and a rock of offense,
even to them which stumble at the word, being disobe-
dient . . . (1 Peter 2:6-8).

The Cult of the "Saints"

The designation *Saint* Peter or *Saint* Paul, as though *saint* is a title
reserved for a select few, is another error of Catholicism that robs
the individual Christian of his position and confidence in Christ. It
is quite clear from the epistles that "saints" is a title for all true
Christians—each of whom has been sanctified by God (set apart for
His purposes). Paul's epistles, for example, addressed the ordinary
Christians then living to whom they were written as "saints": the
"saints" at Corinth (1 Corinthians 1:2; 2 Corinthians 1:1), "to the
saints which are at Ephesus" (Ephesians 1:1), "to the saints . . .
which are at Colosse" (Colossians 1:2).

Nevertheless, the belief had grown that "saint" was a special title
bestowed after death by the church upon a few super-Christians.
The faith of believers during the persecutions was fortified by the
accounts of the noble martyrs who had died true to their beliefs, and
thus was born the cult of the saints. These heroes and heroines of the
faith began to be revered and petitioned for protection and intervention in this life and for assistance in gaining heaven in the next. As a
Catholic priest and historian, Hughes explains:

> The oldest of all the feasts were the annual commemo-
> rations of the martyrs—reunions of the local church, at
> the tombs of the most distinguished members, those who
> had testified to the faith with life itself. . . .
> A practice so natural grew speedily, and though the
> martyr cults were in their essence local things, some of
> the more noted of these Christian heroes—St. Lawrence
> of Rome for example, St. Cyprian of Carthage—soon
> won a wider renown, and honours in churches other than
> their own.

With the Peace of Constantine . . . heroism which had found its crown in martyrdom now developed in the . . . austerity of the new monasticism; and the next saints to be honoured liturgically after death, their prayers officially besought, were the ascetics, the first of them all in time the great St. Martin of Tours who died in 397.[20]

The hierarchy in control must have recognized that any attempt to petition or communicate with the dead was absolutely forbidden in the Bible.[21] Violation of that precept brought judgment. For example, God had delivered King Saul to death at the hands of his enemies because of his attempt to communicate with the spirit of the dead prophet Samuel (1 Chronicles 10:13,14). The specialists in this forbidden art of necromancy were called mediums and wizards, and Saul had previously put them all "out of the land" (1 Samuel 28:3), and rightly so. The prophets repeatedly warned God's people against necromancy. Isaiah had chided Israel with the reminder that to appeal to the dead was a denial of God's concern for them and of His willingness to hear their prayers:

> And when they say to you, "Consult the mediums and the spiritists who whisper and mutter," should not a people consult their God? Should they consult the dead on behalf of the living? (Isaiah 8:19 NASB).

In spite of the clear teaching of Scripture, however, the church was willing to accommodate and even encourage popular superstitions in order to maintain its power over the masses. Chadwick explains how the cult of saints was a natural outgrowth of a paganized Christianity influenced by the social structure of that day:

> In ancient society success depended much on possessing a patron whose word to the right official could obtain for one a well paid post, or secure one's liberty when there was trouble with the police or the tax authorities, or even influence the courts if one was a litigant.

The development, from the third century onwards, of the veneration of the saints as "patrons" whose "suffrage" would be influential in heaven, was a natural transfer to the celestial sphere of the social situation on earth.[22]

The cult of the saints was turned into profit by the sale of relics that had supposedly belonged to, or been associated with, these heroic figures. The alleged preserved tears of the Virgin Mary, fragments of the "true cross" (of which there were eventually enough in Europe to build a cathedral), the very "toenail clippings" from the apostles (at least a barrel full of Peter's alone) became items of merchandise whereby the faithful evidenced their misinformed devotion.[23] By the early fifth century, as one historian points out:

Traffic in relics was increasing whether "prestige objects" such as those of St. Stephen which Paulus Orisius brought back with him from Palestine for Augustine in 416, or more ordinary remains of saints, such as those of St. Alban in his shrine on the hill outside Verulamium. This trade was already becoming an abuse, but it was a sign of the times.[24]

The Papacy: Exceeding Rome's Imperial Power

Contrary to the arguments of those who would persuade us to devote ourselves to the Christianization of today's world as part of the Great Commission, the Christianization of the Roman Empire was not followed by political/economic prosperity, but by progressive deterioration. As the empire broke up it was never again ruled by a central government located in Rome. It was ruled instead by vassals and demi-emperors who retained control over parts of the disintegrating power structure. Unlike the civil and military authority that survived only by breaking into pieces and dispersing, the ecclesiastical authority—the Roman Catholic Church and its pope— retained its central location and power, which it continued to wield from the original headquarters of the empire in Rome. As Frend put it:

> Meantime, however, the hub of the wheel, the institution of the papacy, survived. It had not fallen with pagan Rome, and through the first decades of the fifth century, despite the aberrations of Pope Zosimus's pontificate, it gradually extended its authority over the surviving churches in the West.[25]

The vacuum created by the breakdown of the western empire had to be filled by the church, the only Roman institution capable of doing so. In their now thoroughly politicized role, the new Roman pontiffs progressively took upon themselves not only the titles but much of the flavor and function of emperor as the papacy stepped into the gap left in the West by the collapsing imperial power.[26] Unquestionably, the scepter of Roman emperors passed to the popes. R. W. Southern points out that "The dominating ideal in the rebuilding was that the unitary authority of the Empire should be replaced by the unitary authority of the papacy." He describes the succeeding centuries as:

> . . . the period in western European history when the church could reasonably claim to be the one true state, and when men (however much they might differ about the nature of ecclesiastical and secular power) acted on the assumption that the church had an overriding political authority.
> During the whole medieval period there was in Rome a single spiritual and temporal authority exercising powers which in the end exceeded those that had ever lain within the grasp of a Roman Emperor.[27]

The Vatican built its power structure upon the ghost of the fallen Roman Empire. In many ways the church filled a necessary social and political function. Whatever there was of education, care of the sick, response to social concerns, a moral code, or otherworldly hope was kept alive through the church. It is hardly surprising that her regime was accepted. Most of all, however, it was, as today's Catholic catechisms still maintain, the belief that the church was "the gate to heaven"[28] that made every knee bow to her. As Walter James reminds us:

> The Papacy controlled the gateway to heaven which all the faithful, including their rulers, hoped earnestly to enter. Few in those days doubted the truth of this and it gave the Popes a moral authority which has never been wielded since.
> A Pope like Innocent III held all Europe in his net. . . . through the Church, its bishops, priests, monks and friars, all now closely bound to Rome, the Papacy was able to create in Europe a unity of action and opinion which has not been repeated.[29]

The Magnificent "Whore"

Even temporal rulers were forced, no matter how unwillingly, to bow the knee to the pope. The all-pervasive power which the church wielded over the masses of people, together with its great wealth, made the church a formidable force that even kings found easier to join in partnership than to fight. More compelling yet, however, was the universally accepted belief that the church could bar the gate of heaven to any who opposed her. The church's almost irresistible power had already been demonstrated repeatedly even before the empire's collapse.

Consider, for example, the public humiliation of Emperor Theodosius in 390 by Ambrose, who was not even pope but the bishop of Milan (where the emperor's palace was located). In retaliation for rioting in Thessalonica, Theodosius had arranged the massacre of some 7000 citizens, including women and children, gathered in a public amphitheater. In order to escape excommunication, the emperor obeyed Bishop Ambrose's demand for a humiliating public penance.[30] Not only the common people, but the influential, military heroes, and even emperors quailed at threats of excommunication, convinced that the church held the keys to heaven and hell. As Colman J. Barry reminds us:

> Ambrose in great part established the Western principle that there is one fundamental restriction on traditional autocratic power, as he said, "the emperor is within the Church, not over the Church."[31]

During the Middle Ages the awesome power the popes wielded "over the kings of the earth" continued to grow. Thus was established that magnificent "whore" portrayed by John in Revelation 17—headquartered in a city located upon seven hills (verse 9) and which "reigneth over the kings of the earth" (verse 18). The identification is unmistakable. John's vision in Revelation 17 was being fulfilled in remarkable fashion. Picture the humbled emperor Henry IV waiting barefoot in the snows at Canossa to make his peace at last with Pope Gregory VII in 1077. Within a hundred years that pope's dream had been realized. A monolithic superstructure had effectively bound together the governmental and moral framework of medieval society so that, in retrospect, one could see mirrored in the twelfth century under the Catholic Church an imperial vision that had been lost in the fifth.

It is remarkable but true—and a further fulfillment of biblical prophecy—that the Roman Catholic pope, successor to the ancient Roman emperors, continues to wield similar power today. Most nations—including the United States—maintain an ambassador and diplomatic relations with the Vatican. Even the Soviet Union "has maintained high-level contacts with the Vatican over the last two decades," and aides to the pope and Gorbachev have been negotiating to set up a meeting between these two powerful heads of state.[32] Like other secular rulers, Gorbachev is driven by necessity—he knows and respects the power of the Vatican.

In contrast to the less than 60 million Lutherans worldwide, the pope rules over more than 800 million Catholics, nearly three times as many subjects as Gorbachev rules. There can be no doubt to the identity of the richly clad woman sitting upon the "scarlet-colored beast" in Revelation 17—the "harlot . . . with whom the kings of the earth have committed fornication" (verses 2, 5). The *Catholic Encyclopedia* states:

> It is within the city of Rome, called the city of seven hills, that the entire area of Vatican State proper is now confined.[33]

The very existence, size, and influence of the Roman Catholic Church today is almost as remarkable a fulfillment of prophecy as the preservation of Israel and her return to Palestine. The Bible also prophesies that in the "last days" the secular Roman Empire will be revived and will comprise ten nations in Western Europe. It will be ruled over by the Antichrist, who will also be worshiped as the god of a world religion.

There seems little doubt that this false and abominable last-days religious system, called "Mystery Babylon" (Revelation 17:5), will have its headquarters at the Vatican. The joint histories of the Roman Empire and the Roman Catholic Church provide a fascinating preview of what John in Revelation foretells as yet to come.

The Roman Catholic Church's claim to be the gateway to heaven, its doctrine of purgatory, and its rejection of the rapture stifled the hope of heaven for centuries. Its total dominance of theological beliefs for more than 1000 years through excommunication, torture, and death led to ecclesiastical and moral corruption of such proportions that even the secular world recoiled in shame and horror. Such was the unlikely soil in which the seeds of the Reformation and the eventual recovery of the "blessed hope" would be planted.

7

Babylon the Great

Whether or not the *Donation of Constantine* is a forgery (as most historians have concluded) is immaterial. Significant is the fact that the popes and hierarchy of the Roman Catholic Church circulated it during the Middle Ages as one means of legitimizing their possessions and power and the pomp surrounding them. The *Donation* declared that Constantine had moved the capital of the Roman Empire to Constantinople in the east and deeded the western empire, with all the attendant imperial authority, to Pope Sylvester in order to "exalt the most holy See of blessed Peter in glory above our own Empire and earthly throne, ascribing to it power and glorious majesty and strength and Imperial honor." It further declared:

> And we command and decree that he [the Bishop of Rome] should have primacy over the four principal Sees of Antioch, Alexandria, Constantinople and Jerusalem, as well as over all the Churches of God throughout the whole world; and the Pontiff who occupies at any given moment the See of that same most holy Roman Church shall rank as the highest and chief among all the priests of the whole world and by his decision all things are to be arranged concerning the worship of God or the security of the faith of Christians.
>
> In recompense for this we concede to . . . the Pontiffs

147

who will preside over the See of blessed Peter until the
end of the world . . . our Imperial palace of the La-
teran . . . the crown of our head . . . [and] the tiara; also
the shoulder covering . . . the purple cloak and the crim-
son tunic and all our Imperial garments. . . .

We confer on them also the Imperial sceptres . . . the
spears and standards . . . the banners and various Imperial decorations and all the prerogatives of our supreme
Imperial position and the glory of our authority. . . . [and]
the city of Rome and all the provinces, districts and cities
of Italy and the Western regions, relinquishing them to
the authority of himself and his successors as Pontiffs by
a definite Imperial grant. . . .

Disintegration and Revival

The empire that had been handed to the popes, however, was
doomed to disintegrate and remain in a state of flux for centuries
under the onslaught of numerous invasions and realignments of
power. As Frend reminds us: "By 450 Britain had been lost irre-
trievably, North Africa had fallen to the Arian Vandals, and there
were Arian rulers administering much of Gaul and Spain. On the
Rhineland where the barbarians had settled, Christianity was in
retreat." Frend goes on to point out:

It would take centuries before Western Europe reached
the level of prosperity attained in the last quarter of the
fourth century.

Some time around the fall of Rome the long Indian
summer of the Western Christian and classical world
moved into the winter of the Dark Ages. Victory had
gone to the Germanic invaders and to Augustinian theology.[1]

In spite of the disintegration of the empire, the popes held onto
and even expanded their power to encompass a kingdom far beyond

the wildest dreams of the Roman emperors whom they had succeeded. Eventually the "Holy Roman Empire," which had claimed to be the kingdom of God, would even experience a glorious and lasting revival. It presents a dim picture from history of what is yet to occur under the Antichrist, in renewed partnership with the false church.

Driven from Rome by an uprising, Pope Leo III had fled to the Frankish court of Charlemagne, whose armies recovered Rome and restored him to the papal throne. While Charlemagne attended Mass in St. Peter's on Christmas day of A.D. 800, the pope placed a crown on his head and proclaimed him emperor of the West. The title was eventually recognized both by the eastern emperor in Constantinople and the Caliph of Baghdad. The pope's move was a shrewd one. As Maurice Keen reminds us:

> The restoration of the worldwide dominion of Rome
> was the dream not only of medieval popes and emperors
> but also of many of their subjects and servants.[2]

Charlemagne's power had threatened to overshadow the authority of the papacy. After his coronation in St. Peter's, however, in solid partnership with the pope, Charlemagne "worked for some forty years to create a Christian commonwealth such as St. Augustine had earlier outlined."[3] The emperor's effective military campaigns in northern Europe were accompanied by the forcible conversions of the heathen and thereby enlarged the Roman Catholic domain.

One encyclopedia declares: "The ideal of the Universal Church and the Universal Empire . . . working together in harmony, which the Church had cherished since the fall of the old Roman Empire in the West, was now given a semblance of reality."[4] Charlemagne expressed his view of "church and state" in a letter to Pope Leo III:

> It is our part . . . to defend by armed strength the holy
> Church of Christ everywhere from the outward onslaught
> of the pagans and the ravages of the infidels, and to
> strengthen within it the knowledge of the Catholic Faith.

It is your part, most holy Father, to help our armies
with your hands lifted up to God like Moses, so that by
your intercession and by the leadership and gift of God
the Christian people may everywhere and always have
the victory over the enemies of His Holy Name and that
the name of our Lord Jesus Christ may be glorified
throughout the whole world.[5]

"The Great Dream Broke on the Nature of Man"

To many the revival of the "Holy Roman Empire" was proof that
the millennium had arrived. In the ensuing years, as never before,
man's ideals seemed to approximate ever more closely the world he
saw about him. The church embraced and governed the whole of
society. As Southern reminds us, the medieval church "had all the
apparatus of the state: laws and law courts, taxes and tax-collectors,
a great administrative machine, power of life and death over the
citizens of Christendom and their enemies within and without. . . .
Popes claimed the sole right of initiating and directing wars against
the unbelievers. They raised armies, conducted campaigns, and
made treaties of peace in defence of their territorial interests."[6]
Apparently unaware of John's apocalyptic vision of the "great
whore" on the scarlet beast, Pope Innocent III (1198-1216) fur-
thered its fulfillment by asserting in no uncertain terms the authority of the church over all secular powers:

Just as God, founder of the universe, has constituted
two large luminaries in the firmament of Heaven, a major
one to dominate the day and a minor one to dominate the
night, so he has established in the firmament of the
Universal Church, which is signified by the name of
Heaven, two great dignities, a major one to preside, so to
speak, over the days of the souls, and a minor one to
preside over the nights of the bodies. . . .

Thus, as the moon receives its light from the sun and
for this very reason is minor both in quantity and in

quality . . . so the royal power derives from the Pontifical
authority the splendor of its dignity. . . . [7]
    By the grace of God, a true peace and firm concord
now exist between Church and Empire. . . . The state of
the world, which is falling into ruins, will be restored by
our diligence and care. . . . for the pontifical authority
and the royal power . . . fully suffice for this purpose. . . . [8]

Although the church claimed to be preparing men for heaven, the
pope's vision was clearly directed at things earthly. The church
pretended to represent spiritual values while it amassed material
possessions and power. Rather than looking forward to the millennial kingdom which Christ Himself would return to establish, the
church saw itself as that kingdom ruled by the supreme pontiffs and
wielding its power over the kings of the earth. Moreover, that
kingdom was unashamedly earthly, completely given to the passions
of the body and the things of this life while claiming to be fitting
souls for heaven.

There was no attempt to build a genuine kingdom of God, or even
to improve this world. The monks withdrew from the world, while
the rest, including many of the priests and popes, lived for its
enjoyments. And if, as sometimes was admitted, sins were committed in the process, the church existed to provide absolution—
thereby giving it a much-feared power to hold over the heads of men
and even kings. Barring the door to heaven against those who might
otherwise have entered through the One who had said, "I am the
door; by me if any man enter in, he shall be saved" (John 10:9), the
church opened it only for a fee. Christ's rebuke of the rabbis in His
day was now appropriate for the church that claimed to represent
Him:

> But woe unto you, scribes and Pharisees, hypocrites!
> For ye shut up the kingdom of heaven against men; for ye
> neither go in yourselves, neither suffer ye them that are
> entering to go in.
>   Woe unto you, scribes and Pharisees, hypocrites! For

152 · *Babylon the Great*

ye devour widows' houses, and for a pretense make long
prayer; therefore ye shall receive the greater damnation.
Woe unto you, scribes and Pharisees, hypocrites! For
ye compass sea and land to make one proselyte, and when
he is made, ye make him twofold more the child of hell
than yourselves (Matthew 23:13-15).

While he was greatly revered, much of Augustine's theology,
which many blamed for the earlier collapse of the Roman Empire,
was no longer honored. He had written his *City of God* (with its call
to Christians as strangers on earth to find their hope in heavenly
citizenship) in response to the sacking of Rome on August 24, 410,
by a Gothic army led by the barbarian chieftain Alaric. Rome had
not been violated by an enemy in almost 800 years of pagan rule, and
now—see what befalls it under Christian emperors! Such had been
the disillusioned and angry cry in the streets. Pagans had demanded
of Christians:

> Tell us the reason for Christ's coming; tell us what
> benefit it has been to the human race. Have not matters
> been worse upon earth since Christ came, and was it not
> better in the old days than it is now?[9]

With the revival of the Holy Roman Empire the "good old days"
had returned at last and were even being exceeded. Such had long
been the dream which the church had fostered. Premillennialism
with its hope of the rapture had fallen by the wayside centuries ago.
After all, Christ had not returned and that "little while" had long
expired. Amillennialism, long the undisputed theology, was becoming optimistic enough to be called postmillenialism even though that
belief would not be formalized until 1700. Barry observes: "The
early Christian conviction that Christ's second coming was imminent faded little by little.... Under the pressures of life in the
world, Christianity became Christian culture in the world, an integral part of the whole."[10]

It appeared to many that at long last the vision of St. Ambrose of
Milan, expressed in his oration on the death of the elder Theodosius,

was being realized. He had held out the hope that the Roman Empire, because of the piety of its rulers, would perpetually reign over the world in a partnership with the church, each with special power and authority from God, each serving to guarantee the safety and well-being of the other.

That hope had been dashed with the sacking of Rome, but now it had been revived—and this time it seemed that it would not fail. Riding the crest of success, Pope Boniface VIII reiterated Innocent III's assertion of supreme power over temporal rulers. In his *Bull Unam Sanctam* (1302) he declared:

> Wherefore both [swords] are in the power of the Church, namely the spiritual and material swords; the one, indeed, to be wielded for the Church, the other by the Church; the former by the priest, the latter by the hand of kings and knights, but at the will and sufferance of the priest.
>
> For it is necessary that one sword should be under another and that the temporal authority should be subjected to the spiritual.[11]

Such power was never intended for the church. The sad result was a growing corruption in the church which, over the next few centuries, eventually reached a crescendo. The administration of Roman Catholicism's vast world system was, unfortunately, guided by men with the same propensities for avarice and soft living as the general populace. As Will Durant observed, "The great dream broke on the nature of man."[12]

The Mounting Discontent

Increasingly, the charge leveled against pontiffs, prelates, and priests was that of greed and moral corruption. Machiavelli, in casting about for an example of a successful prince who really knew how to utilize the power available to him to get his own way and augment his position, found his exemplar in Pope Alexander VI (1492-1503), who "did nothing else but deceive men, he thought of nothing else, and found the occasion for it; no man was ever more able to give assurance, or affirmed things with stronger oaths, and no man observed them less. . . ."[13] Of Pope John XII (955-964), Liutprand of Cremona declared:

> Pope John is the enemy of all things. . . . the palace of the Lateran, that once sheltered saints and is now a harlot's brothel, will never forget his union with his father's wench, the sister of the other concubine Stephania. . . .
>
> Women . . . fear to come and pray at the thresholds of the holy apostles, for they have heard how John a little time ago took women pilgrims by force to his bed, wives, widows and virgins alike. . . .[14]

By the fourteenth century the church had lost all credibility as an arbiter and example of Christlike living. With deep shame a Dominican lashed out at his brother priests: "Those who should be fathers of the poor are . . . consumed in gluttony and drunkenness. . . ."[15] One bishop boasted of his sexual relations with abbesses and nuns and claimed to have fathered 14 bastards in 22 months "whom he had provided with ecclesiastical benefices."[16] England's John Colet had been shocked at the levity and ungodliness of the pope and cardinals when he visited Rome. From his pulpit in London's St. Paul's Cathedral, of which he was dean, Colet thundered his disapproval of the wickedness of his fellow leaders in the Catholic Church, which he dearly loved:

> Oh, the abominable impiety of those miserable priests, of whom this age contains a great multitude, who fear not to rush from the bosom of some foul harlot into the temple of the Church, to the altars of Christ, to the mysteries of God![17]

The world was treated to the brazen spectacle of wars fought on the revenues realized from the sale of ecclesiastical offices, and of illegitimate papal progeny being enriched from the same source. No less scandalous was the commissioning of great works of art and the restoration of St. Peter's itself by the sale of indulgences to those too poor ever to make a pilgrimage to Rome or gaze at a Michelangelo. And to maintain its power over the masses it was necessary to keep them in ignorance of the mysteries of grace. To this end the Mass was recited in Latin and the Scriptures kept from the common people. Among the pronouncements of the Synod of Toulouse (1229), for example, we find:

> Lay people are not permitted to possess the books of the Old and New Testament, only the Psalter, Breviary, or the Little Office of the Blessed Virgin, and these books not in the vernacular language.[18]

There were even two rival papacies between 1378-1414, which split the loyalty of Europe and created the unbearable financial burden of supporting two royal ecclesiastical courts. Bad-tempered and arrogant Pope Urban VI held sway in Rome, while Pope Clement VII was ensconced in a second luxurious papal palace in Avignon, France. Voted in by the same body of cardinals, each claimed to be the true successor of Peter and, predictably, fought with one another. So the litany of offenses against piety reached a crescendo in the fifteenth century. Consider Petrarch's description of the papal court at Avignon:

> I am now living in France, in the Babylon of the West. The sun, in its travels, sees nothing more hideous than this place on the shores of the wild Rhone. . . .
> Here reign the successors of the poor fishermen of Galilee . . . loaded with gold and clad in purple, boasting of the spoils of princes and nations . . . luxurious palaces and heights crowned with fortifications, instead of a boat turned downwards for shelter. . . .
> Instead of holy solitude we find a criminal host and crowds of the most infamous satellites; instead of soberness, licentious banquets . . . instead of the bare feet of

the apostles . . . horses decked in gold and fed on gold, soon to be shod with gold, if the Lord does not check this slavish luxury.[19]

Love of Money Is the Root of All Evil

Vast amounts of money were required to maintain the church's high living and sprawling empire—and the methods used to collect the necessary revenues became the scandal of Europe. Bribery was a way of life at the Vatican, and even cardinals obtained their elevation to that high office through payment of a required fee. Before he had become pope, Aeneas Sylvius had written that anything could be bought in Rome and that without money the church would do nothing.[20] In shame Nicholas Clemanges declared:

> The popes appoint their "collectors" in every province, those, namely, whom they know to be most skillful in extracting money, owing to peculiar energy, diligence or harshness of temper, those in short who will neither spare nor except but would squeeze gold from a stone.
> To these the popes grant, moreover, the power of anathematizing anyone, even prelates, and of expelling from the communion of the faithful, everyone who does not, within a fixed period, satisfy their demands for money.[21]

For centuries ecclesiastical offices had not been allotted on the basis of a worthy life, ability, and spiritual maturity, but were sold to the highest bidder. Persons capable of enriching the church, though themselves morally bankrupt, were often appointed to multiple benefices. Each appointment required a substantial contribution of money or land, with little concern for the fact that the local parish or diocese rarely saw its spiritually unqualified and absentee leaders.

The church devised myriad ingenious ways of tapping the pocketbooks of the deluded souls whom it had convinced that salvation could only be acquired through its sacraments—of course, for a designated fee. The poverty of souls that resulted produced great wealth for those who wrote the rules. The same profitable formula has been repeated times without number by an endless list of religious leaders and cults. Oral Roberts' "seed faith" doctrine, now operational throughout most of the charismatic movement, is simply a Protestant variation on Catholicism's time-tested money-raising methods. Although it does not go so far as to offer salvation, this teaching has convinced multitudes that their monetary "gift to God's work" plays an integral part in obtaining answers to their prayers for health, success, and prosperity.

The high-pressure fund-raising techniques not only of Roberts but of some other TV evangelists (and some pastors as well), though more innovative, are no more successful and play upon similar fears to those exploited by Roman Catholicism's schemes from the Middle Ages. Some things never change. Today's Vatican officials, however, have developed far more sophisticated means of engaging in questionable finance while maintaining a front of piety to the world. Numerous exposés have been written concerning the modern church's shady banking deals, its connection to Italy's infamous P-2 secret Masonic Lodge and Mafia, and even the probable murder of Pope John Paul I to prevent the reforms he had intended. There were more than 100 Masons within the Vatican staff, none of whom has been purged since their exposure by the press.[22]

It is ironic that the present pope, while taking the name John Paul II, far from carrying out the reforms intended by John Paul I, has continued instead the church's corrupt policies. Moreover, he shelters within the Vatican, if not the murderers, then three who were accessories to and covered up the murder of his predecessor—along with other corrupt officials whom John Paul I had determined to remove, including some who have been indicted by civil author-ities and would be arrested were it not for the present pope's protection.[23]

Selling Salvation

For both ingenuity and infamy, no money-grabbing scheme in all of history comes close to the sale of indulgences, which became a primary source of ready cash for the popes during that period leading up to the Reformation. The foundation was laid in A.D. 593 when Pope Gregory I proposed the unbiblical but eventually very profitable idea that there was a place called "purgatory," in which the spirits of the dead had to suffer in order to be purged of their sins and fully delivered from "the debt of eternal punishment." Having proven to be useful, this fabrication was declared to be a dogma of the Roman Catholic Church by the Council of Florence in 1439 and remains an important part of Catholicism today.

Thus those who claimed to represent Christ and to lead His "one true church" had, through the traditions they had adopted, departed so far from the Scriptures upon which Christianity was based as to declare dogmatically that Christ's death upon the cross for our sins did not sufficiently cleanse the soul for entrance to heaven. In addition to what Christ endured, we must suffer for our sins as well—in this life, and also after death in "purgatory." Yet the one who, it is claimed, was the first pope declared: "For Christ also hath once [for all] suffered for sins, the just for the unjust, that he might bring us to God [i.e. to heaven]" (1 Peter 3:18).

Numerous Scriptures make it clear that those who have believed on Christ and received Him as their Savior and Lord have been completely and forever purged of the guilt and eternal consequences of sin—a purging, moreover, which could never be accomplished even in part by us, but only by Christ alone. Many Scriptures attest to the sufficiency of this cleansing, such as the following: "The blood of Jesus Christ his Son *cleanseth us from all sin*" (1 John 1:7); "when he had by himself *purged our sins*" (Hebrews 1:3). Yet in heretical rejection of such inspired assurance and the repeated reminder that Christ has "washed us from our sins in his own blood" (Revelation 1:5), modern Catholic catechisms declare:

> In this life we can satisfy for the temporal punishment due to sin by Prayer, Fasting, Almsdeeds, etc.[24]
>
> Purgatory is the state in which those suffer for a time who die guilty of venial sins, or who die without having fully satisfied for the punishment due to their forgiven sins.[25]

Both the Bible and a person's God-given sense of justice cry out against the teaching that "forgiven sins" require further "punishment." Yet Karl Keating, one of Catholicism's top apologists, argues: "Christ's sufferings, although fully satisfactory on behalf of our sins, leave us under a debt of honour, as it were, to repay them by sufferings of our own. . . . it is not contrary to the Redemption to say we must suffer for our sins; it is a matter of justice."[26] It is a testimony to the persuasive power of Catholicism that Keating, who is a lawyer, would embrace in the name of God's justice the very injustice that even man's laws are designed to prevent: double payment for the same crime.

Christ's triumphant cry upon the cross, "It is finished!" is an accounting term in the New Testament Greek, meaning that the debt was paid in full and justice was fully satisfied. All that remains is to believe the testimony of Scripture and to receive the pardon that is freely offered by God's grace on the basis of the debt having been fully paid on our behalf by Christ. To teach that there is yet some further payment to be made through temporal suffering of some undefined kind, either on this earth or in a place called purgatory, is a clear contradiction both of logic and Scripture. Moreover, if Christ was not able to pay fully for our sins, then surely we would not be able to accomplish what He could not.

Purgatory was conveniently invented in order to extend the church's power over the souls of men. Standing between mankind and the One who said, "Come unto *me* . . . *I* am the way," the church would only open the door to heaven to those who joined its ranks, obeyed its precepts, and filled its coffers. The doctrine of purgatory was only a logical further extension of an intricate system of grace-dispensing "sacraments" which popes, cardinals, bishops, and priests had been gradually developing for centuries. As a result, the Roman Catholic Church has replaced Christ as the means of salvation and has grown wealthy in the process of merchandising forgiveness of sins.

How could such clearly unbiblical doctrines become accepted? A major reason was that fewer and fewer Christians took seriously the Berean (Acts 17:11) responsibility and privilege of diligently studying the Word of God for themselves in order to verify the teachings of church leaders. As a result of such neglect, the practice was eventually forbidden. Operating through its hierarchy of leaders, the church claimed to be the sole interpreter of Scripture, custodian of the faith, and the necessary dispenser of salvation through its administration of the "sacraments," and no one was allowed to question its dogmas. *The Convert's Catechism of Catholic Doctrine*[27] (like any other modern Catholic catechism) makes it clear that today's church maintains the same unbiblical and destructive power over the minds and souls of men:

> Jesus Christ made His Church the custodian and interpreter of Revelation (p. 14).
> The Catholic Church is the guardian of revealed truth as contained in divine Tradition and Sacred Scripture. . . . Man can obtain a knowledge of God's word [only] from the Catholic Church and through its duly constituted channels (pp. 34, 36).

While the international intrigue, corruption, and cover-up engaged in by the Roman Catholic Church and its present pope are staggering, the long-standing theological errors it continues to perpetuate are no less evil. The latter are, in fact, far more costly in terms of the untold millions whom Catholicism has kept in spiritual darkness and led into eternal separation from God.

The Incredible Doctrine of Indulgences

The idea of "indulgences" was invented by Alexander of Hales in the thirteenth century. Incalculable wealth was raked in by the church through the fees charged to pilgrims when Pope Boniface III proclaimed the Great Jubilee in which a "plenary indulgence (the complete remission of the temporal penalties of sin) was promised to all who repented, confessed, and visited daily for fifteen days the basilicas of St. Peter and St. Paul [in Rome]." As William Canton points out: "All that year 1300 there were never fewer than 200,000 pilgrims in the holy city [Rome]; and the numbers often exceeded 2 million."[28] Nothing sells so well as phony forgiveness of sins.

The doctrine of indulgences as it stands today was finally declared a dogma by Pope Clement VI in 1343. Clement reasoned that "one drop of Christ's blood would have sufficed for the redemption of the whole human race." The remainder of that blood shed on the cross, its virtue "increased by the merits of the Blessed Virgin and the supererogatory works of the saints," constitutes "a treasure which . . . has been committed by God to . . . St. Peter and his successors, to be used for the full or partial remission of the temporal punishments of the sins of the faithful who have repented and confessed."[29] By papal bull in 1476 Pope Sixtus IV "extended this privilege to souls in purgatory [reducing their time of suffering there], provided their living relatives purchased indulgences for them."[30]

Here we see the illogical and heretical teaching that while one drop of the blood of Christ is sufficient for redemption, all of the rest of His blood is not sufficient to deliver the redeemed from temporal punishment in this world or in purgatory. This is a blasphemous denial of the clear teaching of Scripture. No less blasphemous is the claim that the shedding of Christ's blood in death upon the cross is made more meritorious by the good works of the saints—and that it is, in fact, of no value unless it is somehow dispensed and applied sacramentally by the Catholic priesthood. And, of course, for that service a fee must be paid.

The twin doctrines of purgatory and indulgences actually contradict one another. After claiming that (in addition to what Christ suffered in our place) suffering is required of us, the Catholic Church offers to reduce our time in purgatory *without suffering* in exchange for repeating so many "Hail Marys" or participating in other rituals and sacraments, such as the repetition of the Mass. At the time of the Reformation, indulgences were sold outright for cash with nothing further required.

Obviously, one's spiritual fate ultimately hinged upon the size of one's pocketbook. For the meek and the poor, purgatory was therefore a far greater terror than for those who could afford to sin on a grander scale. Only too happy to believe the church's false promises, sinners lined up to buy indulgences and thus their way into heaven. It was pure business, and it boomed!

The practical effect was increasingly to drain local areas of needed funds and channel them to Rome for the pope's wars and projects. Resentment grew as the economic facts slowly took hold. Anger against this evil invention that pretended to shorten the torments of purgatory for a price became particularly virulent in Germany where the economy was more prosperous and the people more independent than elsewhere in Europe.

At the same time a growing number of would-be reformers inside the church had their theological concerns. From their study of the Scriptures, they began to see that to ascribe merit to purgatorial suffering and indulgences and to make these inventions play a part in the redemption of mankind was an insult both to Almighty God and to the Sin-bearer Himself. These twin dogmas, which had been unknown to the early church, were a mockery of all that the cross had accomplished. There were, of course, many other doctrinal concerns, but it was primarily the issue of indulgences which finally opened the floodgates and swept Europe inevitably upon the pathway of reform.

Great courage born of deep conviction and motivated by God's love was required of those who prepared the way for the Reformation. Anyone daring to question the hierarchy in control of the Roman Catholic Church risked not only excommunication but life itself. This was in fact the price that many would pay in the battle for truth and freedom of conscience that would reach its climax during the sixteenth century.

Leaving the church was not the general desire of the Catholic priests whose consciences were troubled by unbiblical practices. They fervently hoped it could be reformed from within. All that was needed was for the Bible, instead of the church hierarchy, to be accepted once again as the final authority. Sincere submission to God's Word would eventually restore the true faith and dissolve differences. Thus the primary cry of the reformers was *sola scriptura* (Scripture alone). It seemed so simple.

8

The Reformation

England's John Wycliffe (1329-84) was among the first to take up the cry of submission solely to the Word of God. Articulate, powerful, "the morning star of the Reformation," Wycliffe argued from Scripture that Christ, not the pope, was the true head of the church and that the Bible, not the church, was the highest authority. He produced the first Bible in English so that his countrymen could read it in their own language and understand it for themselves. Wycliffe also formed a group of evangelists, the Lollards, to preach the gospel directly from Scripture all over England. Although Parliament condemned his views in 1382 and in 1401 prescribed the death penalty for preaching the gospel, Wycliffe himself escaped martyrdom.[1]

On the continent, John Huss (1369-1415), rector of Prague University, was excommunicated by Rome for preaching the tenets of Wycliffe: personal relationship with Christ and access through Him to God for all believers, and the necessity for church leaders to submit to the authority of Scripture. Huss' outspoken opposition in 1412 to the sale of indulgences in Prague to finance a papal war with the King of Naples brought the full force of the pope's wrath against him. In 1414 Huss was summoned to Constance, Germany, to answer to the General Council convened there for the purpose of considering ecclesiastical reform. Though in possession of a safe conduct from Emperor Sigismund of Bohemia, Huss was arrested and thrown into prison.

Blessed Are Ye...

During his lengthy trial, Huss' forceful arguments, supported by Scripture, posed a threat to the Roman Catholic Church: that salvation was by grace, through faith, and that by the works of the flesh no man could be justified; and that a holy life must of necessity be the mark of a man pleasing to God no matter what his ecclesiastical honors or powers. The first argument, by implication, would have done away with a whole system of needless intermediaries (priests, bishops, cardinals, and popes) and the lucrative sale of salvation for money; and the second would have required the removal of the major part of the Catholic priests and hierarchy on moral grounds.

The very existence of the Catholic Church depended upon the suppression of such ideas. Huss was condemned, degraded, his soul committed to the devil, and his body to the flames. Yet in that very diocese of Constance the priests who represented the religious system that condemned Huss were fathering some 1500 illegitimate babies each year—to say nothing of the widespread homosexuality. Much of the blame must be placed upon the church itself for the imposition of a lifestyle that violates both Scripture ("A bishop [or elder] then must be blameless, the husband of one wife . . . of good behavior"—1 Timothy 3:2) and mankind's natural God-given sex drive. The church showed its disapproval of such immorality not by removing the offending priests but by raising more money from concubinage fees and crib taxes. Two weeks before his July 6, 1415, martyrdom Huss wrote from prison:

> I am greatly consoled by that saying of Christ, "Blessed are ye when men shall hate you" . . . it bids us rejoice in these tribulations. . . . It is easy to read it aloud and expound it, but difficult to live out. . . .
>
> O most Holy Christ, draw me, weak as I am, after Thyself, for if Thou dost not draw us we cannot follow Thee. . . . Give me a fearless heart, a right faith, a firm hope, a perfect love, that for Thy sake I may lay down my life with patience and joy. Amen.[2]

In Florence the consciences of even the worldly rich were pricked in the 1490s. Under the fiery oratory of the Dominican Girolamo Savonarola, who justifiably called the Roman Catholic Church a "harlot" ready to sell salvation for money,[3] the townspeople pledged to reform their own lives. In a dramatic transformation that would be the envy of those who advocate the Christianization of today's cities, the populace responded to the impassioned call for an ascetic godliness. For a brief, frenzied moment in Florence's decadent history, children went from house to house to collect for burning the "vanities" which Savonarola had denounced.

The enthusiasm of the moment soon wore off, however, and the natural bent of the unregenerate human heart reasserted itself. Only those who are born of the Spirit and truly love the Lord will be able to keep His commandments. The Christianized reconstruction of today's world being advocated by some evangelical leaders will be no more successful than the futile and fleeting reconstruction of Florentine society under Savonarola.

When he dared to reprove Pope Alexander VI for his wickedness, the fiery monk—who had already been forbidden the pulpit—was excommunicated and condemned to death. Savonarola was tried, hanged, and then burned to the wild acclaim of a populace that had only recently burned "vanities" under his direction but had quickly grown weary of professing a holiness for which it had no real heart.

The Final Straw

Germany had been growing restless under the heel of the popes, though not so much for spiritual reasons, which actually mattered little. Religion had become more form than substance. It was the continual financial drain of funds from Germany to Rome that galled. The crisis came to a head when Pope Leo X (1513-21) made one more corrupt arrangement that drained additional huge sums of money from Germany. Leo, the son of Lorenzo the Magnificent, had remarked to his brother upon his elevation to the throne of St. Peter: "God has given us the papacy; let us enjoy it." Leo was in need of more funds for one of his pet projects: repairing and expanding

St. Peter's cathedral—a monument to the wealth and corruption of Roman Catholicism that still stands in awesome splendor today.

In the fateful year of 1514, a certain Archbishop Albert, already in control of two provinces under the auspices of the Roman church, cast covetous eyes on a third, the vacant archbishopric of Mainz. In order to overcome the technicality of canon law, which forbade holding multiple offices, Albert—who was also a prince of the House of Hohenzollern—paid Pope Leo X a princely sum for the special "dispensation" that would legalize his ambitious designs. In addition to the regular fee for such an office, Leo exacted a promise from Albert for the payment of a very large sum of money and helped him make that payment by arranging a loan from the wealthy Fugger banking family in Augsburg.

Pope Leo X then issued a papal bull authorizing the sale of indulgences in Saxony, under which half of the money (after commissions) went to Albert and the other half to the Fuggers, thus providing a means satisfactory to the bankers for repaying the loan. It was a blatant financial arrangement, the source of funds being the shrinking pocketbooks of the poor souls who believed they were thereby purchasing valid forgiveness of their sins and a shortened time in purgatory. Albert put the program in the capable hands of a Dominican monk named Johann Tetzel, whose high-pressure sales tactics made the whole scheme work. Agents of the Fuggers traveled with Tetzel and the other indulgence peddlers working under him to make certain that the agreed-upon 50 percent from each sale went to the bank. Tetzel himself was paid about $1,000 per month plus expenses, which was an incredibly huge sum in those days but was paid without grudging because of his unusual talents.

In 1517 Tetzel arrived at Juterbock and word of the booming indulgence sales soon came to the ears of a contentious former Augustinian friar, now lecturing professor at the nearby University of Wittenberg. Martin Luther's famous Ninety-Five Theses, which were nailed in anger to the door of the Castle Church in Wittenberg on October 31, 1517, were mainly an attack against the abuses of the indulgence system such as Tetzel represented, though not against the doctrine of indulgences itself. Luther had not yet gone that far in his thinking, but would soon be forced to break completely with Rome when it refused all appeals for reformation.

Martin Luther

From initial outrage at the extravagant promises and blasphemous merchandising of remission of sins by Johann Tetzel, the Vatican's master indulgence peddler, Luther's quarrel with the church he loved grew to include the smoldering issue of the supreme authority of the Scriptures in contrast to that claimed by popes, councils, decrees, and traditions. In his fiery debate with Meister Eck at Leipzig, Luther declared that "A simple layman armed with Scripture is to be believed above a pope or a council without it."[4]

When accused of spiritual pride in elevating his own opinions over those of the church, Luther responded:

> God once spoke through the mouth of an ass. . . . I am bound, not only to assert, but to defend the truth with my blood and death. I want to believe freely and be a slave to the authority of no one, whether council, university, or pope.
>
> I will confidently confess what appears to me to be true, whether it has been asserted by a Catholic or a heretic, whether it has been approved or reproved by a council.[5]

Summoned to Rome by Pope Leo X, Luther hesitated long enough for the pope, under pressure from the mounting discontent in Germany, to retract the order. Slightly more than a year after Luther had nailed his Ninety-five Theses to the Wittenberg door, the pope, in an effort at conciliation, officially repudiated many of the extreme claims his indulgence salesmen were making. He admitted that indulgences "forgave neither sins nor guilt" and that his power as pope "was limited to . . . beseeching God to apply to a dead soul the surplus merits of Christ and the saints."[6]

There were, of course, no refunds to those who had paid their money in reliance upon previous indulgence dogma nor any explanation as to why the latest pronouncements should be looked upon as any more accurate than those being "corrected." Nor was there any acknowledgement that Scripture (such as Hebrews 9:27—"it is appointed unto men once to die, but after this the judgment") clearly contradicted the idea that the condition of the dead could be changed. When ordered to recant at the Diet of Worms, Luther's answer again pivoted on Holy Writ:

> [I cannot] unless I am convicted by scripture and plain reason. I do not accept the authority of popes and councils, for they have contradicted each other—my conscience is captive to the Word of God.
>
> I cannot and I will not recant anything, for to go against conscience is neither right nor safe. God help me. Amen.[7]

Excommunication and the public burning of Luther's writings were, as expected, the initial reprisal from Pope Leo X. Luther's response was *An Open Letter to the Christian Nobility*. In clear terms he stated what the church must do to rid itself of its three major errors: It must remove the distinction between clergy and laity and thus restore to the individual Christian his rightful priesthood; it must acknowledge every Christian's right to interpret the Scriptures according to his conscience; and lastly, it must restore to Scripture the final authority which the church had so long usurped.

In his conscience Luther had gone beyond the point of no return. In the complete break that followed, however, Luther was never able to rid himself of all that needed to be discarded. Much that was Romish—such as baptismal regeneration and the baptism of infants—remained and is still part of Lutheranism today. Moreover, it was not long until the same lax moral standards were evident among Luther's followers that had been such an outrage in the Catholic Church and had been a major catalyst sparking the Reformation. Nor was Martin Luther, great man that he was, able to free his mind of Catholicism's endemic anti-Semitism.

The Failure of Christianization

In his conflict with the pope, Luther unfortunately allied himself with the German princes, who were only too happy to adopt Lutheranism as justification for applying to their own selfish purposes the wealth which once flowed to Rome. Along with much that was good and fundamental to saving faith in Christ alone without ecclesiastical intermediaries, Lutheranism, which had opposed the corruption of a church wielding imperial power, easily accommodated itself to a new union of church and state. For all of the good intentions of its leaders, the Protestant Reformation quickly found itself entangled in the very partnership with imperial power which had accelerated the downward course of the Roman Catholic Church. As Will Durant observes in his history of the Reformation:

> Theoretically Church and state remained independent; actually the [new Protestant] Church became subject to the state.
> The Lutheran movement, which thought to submit all life to theology, unwittingly, unwillingly, advanced that pervasive secularization which is a basic theme of modern life.[8]

Far from being a single entity, sixteenth-century Germany embodied some 250 separate principalities, each ruled by a prince who had the prerogative of deciding his territory's own religious affairs. Hailed by the "Protestants" as a major victory for the reformed religion, the Smalcaldic League of 1531 united nine German princes and their territories to defend Protestantism against a threatened attack by the pope's imperial forces. Europe would soon be divided (as it remains today) between monarchs and territories loyal either to Protestantism or Catholicism, and bloody, destructive wars would be fought over that issue. Forsaking his earlier commitment to nonviolence and his protestations on behalf of individual liberty of conscience, Luther decided that the sword was indispensable not only for protection from the pope but for enforcement of the new truth. He was acknowledging that the Reformation which had been inspired by the steadfast faith of martyrs must now look for protection to the sword wielded by earthly powers.

In the Peasants' War (1524-26) the princes, with Luther's encouragement, slaughtered nearly 130,000 to suppress an uprising for which in many ways their own greed had been largely responsible. Defeated, the peasants would pragmatically give halfhearted allegiance to a state church that today still prevents so many in Protestant Europe from knowing that personal relationship with Christ which Luther complained was denied under Catholicism.

On their part, the princes approved the new religion not so much out of genuine concern for truth but because it upheld their power and gave them their share of confiscated church properties. Luther's staunch friend Melanchthon sadly declared that "under cover of the Gospel the princes were only intent on the plunder of the churches." The same observations would have to be made a few years later when in less-violent Presbyterian form the Reformation, under the leadership of John Knox, came to Scotland. As Durant observed:

> Now that the nobles were allowed to reject purgatory as a myth, they claimed to have been cheated in some part of their patrimony by ancestral donations of land or money to pay priests to say Masses for the dead, who, on the new theology, were irrevocably saved or damned before the creation of the world.
>
> So the appropriation of ecclesiastical property could be pleasantly phrased as the restoration of stolen goods. Most of the Scottish monasteries were closed, and their wealth was taken by the nobles.[9]

As age closed in on Luther, the new superstructure he had created required the same apologies which his conscience would no longer allow him to give for the Catholic Church. He was now defending the role of military power to enforce Protestantism with the same vigor with which he had condemned its use for maintaining Catholicism. Seemingly forgotten were the words of Christ to Pilate: "My kingdom is not of this world; if my kingdom were of this world, then

would my servants fight . . ." (John 18:36). In fact it had become
very difficult for anyone to hear His voice above the rattle of muskets
and the roar of cannons as Protestants and Catholics fought among
themselves and one another.

In defense of the new authoritarianism and partnership with
earthly powers, Luther argued: "The hand that wields the secular
sword is not a human hand but the hand of God. It is God, not man,
Who hangs, and breaks on the wheel, and decapitates, and flogs; it is
God who wages war." Durant perceptively concludes:

> In this exaltation of the state as now the sole source of
> order lay the seeds of the absolutist philosophies of
> Hobbes and Hegel, and a premonition of Imperial Ger-
> many.[10]

John Calvin

One of the boldest experiments to come out of the Reformation,
though it ultimately failed like other similar attempts, was the
theocracy established by John Calvin in Geneva, the city to which he
moved in 1536 at the age of 27. The character of the man could
scarcely be faulted. One senses the deep frustration as Pope Pius IV
declares: "The strength of that heretic consisted in this, that money
never had the slightest charm for him. If I had such servants my
dominion would extend from sea to sea."[11] His marriage relationship was chaste, affectionate, and loyal. On a modest salary of 100
crowns per year he lived frugally and selflessly and labored tire-
lessly to establish a kingdom given over to godly rule and simple
living. For his enemies, Calvin's unremitting incorruptibility was
galling indeed.

Calvin's genius was an exalted and consuming appreciation of
God's glory. His was truly a God-centered outlook. And the more a
person understood of this God of majesty the greater the sense of
one's own shortcomings. He spelled it out lucidly and with compelling conviction in *The Institutes of the Christian Religion*, written
originally as an appeal to Francis, king of France, to give a fair

audience to the beliefs and aspirations of the French Protestants. Ultimately it became the definitive apologia for the Protestant doctrine in general and predestination in particular. The political connection, however, was not absent even in this. Calvin hoped to gain the support of Catholic Francis, who was then in the process of attempting to make a military alliance with the Lutheran princes against the Catholic Emperor Charles V.

Calvin's reasoning and style were profound—and convincing to those of his day who saw that, in its practical outworking, "Lutheran faith" seemed in too many instances to fall short of God's standards of holy living. Luther himself had written in disgust that "peasants, citizens, nobles, all are more covetous and undisciplined than they were under the Papacy."[12] That admission, of course, gave the Catholics great comfort; but to Calvin, the reason why neither Catholicism nor Protestantism, but only God's grace, could produce holy lives seemed clear:

> The mind of man has been so completely estranged from God's righteousness that it conceives, desires, and undertakes, only that which is impious, perverted, foul, impure, and infamous.[13]

It is a wonder how Calvin found the time to write so profoundly and prolifically. Certainly his writings not only contrast with the fluff of self-centered psychologizing present in so much that passes for Christian teaching today, but they convict us of our shallowness and sin as they convicted readers in Calvin's day. Having convinced us of our own depravity and need to cry out for God's mercy as the only basis of hope, however, he went on to limit that mercy through his doctrine of predestination, the central teaching of Calvinism:

> As Scripture, then, clearly shows, we say that God once established by his eternal and unchangeable plan those whom he long before determined once for all to receive into salvation, and those whom, on the other hand, he would devote to destruction.

We assert that, with respect to the elect, this plan was
founded upon his freely given mercy, without regard to
human worth; but by his just and irreprehensible but
incomprehensible judgment he has barred the door of life
to those whom he has given over to damnation.[14]

Godliness By Coercion

None can quarrel with the teaching that God has the *right* as
Creator and Lord of the universe to do with man what He wills, nor
with the *justice* of sending us all to hell, for that is what our sin
merits. However, Scripture clearly tells us that God is "not willing
that any should perish" (2 Peter 3:9), but that He desires "*all men* to
be saved, and to come unto the knowledge of the truth" (1 Timothy 2:4). Christ's declaration to Nicodemus that God had not sent
His Son into the world "to condemn the world, but that *the world
through him might be saved*" (John 3:17) seems conclusive. It
certainly leaves no room for the idea that God has determined to
deliberately leave some men in their sins. Calvinism thus presents
serious contradictions, but we must defer that concern until a later
chapter.

If God had willed the evil which abounds everywhere, Calvin
would have none of it under his jurisdiction. He valiantly attempted
to force the Genevans to live according to biblical standards without
regard to whether they had been predestined to such a life or not.
The godliness that he taught could only come by God Himself
dispensing "irresistible grace," Calvin was determined to produce
by coercion. Unity of faith even for those who had no faith was to
become a matter of legal prescription.

Supreme over both civil and religious affairs in Geneva was the
city council, over which Calvin, in turn, exercised complete control.
Agreement with the council's confession of faith was a requirement
for citizenship. Conformity to its social and moral decrees was a
condition of continuance. So attractive was the resultant piety and
prosperity of the city, however, that dissenters flocked there from all
over Europe. A pastor visiting from Lutheran Germany in 1610
expressed in extravagant terms what he observed:

There is in that city not only the perfect institute of a
perfect republic, but, as a special ornament, a moral
discipline which makes weekly investigations into the
conduct, and even the smallest transgressions, of the
citizens. . . .
All cursing and swearing, gambling, luxury, strife,
hatred, fraud, etc. are forbidden, while greater sins are
hardly heard of. What a glorious ornament of the Christian religion is such a purity of morals!
We must lament with tears what is wanting with us
[Germans], and almost totally neglected. If it were not
for the difference of religion, I would have been chained
to Geneva forever.[15]

"Conduct was to be guided as carefully as belief," Durant writes,
"for good conduct was the goal of right belief. Calvin himself,
austere and severe, dreamed of a community so well regulated that
its virtue would prove his theology, and would shame the Catholicism that had produced or tolerated the luxury and laxity of Rome."[16]

Some of the strictures enforced in Geneva would seem in our day
to border on the ludicrous. A child's goodnight kiss, an overabun-
dance of dishes at the table, a too-elevated headdress, an excessive
display of lace, a proscribed color in dress—all were fair subjects of
debate and punishment.[17] In some ways Gorbachev's Soviet Russia,
especially now under *glasnost*, seems preferable to Calvin's Geneva:

In a class by themselves stood crimes against Calvin. It was a crime to laugh at Calvin's sermons; it was a
crime to argue with Calvin in the street. But to enter
into theological controversy with Calvin might turn out
to be a very grave crime. . . . [In fact] the regulations
were almost incapable of being kept.
Everybody was compelled to attend church. . . . No
one could leave the town without giving reasons acceptable to the Council. Bands of the faithful had

power to enter the houses, put servants through their catechisms, order parents to send their children to school. . . .

Torture added a customary terror to the criminal trials, and the smallest deviation from orthodoxy was dealt with at once. In sixty years one hundred and fif⁺ᵛ heretics were burnt in Geneva. . . . fathers and mothers accused their children not of minor offences merely, but of crimes, and informers were everywhere.[18]

Never had a society been ruled by such a minutia of laws. Moral lapses were pursued with the greatest rigor. In the council's heyday, over 400 persons were indicted for moral offenses in the course of one year in Geneva. Punishments were spelled out with awesome severity—from banishment to beheading. Blasphemy, idolatry, and adultery were capital offenses.[19] One of those beheaded was a child who was convicted of striking his parent.[20] A man named Gruet was tortured for three years, "confessed" at last, and was executed in 1547 for having attached a disrespectful placard to Calvin's pulpit at St. Peter's.

A Valiant Attempt to Reconstruct Society

The obedience that God, according to Calvinism, could have predestined but chose not to, Calvin was determined to effect, not by grace but by the severest imposition of law. The once noble cry of *sola scriptura* had somehow metamorphosed into *sola Calvinism*. Once again the Bible could only be interpreted by the ruling ecclesiastical authority:

The new clergy . . . became under Calvin more powerful than any priesthood since ancient Israel. The real law of a Christian state, said Calvin, must be the Bible; the clergy are the proper interpreters of that law; civil governments are subject to that law, and must enforce it as so interpreted. . . .

Calvin was as thorough as any pope in rejecting individualism of belief. [He] . . . completely repudiated that principle of private judgment with which the new religion had begun.

He had seen the fragmentation of the Reformation into a hundred sects, and foresaw more; in Geneva he would have none of them. There a body of learned divines would formulate an authoritative creed; those Genevans who could not accept it would have to seek other habitats.

Persistent absence from Protestant services, or continued refusal to take the Eucharist, was a punishable offense. Heresy again became an insult to God and treason to the state, and was to be punished with death. Catholicism, which had preached this view of heresy, became heresy in its turn.[21]

Michael Servetus, who had escaped after being arrested by the Catholic Inquisition in Lyon, was burned at the stake in Calvin's Protestant Geneva for denying the Trinity. Of the tract Calvin wrote to justify the execution of Servetus (*The defence of the orthodox faith in the Sacred Trinity*), R. Tudor Jones comments:

It is Calvin at his most chilling. The document is as frightening in its way as Luther's tract against the rebellious peasants.[22]

Great man that he undoubtedly was, Calvin obviously misunderstood something vital. He was not willing to allow the same freedom that God clearly allows. Calvin did not believe that man had the power to choose to obey God, to choose to do good—but his attempt to force men to behave would have to be called a failure. Paul had presented the human dilemma with these words: "To will is present with me, but how to perform that which is good I find not" (Romans 7:18). It was not that man could not see the truth and even desire to do it, but that he lacked the power which only God could supply. Nor could that power be generated by imposition of law, but by grace and love and the filling of the

Holy Spirit. While Calvin had a great love for God, he showed little grace in his dealings with his fellows on God's behalf.

Like Luther, Calvin also fell back upon the power of godless rulers, a practice which the reformers had condemned in Rome. Why the secular sword should be called upon to force upon the unwilling what God chose not to effect by "predestination" and "irresistible grace" was not explained. A letter dated October 22, 1548, to Lord Protector Somerset, corrupt adviser to King Edward VI of England, is especially revealing. Calvin refers to those who oppose Edward as "obstinate adherents to the superstitions of the Roman Antichrist." He goes on to provide the following advice on how to deal both with rebels against the crown and doctrinal heretics:

> [They] well deserve to be repressed by the sword which is committed to you, seeing that they attack not the King only, but God who has seated him upon the throne, and has entrusted to you the protection as well of his person as of his majesty.[23]

It was worse than ironic that the two chief reformers were so adamant in their imposition upon the Protestants of the very authoritarianism which Catholicism had so long wielded and which had been a chief cause of the Reformation. While Luther and Calvin fell into the same error as the popes of making alliances with secular authorities, never would a Protestant church or denomination, however, wield power *over* the kings of the earth as Catholicism had and still continued to do. For one thing, the Protestants had no pope, nor did the Protestant churches claim to be the gateway to heaven, but pointed men to Christ as "the way, the truth and the life." It was up to each individual to work out his own salvation "with fear and trembling" (Philippians 2:12)— fear of God, not of an ecclesiastical authority.

Never has such a valiant attempt been made to effect a "reconstruction" of society as under the efficient direction of Calvin. Nor could anyone be better qualified than he or find circumstances so much in favor of the desired goal. Yet Christianization failed even in the small area of Geneva for the same reasons that any such attempt must fail today as well. Only a small percentage of mankind is willing ("predestined," according to Calvin) to come to Christ in repentance and to be born again by the Spirit of God—but only thus can one live in obedience to God's laws. Many Scriptures make this very clear, among them the following:

> For what the law could not do, in that it was weak through the flesh, God sending his own Son in the likeness of sinful flesh, and for sin, condemned sin in the flesh, that the righteousness of the law might be fulfilled in us, who walk not after the flesh, but after the Spirit. . . .
> Because the carnal mind is enmity against God, for it is not subject to the law of God, neither indeed can be. So then they that are in the flesh cannot please God.
> But ye are not in the flesh, but in the Spirit, if so be that the Spirit of God dwell in you. Now if any man have not the Spirit of Christ, he is none of his (Romans 8:3-9).

Sheep Cannot Keep Peace in the Jungle

The sinfulness of man created an impossible dilemma. Those who seek to Christianize today's world by joining forces with the ungodly, no matter how good the cause, could well find themselves confronted with similar problems. The heart of even "Christianized" man is still "deceitful above all things, and desperately wicked" (Jeremiah 17:9). As Roland H. Bainton points out in his life of Martin Luther, ". . . coercion can never be eliminated because society can never be Christianized."[24]

Yet riding this dead horse to victory is the new vision that is sweeping the evangelical church in America today. Oddly enough, this impossible goal of Christianizing the world is now being presented as the long overlooked true intent of the Great Commission. Today's church, we are told, must take over society, as the Catholic

Church accomplished and the Reformers attempted, if it is to fulfill "its God-ordained leadership role . . . [and] cause 'God's will to be done on earth as it is in heaven.' "[25]

Bainton goes on to quote a still-militant yet disillusioned Luther, whose words ought to be heeded by those who today seek the same "reconstruction" of society that failed not only for the reformers but on so many other occasions throughout history:

> The world and the masses are and always will be unchristian, although they are baptized and nominally Christian.
>
> Hence a man who would venture to govern an entire community or the world with the gospel would be like a shepherd who should place in one fold wolves, lions, eagles, and sheep. The sheep would keep the peace, but they would not last long. The world cannot be ruled with a rosary.[26]

It does not bode well that the Reconstructionists, whose influence in the church is growing rapidly, have Calvin as their faultless hero and hope to model Christianized society after his failed Geneva experiment.

9

Dare We Forget?

In spite of the many extremes and inconsistencies, much good was accomplished by the Reformation. There were thousands of people who never went along with the excesses of Luther or Calvin or condoned the unholy alliance between church and state. Many Christians also recognized and repudiated the elements of Romanism which much of Protestantism still retained. Eventually out of the independent groups they formed came the Baptists and various Brethren and "Free" churches, which in turn spawned the evangelical movement that dominates American Protestantism today. E.H. Broadbent writes:

> It is often thought that when the Reformation was established, Europe was divided into Protestants on the one hand and Roman Catholics on the other. The large numbers of Christians are overlooked who did not belong to either party, but who . . . met as independent churches, not relying . . . on the support of the civil power. . . . They were so numerous that both the State Church parties feared they might come to threaten their own power and even existence.
>
> The reason that so important a movement occupies so small a place in the history of those times is that by the relentless use of the power of the State the great Churches, Catholic and Protestant, were able . . . to destroy much of

the literature of the brethren [as most were called] . . .
writing their history to represent them as holding doctrines which they repudiated. . . .[1]

The Reformation had done away with purgatory, indulgences,
images, prayers to and for the dead, the cult of the saints, and much
of the corruption that inevitably accompanies the elevation of and
submission to an elite hierarchy. In general, only two ordinances
remained: baptism and the Eucharist (the latter becoming known
also as "communion" or "the Lord's supper"). Both of these were
the cause of continuing controversy and division within the Reformation and contributed to the spectacle of wars and martyrdom
among the Protestants themselves. Unity of faith, even for those
who professed the same faith, was not easy to achieve.

The "Free Church" Movement

Baptism caused the greatest controversy within Protestantism.
Catholicism's infant baptism was retained among both Lutherans
and Calvinists as well as by Anglicans and Presbyterians in England
and Scotland. There were many, however, who saw clearly that
baptism was only for *believers* who had personally received Christ
as Lord and Savior ("If thou believest with all thine heart"—Acts
8:36-39) and were thereby making public confession of that fact.
They saw from experience that infant baptism led to the false belief
that a person was, by virtue of the baptism, in some sense a
Christian. Even though Confirmation was required later in life, it
became in many cases a mere formality. Most of those who repudiated infant baptism and submitted to baptism as believers in Christ
were called Anabaptists (or "rebaptized ones"). Terrible was their
suffering at the hands of both the Catholics and Protestants.

With what a tremendous sense of *déjà vu* the new class of martyrs
must have viewed their world. The Anabaptists desired only what
the Reformation had originally proclaimed: the freedom to worship
in simplicity apart from all political factions and machinations and
to conduct their lives in humility and mutual charity. The nonpolit-
ical nature of the "brethren," as they preferred to be called, took

pacifism to its extreme conclusion. No matter what outrages were committed against their persons or properties, they refused (with few exceptions) to lift the sword or go to law in their own defense.

To these "independent" Christians, the mutual charity taught in Scripture implied a sharing of goods, albeit a voluntary one. It must have been particularly convicting for both the Lutheran and Catholic Churches to see a community of believers so uninterested in either power or the accumulation of wealth. Such were the very weaknesses which had shamed Rome before the world and to which the Lutheran Church, under the patronage of the State and its powerful princes, was fast accommodating itself.

Almost unique at that time was the Anabaptists' fervent expectation of the return of Christ. It helped make the pain of loss more bearable—whether of earthly goods or of life itself. Moreover, their revival of the forgotten hope of Christ's imminent return contributed in no small way to the circumspect manner and purity of life that characterized the Anabaptist movement as a whole. Though fervent in their expectation of the establishment of a heavenly kingdom on earth, they were adamant that it was to be initiated by Christ and not by their own efforts in His absence.

Far from perfect, however, the Anabaptists had their heresies (some denied the Trinity and were involved in polygamy) and made at least one attempt to establish an earthly kingdom. In 1534 a splinter group forcibly installed itself as a military theocracy in Munster in Westphalia. Grandiose plans for a New Jerusalem were set in motion and all Lutherans and Catholics were given the option of rebaptism or banishment.

John of Leyden, a former tailor, was crowned "King of the people of God in the New Temple" in a ceremony marked by all the panoply and symbolism of royal office. His robes were selected from among the sumptuous garments left behind by the banished dissenters. The death penalty was imposed by the new monarch for a series of trivial offenses. One of them, significantly, was "complaining."

Success seemed assured as a steady flood of poor and dispossessed, attracted by the radical communism, streamed in to strengthen the garrison for the coming conflict. In June of 1534, however, the grand experiment in kingdom living was betrayed from within and the bishop's troops stormed the city. Not one of its brave but deluded defenders was spared.

Transubstantiation

While baptism had remained much the same, radical changes were made by the Reformers in the understanding and practice of the Eucharist. It was the one other sacrament which the Protestants carried over from their common backgrounds in what they had all previously considered to be "the only true church." The major change in the Eucharist was the Reformation's repudiation of Catholicism's doctrine of *transubstantiation*: "that by the consecration of the bread and wine a change is brought about of the whole substance of the bread into the substance of the body of Christ our Lord, and of the whole substance of the wine into the substance of His blood."[2] This was no mere theological technicality, but one of the most serious issues involved in the Reformation—and one upon which neither side would compromise.

Why was transubstantiation so important that its rejection was most often the specific charge leveled against those burned at the stake? It was because of the Catholic doctrine that the sacrifice of Christ could only suffice for sins which preceded it in time. Thus, each sin necessitated another offering of Christ, even as in Old Testament times animal sacrifices were repeatedly offered. Since Christ is not literally being crucified again and again on Calvary, this resacrifice was possible only if the Eucharist contained His actual body and blood. Hence the dogma of transubstantiation.

Scripture anticipates such heresy. Hebrews 10:1-18, for example, declares that the fact that the Old Testament offerings had to be repeated was proof that they "could not take away sins." Christ's "one sacrifice for sins forever" is then presented in contrast. That this sacrifice was only offered *once* and never needed to be repeated is given as proof that it was accepted by God as full atonement for man's sin. The argument ends with this conclusion: "There is no more offering for sin." Clearly the alleged reoffering of Christ in the Catholic Mass is condemned as fraudulent by such Scriptures.

Hebrews 6:4-6 presents the same argument in different form. It declares that if it were possible to lose one's salvation it would therefore be impossible to be saved again, because this would require that Christ be recrucified with each lapse in faith. If His sacrifice upon the cross was not sufficient to *keep* one saved then He would have to be crucified again—and again and again. Yet Catholicism claims that the Mass accomplishes the very resacrifice of Christ which Scripture repudiates. The dogma of transubstantiation thus represents a denial of the true gospel of Christ whereby we are saved through faith in His death, burial, and resurrection as real events which, having occurred once at a particular place and time in history, fully accomplished the remission of our sins.

According to Hebrews 6:4-6, the teaching that Christ needs to be sacrificed more than once holds the Son of God up "to an open shame." Surely it would have been foolish in the extreme for Him to offer Himself on the cross to procure a salvation that we could never obtain ourselves, but which it was thereafter up to us to keep by living a good life. Since every recipient of such salvation would inevitably lose it through sinning, Christ would have died in vain, for no matter how many times He was sacrificed it would never be enough.

No wonder that Roman Catholic doctrine does not specify how many Masses must be performed in order to release one soul from purgatory. Even the pope has no assurance on this point, either for himself or for those who trust in him.

The Council of Trent

The Council of Trent met in a number of sessions between 1545 and 1563 to formulate Catholicism's official response to the escalating Protestant Reformation. Essentially the council rejected everything the Reformation stood for and reaffirmed the doctrines that had been at issue. The reformers' cry of *sola scriptura*, the priesthood of all believers, and salvation by faith alone were condemned as heresies worthy of death. The Bible was declared to be insufficient unless supplemented with church tradition and new dogmas. Faith alone could not save without good works and the rituals and mediation of the church and purification of a person's sins through his own suffering on earth and in purgatory. As for that key doctrine of indulgences that had precipitated the Reformation, the council decreed:

> If anyone says that after the reception of the grace of justification the guilt is so remitted and the debt of eternal punishment so blotted out to every repentant sinner, that no debt of temporal punishment remains to be discharged either in this world or in purgatory before the gates of heaven can be opened, let him be anathema.[3]
>
> [We affirm] that there is a purgatory, and that the souls there detained are aided by the suffrages of the faithful and . . . [that] the bishops shall see to it that the suffrages of the living, that is, the sacrifice of the mass, prayers, alms and other works of piety which they have been accustomed to perform for the faithful departed, be piously and devoutly discharged in accordance with the laws of the Church. . . .[4]

It was reaffirmed that the cross of Christ was insufficient to deal fully with sin. That sacrifice had to be repeated endlessly by the Catholic priesthood and supplemented by the sacraments of the church, without which no one could enter heaven. One judgment was repeatedly pronounced by the council upon any failing to accept each and all of its *Canons and Decrees*: ". . . let him be anathema [eternally damned]."[5]

The Canons and Decrees of the Council of Trent remains the standard in the Roman Catholic Church to the present day. Modern catechisms require that today's Catholic must "accept, without hesitation, and profess all that has been handed down . . . especially by the Sacred Council of Trent. . . ."[6] The "confession of faith" to which any person joining the Catholic Church must subscribe includes the following:

> I accept and hold, in each and every part, all that has been defined and declared by the Sacred Council of Trent

concerning Original Sin and Justification [i.e. "baptism for remission of sins," etc.].

I profess that in the Mass is offered to God a true, real and propitiatory sacrifice for the living and the dead; that in the Holy Sacrament of the Eucharist is really, truly and substantially the Body and blood together with the soul and Divinity of Our Lord Jesus Christ, and that there takes place what the Church calls transubstantiation, that is the change of all the substance of bread into the Body and of all substance of wine into the Blood. I confess also that in receiving under either of these species one receives Jesus Christ, whole and entire. [With this misunderstanding of what it means to "receive Christ" it is difficult to convince a Catholic to believe the simple gospel.]

I firmly hold that Purgatory exists and that the souls detained there can be helped by the prayers of the faithful. Likewise I hold that the saints, who reign with Jesus Christ, should be venerated and invoked, that they offer prayers to God for us and that their relics are to be venerated.

I profess firmly that the images of Jesus Christ and of the Mother of God, ever Virgin, as well as of all the saints should be given due honour and veneration. I also affirm that Jesus Christ left to the Church the faculty to grant Indulgences and that their use is most salutary to the Christian people.[7]

The position given to Mary makes it difficult for the average Catholic to comprehend that Christ paid fully for his sins, that he has eternal life as a free gift through believing the gospel, and that each Christian has full access to God through Christ alone. Catholics feel unworthy to pray directly to Jesus, or to the Father through Christ, having been taught instead to rely upon Mary's mercy and intercession with Father and Son. Take, for example, the rosary. Each time it is repeated, the Apostles' Creed is recited once, the

188 • *Dare We Forget?*

Lord's Prayer six times, and the "Glory be to the Father . . . Son, and to the Holy Spirit . . ." six times. The "Hail Mary," however, is repeated 53 times. Its appeal to "Holy Mary, Mother of God, pray for us sinners, now and at the hour of our death," clearly delineates the primacy of her position in the Catholic heaven and forgiveness of sins. The rosary concludes with:

> Hail, holy Queen, Mother of Mercy! our life, our sweetness, and our hope! To thee do we cry, poor banished children of Eve; to thee do we send up our sighs, mourning and weeping in this valley of tears.
>
> Turn, then, most gracious Advocate, thine eyes of mercy toward us; and after this our exile show unto us the blessed fruit of thy womb, Jesus; O clement, O loving, O sweet Virgin Mary.
>
> Pray for us, O holy mother of God. That we may be made worthy of the promises of Christ.

Rare is the Catholic who has any real assurance of heaven. It will only be reached, if ever, at the end of a long and painful sojourn in purgatory. So much depends upon the sacraments administered by the church, one's condition at the time of death, the faithfulness of surviving relatives in engaging the church to continue Masses for one's soul after death, the intercession of numerous saints, and the influence of Mary. Little if any hope is placed in Christ Himself, the One who came from heaven, who told us about it, who paid for our sins to take us there, and who is Himself the only way to His Father's house of many mansions.

Catholics, Charismatics, and Ecumenism

The battle that was fought by the Catholic Church against the Reformation is still being waged today and with greater effectiveness than ever before. Most Protestants are either uninformed or have forgotten the grave issues involved in the Reformation and have been convinced that a lack of "unity" is the only problem. We are being bombarded with cries for "unity," especially from charismatic leaders, and efforts such as "Pentecost 1988" are working toward that end. Reporting on that event, *Christianity Today* stated that "Protestants, Catholics, Orthodox, and evangelicals set aside their differences to meet in Arlington, Texas, for a 'Gathering of Christians.' "[8] One disgruntled conservative who attended wrote:

> The wrap-up was on Wednesday morning. We sang "The Church's One Foundation"—four stanzas anyway. The verses about "false sons in her pale," and standing against "foe or traitor," and "by heresies distrest," were not among them.[9]

The charismatic movement has been particularly vulnerable to an ecumenical union with Rome ever since Catholics began to "speak in tongues." One can only wonder, however, why most of those who have allegedly been "baptized in the Spirit" become even more enamored with prayers to Mary and various "saints," the reoffering of Christ in "the sacrifice of the Mass," and other serious heresies destructive of the gospel and so contrary to what the Holy Spirit has declared in Scripture.

Charismatic leadership refers to what it considers to be the last-days outpouring of the Holy Spirit in the renewal of His gifts upon the "old line denominations—Episcopal, Presbyterian, Methodist, Lutheran—and [upon] . . . Roman Catholics. . . ." The Charismatic Bible Ministries, founded by Oral Roberts along with most of today's visible charismatic leaders, has as its motto: "Unity and love through signs and wonders." As though faith is believing *anything*, rather than commitment to truth for which we must contend, Paulk suggests that Paul's "unity of the faith" (Ephesians 4:13) has nothing to do with doctrine.[10] Typically, another influential charismatic writer recommends a unity which comes not through commitment to common truth, but through feelings and experiences and presumed miracles:

> [There will be] a deluge of the Holy Spirit's power

upon the whole Church—Roman Catholic and Protestant. The same unity that was in the upper room of the New Testament Church will be found among Christians in every nation. Mass healings will take place worldwide, demons will be cast out, miracles will become the norm.[11]

There can be no doubt that the predominant cry today among many of those who call themselves Christians is "unity." That same seductive theme was the principle weapon with which the Roman Catholic Church attempted to stop the Reformation: "You make schism in Mother Church!" Luther was urged to "keep in mind the unity of the holy, catholic, and apostolic church. . . ." Unity has an emotional appeal, especially for those who wish to be "positive" at all cost. It is today's major weapon in reversing the Reformation.

Charismatics stand at the forefront of the growing move to bring Protestants back in union with Rome. One example of the many significant efforts being made in that direction was the North American Congress on the Holy Spirit and World Evangelization in New Orleans in mid-1987. Of the 35,000 charismatic participants, about 51 percent were Roman Catholics, with priests playing a key role both in leadership and speaking.[12]

When German evangelist Reinhard Bonnke called for those who wanted to receive Christ to stand, to his utter amazement nearly half of those present came to their feet, indicating they did not know Christ personally as Savior and Lord. Yet they had for the past three days been praising God, speaking in tongues, and in every way participating in what was billed as a conference for believers who had already been baptized in the Holy Spirit. Astounded at the response, Bonnke tried to explain that he was only interested in those who had never received eternal life through Christ. Still the multitude remained on its feet.

Vinson Synan, chairman of the Congress, was questioned about this seeming paradox and why there was nothing in all of the talks and workshops to make clear what it meant to be born again and to know Christ personally as Savior and Lord. He reportedly shrugged off the issue as one of those theological differences that might take years to work out and should not be allowed to stand in the way of unity, with the words: "Well, we don't have time to do that!"[13]

Unity at What Cost?

That errors which were considered so serious that the Reformers gave their lives to oppose them are being waved aside by Protestants today for the sake of unity does not bode well for the future. If he were still alive, Luther would be shocked to learn that the Lutheran World Federation, which represents 93% of the world's 58.6 million Lutherans, has its headquarters "at the [WCC] Ecumenical Center, Geneva, Switzerland, and . . . works closely with the World Council of Churches and other ecumenical agencies [headquartered] there."[14] The WCC, of course, has a long history of ignoring truth and doctrine in its pursuit of ecumenism. One is reminded of the ecumenical spirit in Nazi Germany that allowed church leaders to see no wrong in Hitler, though his true intentions should have been plain enough. Of those days Charles Colson writes:

> Churchmen were so enamored with the fledgling ecumenical movement that, to Bonhoeffer's disgust, they refused to censure the German church even after German Christians [the Nazi-front organization] had taken control.[15]

Unfortunately, in the eyes of many Christian leaders today, doctrine is no longer looked upon as the framework for truth but as the enemy of unity and love. Popular charismatic leader Earl Paulk, a presumed evangelical, declares that unity requires "stepping over walls of doctrine that powerfully separate us." Embracing not only Catholics but even Mormons as "brothers and sisters in the faith," Paulk writes:

> What would a meeting be like which brought together liberal evangelicals, such as we are, conservative theologians, represented by Holiness groups and southern

Baptists, and Catholics, Seventh-Day Adventists, and members of the Church of Jesus Christ of Latter-Day Saints?

Many of these groups have become so different that we almost regard them as enemies, rather than as brothers and sisters in the faith. How can we step over these walls that have been built so high?[16]

Popes, cardinals, bishops, and other Catholic leaders are only too pleased to encourage cooperation and demonstrations of unity between Catholics and Protestants. At the same time, however, they busy themselves combating the "dangerous doctrines" of salvation through faith in the finished work of Christ. Roman Catholic apologist Karl Keating is holding workshops across the country to educate Catholics against evangelical teachings and to challenge Protestants. Recently "a committee of Catholic bishops urged the nation's hierarchy . . . to develop a plan of biblical education that would 'counteract the simplicities of biblical fundamentalism.' " The bishops issued a statement in both English and Spanish which complained about the great inroads fundamentalism is making into Catholicism, particularly among Hispanics.[17] There is a high cost to ecumenism, and unfortunately there are Christian leaders who are willing to pay any price for "unity."

Among many so-called Protestants today, the great issues of the Reformation have apparently been forgotten, or are no longer considered important. Describing his feelings as he watched Pope John Paul II perform Mass during his visit to Los Angeles in September 1987, Robert Schuller reportedly said, "I cried through most of the Mass, because there was nothing that he said in words or in theological content that didn't harmonize with my own belief system."[18] Apparently considering the eternal issues of the Reformation now outdated, Schuller advocates pop psychology as the new standard for the church:

Where the sixteenth-century Reformation returned

our focus to sacred Scriptures as the only infallible rule for faith and practice, the new reformation will return our focus to the sacred right of every person to self-esteem![19]

Any departure from the Reformer's *sola scriptura*, even one seemingly so benign and well-intentioned as *Christianity Today's* recently issued "formal call for remonasticization in the [Protestant] church,"[20] can be dangerous. Monasticism originates not in Scripture, but in Catholicism. It contributed greatly to the fall of the Roman Empire and brought many errors and excesses into the church. A revival of monasticism could nudge Protestants further on the road back to Rome.

Whatever his public relations remarks to confuse Protestants, the pope fervently believes that through performance of the sacraments such as the Mass, the Catholic Church, "outside of which nobody can be saved," is enabled to "lead all of good will to heaven with divine certainty."[21] Return of all "separated brethren" to that "one true Church" is the unity being pursued by the Roman pontiff. Apparently willing in the interest of unity to overlook the issues for which thousands were martyred during the Reformation, Schuller recently confided to *Los Angeles Herald Examiner* columnist Father Michael Manning:

It's time for Protestants to go to the shepherd [the pope] and say, "What do we have to do to come home?"[22]

Ecumenism's Ambassador to the World

Pope John Paul II, head of the church that built St. Peter's Cathedral and its magnificent headquarters with funds raised from the sale of indulgences, generally clothes his persistent appeal for "unity" in terms that disguise his intent to bring all back under submission to Rome. Any lesser goal would be a denial of his office and Rome's long-standing assertion that "the only Church of the present day which can prove her claim to be the divine Church established by Jesus Christ is the Catholic Church . . . governed by the Pope, the Bishop of Rome."[23]

On May 3, 1987, Pope John Paul II gave a key speech on his favorite theme: religious unity. The site he chose for this speech was significant: Augsburg, Germany—birthplace in 1530 of the Lutheran Augsburg Confession, which was rejected summarily by the Council of Trent. News wires suggested that the pope had "offered an olive branch to West Germany's predominant Lutherans." In fact, what he actually said was just the opposite.

The pope's proposal that it had been necessary for "religious wars to occur in order to lead the church to reflect on and renew its original values" was simply reaffirming the Catholic Church's rejection of the Reformation. He encouraged Catholics to believe that "God may bring the Christian denominations and churches back together again."[24] By "together" the pope had only one thing in mind—for the "separated brethren" of Protestantism, in abject surrender of everything for which the martyrs died, to rejoin the Catholic Church.

In his farewell speech just before departing Germany for Rome the following day, the pontiff "linked the prospect of a free and united Europe with a Christian unity. . . ." He identified the "major challenges of our times" as "Christian roots in Europe, world peace, [and] the reunification of Christians. . . ." Revealing both his determination and confidence, "John Paul told an ecumenical gathering of Protestant and Greek Orthodox leaders . . . 'The spirit of love can overcome any separation. Let us give thanks for all the steps that have brought us closer to greater unity in recent years.' " Knowing what the Pope means by "unity," the following comment by the *Los Angeles Times* is significant:

> In a rare forecast of success for the ecumenical movement between Catholics and Protestants, he [John Paul] told [German Chancellor Helmut] Kohl in a farewell speech . . . "I am firmly convinced that the vexation of denominational division can, with the necessary patience and endurance, gradually be overcome."[25]

The Importance of Doctrine

We do well to remember the supreme price at which freedom of conscience was purchased. One of the most prized privileges that Christians enjoy today is the right to go to the Bible and decide what it teaches for themselves. Part of what it teaches is, of course, submission to church leaders—but not at the expense of conscience and biblical truth. There must always be that balance. Paul reminds us that "all Scripture is given by inspiration of God . . . for doctrine, for reproof, for correction . . ." (2 Timothy 3:16). Evangelists, authors, pastors, and elders, no matter how prominent, must also be open to correction. If not, a new Protestant popery is the grim alternative.

It is a sign of the times that doctrine is largely neglected today. Serious doctrinal error has not merely "crept" into the church, but is being taught openly by popular church leaders. The necessary correction of such men, rather than being recognized as vital to truth and the spiritual health of the church as a whole, is criticized as divisive. As a result, the cause of truth and the spiritual health of the church is at risk.

God's Word is sermonized, watered down, and played with, but it is rarely used for its intended doctrinal and corrective purpose. "Reprove, rebuke, exhort," Paul reminded Timothy, "with all longsuffering and doctrine. For the time will come when they will not endure sound doctrine . . ." (2 Timothy 4:2,3). We seem to have arrived at that time in church history. A Protestant Reformed Church pastor writes with passion:

> Because of its sublime indifference to doctrine, that is, truth, the charismatic movement is one of the most powerful and effective forces at work in the world today . . . for the uniting of Protestants and Roman Catholics. . . .
>
> Protestant people, tolerating false doctrine . . . do not understand that their ancestors gave up all—*for doctrine*. They do not understand that men of flesh and blood like themselves once dared everything . . . *for doctrine*.

They do not understand anymore the words of Luther's mighty hymn, "Let goods and kindred go/This mortal life also"—*for doctrine.*[26]

How Dare We Forget!

Among the thousands of martyrs who gave their lives for truth and sound doctrine in the cause of the Protestant Reformation, three of the best known were England's bishops Thomas Cranmer, Hugh Latimer, and Nicholas Ridley. Along with many others they were imprisoned in the infamous Tower of London. Under torture and persistent brainwashing, Cranmer, who had been King Henry VIII's yes-man but later became a leader in the English Reformation, vacillated repeatedly. He eventually recanted six times before "rob[bing] his persecutors of their choicest victory as he reasserted for the last time his evangelical faith" and sealed it with the words:

> And forasmuch as my hand offended, writing contrary to my heart, my hand shall first be punished therefor; for may I come to the fire, it shall first be burned. [This vow Cranmer resolutely fulfilled.] And as for the pope, I refuse him as Christ's enemy and Antichrist.[27]

With England's temporary return to Catholicism under Bloody Queen Mary, 288 Protestants were burned at the stake in four years.[28] In that sudden reversal, we hear the voice of Dostoevsky's Grand Inquisitor once again as he stands in the cell door gazing at his silent Prisoner. He has arrested Him for daring, on the very steps of the cathedral, to open the eyes of the blind and, in response to the pleas of its mother, to raise a dead child from its coffin. The Inquisitor remonstrates:

> Why . . . art thou come to hinder us?
> I know not who thou art and care not to know whether it is Thou or only a semblance of Him, but tomorrow I shall condemn Thee and burn Thee at the stake as the worst of heretics.

And the very people who have today kissed Thy feet, tomorrow at the faintest sign from me will rush to heap up the embers of Thy fire.[29]

In his moving *Why Were Our Reformers Burned?* Bishop J.C. Ryle reminds us: "The principle reason why they were burned was that they refused one of the peculiar doctrines of the Roman Church. On that doctrine [of transubstantiation], in almost every case, hinged their life or death. If they admitted it, they might live; if they refused it, they must die." Ryle then quotes "the words of the sentence of condemnation" against numerous martyrs, such as the following pronounced against Bishop Ridley:

> The said Nicholas Ridley affirms, maintains, and stubbornly defends certain opinions, assertions, and heresies, contrary to the Word of God and the received faith of the Church, as in denying the true and natural body and blood of Christ to be in the sacrament of the altar, and secondarily, in affirming the substance of bread and wine to remain after the words of consecration.[30]

Thomas Cranmer, who died under precisely the same sentence, had been the first Protestant archbishop of Canterbury and the author of the first official Protestant Prayer Book. Ironically, the latest archbishop of Canterbury, Lord Ramsey, recently deceased (April 1988), was known for his passion "to unite the world's churches," and to thereby reverse the Reformation through a union with Rome. There are those who seem to forget. Not Bishop Ryle, who wrote in the 1880s with obvious depth of feeling:

> I wish my readers to remember that the burning of the Marian martyrs is an act that the Church of Rome has never repudiated, apologized for, or repented of, down to the present day. . . .
> Never has she repented of her treatment of the Vaudois and the Albigenses; never has she repented of the wholesale murders of the Spanish Inquisition; . . . never has

she repented of the burning of the English Reformers.
We should make a note of that fact and let it sink down
into our minds. Rome never changes.[31]

Today a cross formed by stones in the street and a plaque on the
building facing it mark the spot in front of Oxford's Balliol College
where Cranmer, Ridley, and Latimer were burned. Nearby a weath-
ered monument reminds the few who pay it any attention these days
that those three martyrs, like hundreds of others, "gave their bodies
in opposition to the errors of Rome"—grave errors that are still the
foundation of Catholicism.

Hugh Latimer had been "the most exciting preacher of his generation." He and fellow martyr, London's Bishop Ridley, were bound
back-to-back to one stake. Latimer's last words are perhaps the
most moving utterance of any martyr. With courage and faith
undiminished he cried out to his companion as the flames began to
mount:

Be of good comfort, master Ridley, and play the man.
We shall this day, by God's grace, light such a candle in
England as I trust shall never be put out.[32]

That "candle" is barely flickering today and is in grave danger of
being extinguished. How dare we forget!

10

The Reconstruction Delusion

In our brief survey of church history, we have noted some of the attempts to "Christianize" society through a partnership between the church and worldly powers. Not only have all such efforts failed to produce a sustained increase in general piety, but the end result has invariably been detrimental for the secular world as well as for the church. Admitting such failure, Martin Luther declared: "It is out of the question that there should be a Christian government even over one land . . . since the wicked always outnumber the good."[1] Nevertheless, the false vision of somehow "changing the world for Christ" by infiltrating and eventually "taking over governments for God" is so appealing that many Christians, in their zeal, find it impossible to resist what Colson calls "the greatest temptation today."

The Roman Catholic Church has been living this dream ever since the days of Constantine. We have seen something of the unfortunate results in history past. The Apostle John, inspired of the Holy Spirit, prophesied the phenomenal rise and then collapse and God's judgment of the harlot church after it joins with the Antichrist in establishing a new world order. While its headquarters will be at Rome, this false religious system will represent all churches, denominations, cults, and religions joined in one. Christians today are repeating the proven errors of the past when they attempt to mix religion and politics.

In every nation the Protestant Reformation was perverted by an unbiblical mixture of the holy and profane that came about through a repetition of Catholicism's partnership with worldly governments and affairs. The end product was the state church system of Europe, which today represents a Protestant version of Catholicism's embrace of the ungodly into the bosom of the church. Separation of God's people from the world is an imperative of the faith. Violation of that biblical principle will always be disastrous. Chadwick reminds us:

> [The Catholics] . . . rejected in principle the puritan view of the church as a holy and exclusive community in its empirical reality, and affirmed that the church was like Noah's ark with clean and unclean beasts, or like the field of the parable in which wheat and tares remained side by side until the harvest of the Last Judgement.[2]

Referring to developments after Constantine, Peter Brown writes: "Far from being a source of improvement, this alliance [with the state] was a source of 'greater danger and temptation'. . . . The spread of Christianity in Africa, [for example], by indiscriminately filling the churches, had simply washed away the clear moral landmarks that separated the 'church' from the 'world.' "[3] Luke tells us that the purity and power of the early church was so awesome that unbelievers dared not join it even if they could (Acts 5:13). In contrast, Augustine lamented the sorry details that became commonplace in the Roman Catholic Church worldwide:

> The man who enters [a fourth-century church] is bound to see drunkards, misers, tricksters, gamblers, adulterers, fornicators, people wearing amulets, assiduous clients of sorcerers, astrologers. . . .
> He must be warned that the same crowds that press into the churches on Christian festivals, also fill the theatres on pagan holidays.[4]

The "Ekklesia"—A Called-Out Company of Believers

It is very clear from Genesis to Revelation that God's special people, the children of Israel, are distinct from all other peoples on earth. Beginning with Abraham, God set forth specific conditions that governed His relationship with His chosen people and which, at the same time, would guard them from any worldly influence— injunctions which anciént Israel repeatedly violated and modern Israel has abandoned. Originally, Israel had not only a distinct religion, but its dietary and hygienic laws and entire way of life established for her by God were designed to maintain her separation and prevent any intermingling with the Gentiles. Israel's uniqueness was, of course, obvious to the other nations around her. As God Himself said to His people concerning the laws He gave to them:

> The nations which shall hear all these statutes [shall] say ... "What nation is there so great, who hath God so nigh unto them ... [and] that hath statutes and judgments so righteous as all this law ... ?" (Deuteronomy 4:5-8).

It is therefore not surprising that the church established by Christ is also called "a peculiar [separate, distinct] people" (1 Peter 2:9). The Old Testament injunction to Israel to "come out from among them [the worldly], and be ye separate" (2 Corinthians 6:17) is applied by Paul to the church. Comprised of both Jews and Gentiles, the church is separate and distinct from all the rest of the world, including Israel. Christians, as citizens of heaven, are not to adopt the lifestyles of the unsaved, nor their fleshly ambitions and interests, and are certainly not to marry those who do not belong to Christ. Nor are believers to become partners in business, or in any other way to be "unequally yoked together with unbelievers" (verse 14). Unfortunately, as with modern Israel, the modern church has also largely abandoned the principle of separation.

The Greek word used for church in the New Testament is *ekklesia*, which means a called-out company of people. Jesus called His disciples out of the world to follow Him, through death and resurrection, to a new world; and He warned them that they would be hated by this present world. They, in turn, were to make other disciples, calling them out of the world—and they, in their turn, were to make yet more disciples with the same peculiar calling. That command from the lips of Christ, known as the Great Commission (Matthew 28:16-20), has come down to us today and remains a clarion call to us to make the same kind of disciples also.

In His prayer in John 17, Christ repeatedly referred to the fact that His disciples, though remaining as His witnesses in the world, were not of the world but had been chosen *out of* the world. When the apostles and elders met in that first church council in Jerusalem, Barnabas and Paul declared "what miracles and wonders God had wrought among the Gentiles by them" (Acts 15:12). Most miraculous to them was the fact that Gentiles were being converted. The apostle James then explained that certain Old Testament prophecies were being fulfilled as God was taking *"out of them* [Gentile nations] a people for His name" (verses 14,19). As H. Wayne House and Tommy Ice point out in their valuable book, *Dominion Theology, Blessing or Curse?*:

> Note Revelation 7:9—"a great multitude which no one could count, *from* every *nation* and all tribes and peoples and tongues." The Greek preposition for the English word "from" is *ek*, which means "out of". . . .
>
> In Acts 15:14 when James says that "God first concerned Himself about *taking from among* the Gentiles a people for His name," the *ek* preposition is used . . . also. Further, the word "Gentiles" is the . . . same Greek word used in Matthew 28:19 [the Great Commission] and translated "nations." . . .
>
> So the idea the New Testament teaches is that . . . Christ is calling out of the nations a people for His own name—the Body of Christ. . . . there is no passage which teaches that whole nations will be converted to Christ or that we are to make "Christian nations."[5]

Christ explained that from the mass of people who are pursuing the broad road to destruction, a relatively few are heeding the call to take instead the narrow way that leads to life (Matthew 7:13,14; Luke 13:23,24; etc.). That small company, *called out* from among both Jews and Gentiles by the Holy Spirit in response to the gospel, comprises the church. The Bible clearly teaches that after they have been called out from the world, Christians, though still in the world, are to remain separate from it. What does that mean? While we must leave readers to study and interpret biblical teaching on this vital subject for themselves, we can briefly point out several important basics.

Some vocations (involving work in casinos, brothels, or bars, for example) are obviously not for Christians. In general, however, Christians find themselves living and working side-by-side with the ungodly, whether as employees of private industry or government. Separation is not to be through Christians living in their own closed communities and shunning outsiders, but in the midst of daily and often close contact with the world. If Christ is living in us, then we will think, live, act, and speak more and more as He would in each circumstance as we grow in wisdom and mature in our relationship to Him. The Christian life is not following a set of denominational rules but living in obedience to God's Word under the guidance and empowering of the Holy Spirit, who is continually filling us and expressing Christ through us. That we belong to Him will be obvious, and that difference will set us apart even while we show His compassion and love to the unsaved with whom we have contact.

Unfortunately, the world's idea of successful marketing has influenced the church, causing it to attempt to sell Christianity to the world in the same manner. Many Christians assume that they must use Dale Carnegie-like techniques in representing Christ. In their attempt to be well-liked by the world, they compromise their Christian witness, often without realizing it because worldly standards have become such an intimate part of their thinking. They forget that the world in general never did and still does not respond well to Christ and would crucify Him again if it had the opportunity. As to what that means in our relationship to worldly people, Paul gave us something to ponder prayerfully:

God forbid that I should glory save in the cross of our
Lord Jesus Christ, by whom the world is crucified unto
me and I unto the world (Galatians 6:14).

The New Call to Christianize the World

Such Scriptures fly in the face of today's popular belief that
Christians are to be so closely involved in the world that they will
eventually be running it.[6] As already mentioned, this view, after
being preserved within the generally small Manifested Sons of God
groups on the fanatical fringes of the Pentecostal movement, has
been gaining ground rapidly among charismatics. Similar theories
are being effectively carried into mainstream evangelical churches
by the Coalition on Revival headed by founder Jay Grimstead. In
turn, COR seems to have been heavily influenced by previously
mentioned Reconstructionists such as Gary North and Rousas J.
Rushdoony.

Virtually unknown 20 years ago, Reconstructionism is now significantly affecting the evangelical church. With more than 100 of
their own books published and numerous newsletters and teaching
tapes to their credit, the Reconstructionist leadership is not only
extremely prolific but highly intelligent and aggressive. Bill Moyers,
in a three-part television series aired over public broadcasting
across the country in December 1987, devoted one entire program to
the Reconstructionists and their postmillennialist call for Christians
to take over the world before Christ can return.

What Abraham Kuyper accomplished in Holland (though he was
not a postmillennialist) at the beginning of this century is often cited
as an example of what COR and the Reconstructionist movement
hope to achieve. Under Kuyper's leadership, Christians "controlled
the largest newspaper in the nation, founded the Free University of
Amsterdam to educate in terms of the Christian perspective, established a national Christian Day School movement, founded a new
Christian denomination, founded a political party which controlled
the legislature for over a decade, founded a Christian labor union,
and elected Kuyper to the office of prime minister of the Netherlands for four years."[7] Yet this remarkable accomplishment, which

Grimstead points to as a model of what COR hopes to achieve, eventually left Holland worse off spiritually than it was before. If Reconstructionist/COR theories were correct, then the great success achieved by Kuyper would have become a base for further advancement of the kingdom of God. Instead, there was a complete reversal as in the case of Savonarola's Florence. It is an understatement to say that Holland today is the ultimate antithesis of everything Kuyper and his colleagues stood for and seemed at one point to have accomplished.

Nevertheless, a recurring theme among Reconstructionists is the "glorious goal of worldwide conquest!"[8] Elaborating on that thesis, another writer declares: "We are to pull down the ungodly strongholds of this world, and we are to erect godly institutions in their place. . . ."[9] Yet another repeats the unbiblical call to "Christianize all . . . nations. . . ."[10] David Chilton maintains the rhetoric of conquest with the declaration that "Christianity is destined to take over all the kingdoms of the earth. . . ."[11] Claiming that this is what Christ meant when He told His disciples to go into all the world and preach the gospel, Gary North writes:

> God wants Christians to control the earth on His behalf. . . . [We] want to see a Biblical reconstruction of the United States, so that it can serve as an example to be followed all over the world.[12]

The aim is to Christianize the entire world before Christ returns. Reconstruction author George Grant writes: "The army of God is to conquer the earth, to subdue it, to rule over it, to exercise dominion. Christians are called to war. And it is a war we are expected to win."[13] Chilton writes: "Our goal is world dominion under Christ's lordship, a 'world takeover' if you will. . . . We are the shapers of world history . . . [He has] commissioned us to take over the world."[14] Somehow, calling the *ekklesia* out of the world in preparation for a departure to heaven has metamorphosed into taking over the world and establishing ourselves here. To this end, COR is now implementing specific plans for taking over two test counties in

California. The 12-point Christianization program asks participants to:

> Replace anti-biblical legislation in the county with righteous, sane, biblically oriented legislation. Replace anti-biblical elected officials (city council members, mayors, state senators, school board members, etc.) with biblically oriented candidates.[15]

During its first three centuries the church never entertained the idea of "reconstructing society." Christ had clearly said, "My kingdom is not of this world" (John 18:36). He never said a word about reforming the corrupt Roman regime, never even hinted at infiltrating its bureaucracies, never advocated organized social or political action, nor suggested that his followers lie down in front of the Roman legions or stage a protest march in Rome or Jerusalem. He specifically declared, "I pray not for the world, but for them which thou hast given me . . . *out of the world*" (John 17:9,6).

There were no plans made by Paul or Peter (or anyone else in the early church) to organize mass demonstrations against Roman corruption and its occupation of Palestine—or in favor of establishing "Christian values" throughout the Roman world. In contrast to such ideas, Peter wrote: "Christ also suffered for us, leaving us an example that ye should follow his steps . . . who, when he was reviled, reviled not again; when he suffered, he threatened not, but committed himself to him that judgeth righteously" (1 Peter 2:21-23). In representing Christ to the world, the church was to conduct itself as He consistently had. The time for a "takeover" would come only when He returned in power and glory.

Appropriate Social/Political Action Tempered by Wisdom

The Great Commission involves not social and political action aimed at overturning or reforming governments and institutions, but preaching a gospel that transforms individuals and changes their eternal destiny. While there is a place for lawful and appropriate social and political action, it must not be confused with the Great

Commission. To determine what is lawful, we must distinguish between the rights of governments and those of private citizens. These rights vary in different countries and times, as we have already pointed out. Much of what is lawful in the United States would not be allowed in the Soviet Union, for example, any more than it would have been in the Roman Empire.

On the other hand, Christians are not obliged to obey every government demand. This is clear both from the example of Christ Himself and His apostles, who, in order to obey God, refused to obey the Jewish religious leaders. Christ's resurrection itself was in defiance of the Roman seal placed upon His tomb and the guard stationed there to see that He remained in it. Scripture clearly tells us that no government has any authority except that which comes from God (Romans 13:1), and citizens, therefore, are not bound by any civil laws that violate the will of God for their lives.

No government, for example, has the right to forbid Christians to worship God, to own and read the Bible, or to give Bibles or tracts or otherwise share their faith with others. Nor does any government have the right to cause believers to break God's laws or act contrary to their faith and God-given conscience. The government has the right to see to it that its citizens are educated in a manner that will strengthen the nation's capabilities to survive and grow. It does not, however, have the right, under the cover of education, to attempt to persuade children raised in Christian families to adopt beliefs or practices contrary to the faith of their parents.

Consequently, parents have the right, in obedience to God, to object individually or collectively and to resist the teaching of evolution or other atheistic/humanistic theories or occult or religious (witchcraft, New Age, etc.) beliefs or practices to their children which are contrary to the Christian faith. They have the right to resist immoral teachings in the public schools that present young minds with ideas and temptations that would never otherwise occur to them at their age. Current examples are some facets of sex education, values clarification, the presentation of homosexuality or free sex to children as alternative lifestyles—or any other teachings that deliberately attempt to undermine Christianity in the eyes of children of Christian parents.

Of course, the distinction must be made between trying to force values upon others, and simply standing true to personal convictions in obedience to God. It is one thing to protect our own children from godless influences that are an offense to God and that violate the charge He has given to governments. It is something else to attempt to force biblical values upon a godless world. For example, it may not be necessary to change the curriculum in order to prevent our own children from being adversely affected. The protest or action ought to provide an appropriate remedy (such as exempting the children of Christian parents from certain instructions) rather than attempting to force Christian values upon the population at large.

On the other hand, Christians in America certainly have the right (and it is a right that is not guaranteed by God's laws) to seek political office and to use their voting power to foster their own values. The higher the level of government, however, the less likely it is that the elected official can function as a Christian either in bringing a Christian influence to bear through his office or in maintaining an uncompromising witness for Christ. On lower levels, far more good can be done. For example, if the majority of a local school board is made up of Christians, it could have a more practical effect than could a Christian majority of the president's cabinet.

While Scripture does not specifically encourage it, there is also no prohibition in the Bible against appropriate social action in the interests of godliness. It must, however, be tempered by wisdom and suited to the individual case. There is a significant difference between getting involved in politics to the extent that we are in partnership with the ungodly in running the world—and in taking, individually and collectively, a public stand for righteousness by using the legal means at our disposal. All we do must always give top priority to the eternal destiny of souls and not allow that to be obscured by focusing unduly on temporal concerns, no matter how large they may loom at the moment.

Perverting the Great Commission

We are now being told, however, that "just to get souls saved and discipled for heaven" is only part of the Great Commission, while getting the ungodly to obey biblical principles is the lost secret of "changing the world for Christ." The idea is now being presented that fulfilling the Great Commission doesn't necessarily mean to change people's destiny from hell to heaven. It may merely cause ungodly, hell-bent sinners to live ethical lives in obedience to God's laws for earthly benefits. Gary North explains this new understanding of salvation and the Great Commission:

> ...the postmillennialist does not preach that the whole world will someday be populated exclusively by regenerate people. But... [that] the whole world will experience cultural blessings as a result of the spread of the gospel....[16]
>
> The concern of the evangelical world has been on the saving of souls, and they have long neglected the healing of the institutions of the world. But God's Son died to save (heal) all men, even though He did not die to regenerate all men.
>
> By neglecting the task of healing the KOSMOS—the institutional world order—Christians are denying the comprehensive nature of Christ's salvation.[17]

Nowhere does Scripture use the term "save" in relation to the gospel or the Great Commission in the manner North alleges. Nevertheless, there is a strong move within the church today to give this deceptively appealing cause of "Christianizing" the world, which has failed repeatedly in the past, one more grand try. The hope is to thereby "reform every sphere of life in every nation and place according to the standards of God's Word."[18] In defiance both of logic and Scripture, COR's *Manifesto* declares that the Great Commission enjoins the church, as "the world's teacher, example, salt, and light" to persuade secular societies and their institutions to adopt a Christian lifestyle.[19]

At the Lincoln Memorial on July 4, 1986, in a bold challenge to the rest of the church, 50 members of COR's steering committee and 500 delegates signed its *Manifesto for the Christian Church: Declaration and Covenant.* "It is COR's hope," explained a newsletter, "that every Bible believing church in America and Canada will sign it also . . . [because it represents] God's will for the entire Christian Church at the end of the 20th century."[20] COR literature declares enthusiastically:

> The *Manifesto Covenant*, analogous to Luther's 95 Theses, was "nailed to the Church's Door" by 50 of COR's Steering Committee members.
>
> By God's grace, this event and the unleashing of this document onto the Church and the world will mark a turning point in history wherein the Body of Christ will awaken and take its proper leadership role with the world.
>
> Then, once again, we may see the Church transforming the world and influencing it to conform to Biblical standards . . . [and] every sphere of life on the face of this planet begin to be penetrated, purified and made more whole by Biblical principles. . . .[21]

That statement is both a perversion of the Great Commission and dangerously misleading. The phrase "once again" suggests that what is being proposed has been accomplished successfully in the past. When did the church "transform the world and influence it to conform to biblical standards"? The only time when that might be said to have occurred was during the Middle Ages, when Roman Catholicism ruled the world, reaching the zenith of its power, as we have seen, under Pope Innocent III (1198-1216). Walter James reminds us that in those days "Christianity was undisputed master of the scene,"[22] while Southern writes:

> The ideal church of the twelfth and thirteenth centuries was a society of disciplined and organized clergy directing the thoughts and activities of an obedient and receptive laity—kings, magnates, and peasants alike.[23]

One could hardly hope for the Christian church to have greater control over the world than during the Middle Ages to which Grimstead refers so favorably. Yet we have seen the sad result of that apparent triumph: a partnership with worldly powers producing an authoritarian, corrupt church, with the Reformation falling into the same ditch. Yet the "New Reformation" being proposed—a hoped-for "Christian Reconstruction" of society worldwide—is specifically designed to repeat the same errors.

High Hopes and Disillusionment

Nevertheless, in the flush of their recent apparent successes following Ronald Reagan's landslide victory in 1980, conservative Christians in America have been convinced that voting their candidates into key political offices, marching in protest, and putting pressure on the government through lobbying organizations is the way to forward the cause of Christ. As Gary North has said: "Christians are being challenged by God to reclaim the political realm for Jesus Christ.[24] . . . It is His [Christ's] goal that His earthly followers eventually exercise authority over the earth in His name . . . by becoming knowledgeable and involved in the ordering of earth's governments. . . ."[25] George Grant writes:

> The task of the people of God in politics is to counter the effects of sin with the redemptive work of Christ. We are to take up our inheritance by reclaiming the land. . . .
> In short, we must take authority over the nations with the applied rule of Christ Jesus.[26]

Once again the word "reclaim" used by both North and Grant is misleading—and the methods and goal they suggest are not biblical. An ad for the "Biblical Blueprint Series" of Reconstructionist books refers to "a growing army of registered voters . . . [taking] dominion." In a more recent promotional letter accompanying a color brochure for the same series, North writes (in contrast to Christ's teaching that the world would hate and persecute His followers):

By 2001, you could be president, thanks to the coming
"Second American Revolution" of the late 1990's. . . .
You see, as a Christian and a conservative, you'll be part
of a very popular bunch.

In fact, voters will be insisting that all leaders . . . be
firmly committed to no-nonsense, Christian values. . . .
Christians and conservatives will be swept into most
elective U.S. offices by ridiculous margins. . . .

All across America, Christian experiments, projects,
and all-out campaigns are producing exciting results . . .
showing we can change the world. . . . We've won elec-
tions . . . and we're reaching more voters at every election! . . .

Humanism's house of cards is about to collapse. . . .
[We have] the most dazzling, mind-bending Christian
plan of action since Luther swung his hammer at the
church door in Wittenberg. . . . I invite you to join us in
setting the agenda of world affairs. . . .

It all sounds extremely impressive and enticing. Not, however,
when we remember that without a doubt Christ would be crucified
by today's world if He walked among men once again as the meek
and lowly Lamb of God and, as the Light of the world, called upon
them to repent. Something is wrong, therefore, when those who
claim to be His followers hope to be admired and praised as honored
leaders of those who would crucify their Lord.

The true Christian, having accepted Christ's death in his place
for his sins, recognizes, as Paul said of himself, that he has been
"crucified with Christ" (Galatians 2:20) and has been given a new
life, the very life of his resurrected Lord. It would be a complete
contradiction, then, for those who are united with Christ in His
crucifixion and rejection by the world, to compromise their Christianity by getting voted in by Christ-rejecters to high office in order
to help run this world in partnership with those who despise their
Lord.

Moreover, an in-depth evaluation, which is beyond the scope of
this book, would reveal that the high hopes and original promises of

political involvement by well-meaning Christians have simply not been realized. In attempting to justify political ambitions by Christians, Joseph and Daniel—who were put into high government office by God for His purposes—are often cited as examples. To be honest with the analogy, however, it must be admitted that neither Joseph nor Daniel had any significant long-term effect upon the countries they governed. Egypt eventually enslaved the Israelites and was punished for it; and with the exception of his influence upon three kings, Daniel had little impact upon Babylon, which also was destroyed.

Unlike today's Christians in high office, Daniel was inflexible in his commitment to God and was hated for it. He never compromised one iota, not even in his diet. For that reason he was not popular with the other government officials who were continually plotting to get rid of him. Daniel was in that position by God's definite appointment for a specific purpose, which provides no justification for Christians presently running for political office simply because it is possible to do so. One simply cannot make a biblical case from either Daniel or Joseph to justify a Christian entering politics at the higher levels.

The Perils of Public Office

The perils of public office and the pressure it brings to compromise one's commitment to Christ have been demonstrated repeatedly. Pat Robertson, in spite of his claim that God had called him to run for president, became a recent object lesson. It was sad to see a man who until then had been attempting to win souls for Christ begin to deny, when questioned by reporters or a talk-show host, that he was an evangelist at all. Robertson's contradictions of previous statements and his repeated protests that as president he would never try to push his Christianity upon anyone or let it interfere with his official duties were poignant reminders of the compromise that is demanded by the very nature of political office in a democracy.

Compromise is inevitable if an officeholder is to represent his godless constituents as well as the Christians. Moreover, his ability to speak out for Christ is compromised 24 hours of the day and seven days in the week. The reason is quite obvious. While an accountant, for example, must not force his Christianity upon his fellow employees, he is free off the job to preach the gospel. The president of the United States, however, or a senator or cabinet member is never off the job, but always represents his office and must be very careful not to push his Christianity at any time. It would, therefore, not be a step up, but decidedly a step down for Billy Graham, for example, to become president of the United States, because it would mark the end of his gospel crusades and open witness for Christ.

To mention one more specific example, the performance of Surgeon General C. Everett Koop over the past few years has been a great disappointment. No one attributes this to a flaw in the Christian commitment of Koop, which seems to be above question. Yet he has compromised his Christian faith in his speeches and actions. Of the recent brochure *Understanding AIDS: A Message From The Surgeon General* sent to all postal customers, Judie Brown, president of American Life League, wrote in bitter disillusionment:

> Disinformation abounds and begins promptly. . . . Page 3 carries a discussion of so-called "risky behaviors" that, if studied, provides all manner of permissive activity. For example, he writes: "Sex with someone you don't know well . . . is risky." Does this mean casual sex with someone you know "well" is fine? . . .
>
> He never describes the health benefits of chastity outside of marriage and fidelity within marriage. Rather, he caters to such lifestyles as homosexuality and bisexuality by avoiding even a modest encouragement toward a type of sexual relationship designed by nature for man and woman to become one in marriage. . . .
>
> A certain philosophy with regard to society's sexual behavior, however, is not absent. The surgeon general has done a great disservice to the USA's parents, to the USA's children and, perhaps most obviously, to his own high office.

As a physician of past note, admired by so many of his peers, he has simply become, through the publication of this booklet, Captain Condom![27]

Koop has explained on occasion that he cannot force his evangelical beliefs and lifestyle upon the country, but that he must represent all factions. Perhaps it would have been best then, in a public display of integrity, to resign rather than to compromise by offering, in the face of a most dangerous threat to public morals and health, what he himself believes to be immoral and inadequate solutions. Stating what the surgeon general no doubt believes but was prohibited by his office from declaring, two concerned and qualified Christians have written in an excellent booklet on AIDS:

> The world's solution is no solution at all. It will compound the disaster. Pushing the condom simply encourages promiscuous sex. And the condom is . . . effective only 90% of the time in preventing pregnancy, even though pregnancy can occur only two or three days out of a month.
>
> The transmission of AIDS can occur with *every* sex act on *any* day of the month. When an unwanted pregnancy occurs, abortion can serve as a back-up means of escape. There is no escape from AIDS. When it is contracted, it ultimately means death.
>
> Relying on a condom is like playing Russian roulette.
>
> The only valid hope for stemming the AIDS epidemic is to be found in the Bible. God's Word makes it clear that our hope is not "safe sex" but, rather, moral sex. Sexual union within marriage with one faithful partner is the only way to be sexually active and free from the danger of AIDS.[28]

Not only Koop but others as well have fully demonstrated that the benefits of getting Christians into high office have been greatly overrated. Moreover, through the deepening involvement of the church in politics, are we not sowing the same seeds of destruction as in the fourth century when the church became unequally yoked together with the Roman Empire?

Repeating Constantinian Mistakes?

Christians ought to stand against such evils as homosexuality, abortion, pornography, and the abuse of drugs, and do all they can to limit godless influence in society. At the same time, the Christian must not forget that his primary responsibility to the world is to present it with the gospel. Too often social and political activism becomes a substitute for saving souls. Moreover, Christians must take their stand against moral and social evil as those who are redeemed by the blood of Christ and not join with the ungodly in promoting moralism, a system which is no better than humanism. Unfortunately, conservative Christians have joined forces with and thereby given credibility to such anti-Christians as Mormons and Moonies. One example is the American Freedom Coalition headed by Bob Grant of the lobbying group, Christian Voice. As the *Washington Post* commented:

> Grant and other group [coalition] leaders bristle at criticism of their ties with Moon's movement, saying they are willing to work with any group that shares their conservative goals.
> "One thing about the Unification Church, they are the strongest anti-communist church in the United States," said [Richard] Ichord [former U.S. Representative from Missouri], who operates a Washington lobbying firm. . . .[29]

Much of today's church has ceased to be the *ekklesia* called out of the world and has become part of the world's establishment. Having watched their leaders join the ungodly in good causes, most Christians have lost their sense of separation from the world. The popular trend now among many evangelicals is to be as much like the world as possible in order to gain the acceptance that is currently considered a prerequisite for something called "friendship evangelism"—another new approach to the Great Commission that neither Jesus nor Paul knew anything about. Some Christians are convinced that it takes months or even years to "earn the right to tell someone about Jesus"—hardly a tactic of the early church, which perhaps would not have been persecuted and martyred if it had preached the gospel more "positively."

Many pastors and preachers attempt to adjust their message to make it sound as appealing as possible from a worldly viewpoint in order to increase the response. The Jesus they represent is a self-improvement, success expert who offers a more efficient and psychologically sound route to the same "good life" on this earth that every non-Christian seeks. The loss of heaven's importance, the rapture's relegation to a vague and distantly future role, and the church's identification with the world in its social and political struggles are combining to deaden the commitment of the contemporary Christian to the biblical standards of separation from a godless world.

The belief that Christianity is in the process of taking over the world seems appealing, just as it did in the days of Constantine and his successors. Those who suffered persecution and martyrdom, however, either under the Roman emperors or at the hands of the popes who succeeded them, had a different perspective. And the latter view, though certainly one that has little appeal today, has been vindicated by history. Must we learn the same lessons again at equal cost?

Setting a Godly Example for the World?

Contrary to COR's good intentions, the Bible never assigns the church a "leadership role with the world." The standard of behavior expected of the church is far higher than that expected of the world—and to confuse the two is to destroy both. The Christian is empowered by the Holy Spirit to live a holy, separated, Christ-like life motivated by love for His Lord. The worldling, however, motivated by fear of the consequences of violating civil law and prodded by conscience into recognizing himself as a hopeless sinner in God's eyes, is called upon to repent and receive Christ as his Savior and Lord. The very idea of the church setting a biblical standard for the unconverted secular world to follow is unbiblical and impractical.

The Reconstructionists such as Rushdoony and North, whose influence within the Coalition on Revival is quite apparent, are the same kind of legalists whom Paul refuted in the Galatian epistle. They hope to enforce upon both the church and an unconverted world laws given to Israel as God's peculiar people, but which neither Israel nor any other unregenerate people could keep. As Calvinists, the goal of the Reconstructionists, as we have already noted, is basically to institute worldwide the same legalistic regime with the same extreme consequences for violation of religious codes as that which Calvin imposed upon Geneva. Yet history has proved repeatedly what Paul declared: "For if righteousness comes by the law, then Christ is dead in vain" (Galatians 2:21). House and Ice correctly warn:

> Unfortunately, the only thing the Christian Reconstruction movement will likely produce will be a contribution toward the development of moralism instead of biblical Christianity.
>
> Moralism is fostered when a culture or society believes that being a good Christian means measuring up to a public consciousness of right and wrong.[30]

The goal that God has in mind is not to create a society of nations that keep His laws or a world that obeys biblical principles. The whole world has been declared guilty before God, and the issue now is repentance, justification, and reconciliation. This is what the Book of Romans is all about. Nowhere in the New Testament can we find the teaching that the aim of Christianity or of the Great Commission is to convince the world that it ought to obey God's laws. Israel failed in that attempt—and the new covenant of grace which God has provided for her is for all who will believe. No one can perfectly obey God's laws. What we need is to admit that we are sinners who have broken His laws and receive the remedy God offers in Christ. This is the gospel, and to preach it to the nations is the sole purpose of the Great Commission.

Those who are not indwelt by the Spirit of God are by nature antagonistic to God and unable to obey His laws. Even if they succeeded in doing so, their "obedience" would be motivated by self-interest rather than love for God and thus would not be acceptable to Him. The very foundation, then, of this movement to Christianize the world rests upon false assumptions which the Bible repudiates and which history has repeatedly proved unworkable. Nevertheless, COR's fervent and sincere desire, as Grimstead so often states it, is to realize that:

> the Great Commission involves, not just getting individuals saved, but includes storming the gates of hell and influencing governments and nations to live according to the Bible.[31]
>
> . . . to show [the world] the way to live and conduct its affairs. . . . The world will not know how to live or which direction to go without the Church's biblical influence on its theories, laws, actions, and institutions.[32]

Here again we have a complete disregard for the great differences between the church and the world. Sincerely but subtly the emphasis shifts from converting individual sinners out of the world and preparing them for heaven, to setting a godly example to be followed by a godless, Christ-rejecting world. This is what COR calls "chang[ing] the world by getting God's will to be done, on earth as it is in heaven," before Christ returns.[33]

What Happened to the Cross?

If, as COR says, we are to get the nations of the world to do God's will, we must face the issue: What is it that God wants men to do? That question was asked by a group of Jews who wanted to make Christ their king out of a wrong motivation (so that they would always be fed and healed by Him): "What shall we do that we might work the works of God?" Jesus replied, "This is the work of God, that ye believe on him whom he hath sent" (John 6:28,29). The first "work" God wants anyone to do is to believe on the Lord Jesus Christ—and that involves first and foremost coming to the cross as repentant sinners for whom Christ died and rose again. Until that step has been taken, "all our righteousnesses are as filthy rags" (Isaiah 64:6).

It is true that Christ set an example to be followed—but only by those who belong to Him through being born of and indwelt by God's Spirit. Moreover, the example itself involves the cross as well: "Whosoever will come after me, let him deny himself and take up his cross and follow me" (Mark 8:34). Evangelicals repudiate the suggestion of liberals that Christ gave us a philosophy of life and set a moral example for the world to follow. That teaching is destructive of the gospel and actually prevents men from coming to Christ as repentant and needy sinners, yet it is being revived today in a more subtle form, and not by liberals but by well-intentioned evangelical leaders.

It is commendable that COR calls upon Christians to live in obedience to the Word of God. However, the emphasis upon a full surrender to Christ as Lord is nothing new. What is new, at least for evangelicals (though liberals and social gospel and liberation theology advocates have preached it), is the idea of getting non-Christians to live Christianized lives—and the insistence that the Great Commission requires us to do so. In a typical talk to pastors interested in COR, Grimstead explained:

> . . . we are God's representatives on this planet in our nation and in our cities to get God's will done on earth as it is in heaven, right now before the millennium and before heaven. Now we have differing views about how far we can carry that. Our Postmillennial brothers think they can take it the whole way. We Premillennialists can gain back America and the Western hemisphere or chunks of it.
>
> But one thing we have to agree upon . . . is that our task is to get the view of reality in the Bible and the view of

morality in the Bible imposed upon our culture for the glory of God and the well-being of mankind, Christians and non-Christians alike. And that . . . the Christian church worldwide is responsible for letting the culture disintegrate this far.[34]

Grimstead makes an unbiblical and unreasonable connection between the church and the world from which it is supposed to be separate, and perverts the Great Commission in the process. Far from imposing biblical morality upon the unsaved, the Bible warns that attempting to keep the law will not save and will only breed self-righteousness. It is, moreover, an impossible standard for the non-Christian.

The growing vision of Christianizing the world, and of a "triumphant church" increasing in numbers and power and wealth until it comprises the majority of earth's inhabitants, is very enticing. That goal, however, would not be enticing to the millions down through history who, as part of that *ekklesia*—the "called-out" company—have died a martyr's death for their Christian testimony.

Anneken Jans, a young mother, was among that company. On the eve of her execution in Rotterdam, Netherlands, in 1539, she left a written statement to be given to her infant son when he would be old enough to understand. Here is the counsel of this brave martyr—so out of step with the take-over-the-world mentality of today:

Where you hear of a poor, simple, cast-off little flock which is despised and rejected by the world, join them; for where you hear of the cross, there is Christ.[35]

11

The Great Dominion Myth

Thus far, in discussing the dimming or deferring of the hope of heaven and the issue of a church takeover of the world before Christ can return, we have concentrated mainly upon the Reconstructionists and the Coalition on Revival because they exert an increasing influence among evangelicals and fundamentalists. As for those groups impacting charismatics, we have also mentioned Kingdom Now/Restoration teachers such as Earl Paulk and Rick Godwin. There are, of course, many other groups and individuals of significance in this movement who could be mentioned.

In spite of the commonalities among those involved, there are, as would be expected, differences of opinion and emphasis on certain points. It is not our purpose, however, nor is it necessary to discuss such details. What we need to recognize is the fact that one concept forms the common link between all those who minimize or reject the rapture and teach in some form that the church must take over or Christianize the world. That concept is *dominion*. In fact "dominion theology" is the basic premise for all those who expect to establish the kingdom prior to Christ's return.

Before discussing what is meant by dominion theology, we must understand that it was invented only recently. This teaching is, in fact, so new that R.J. Rushdoony is referred to as "the father of dominion theology." Thus the Reconstructionists are able to take credit for a key theory that has given postmillennialism the spice it needed in order to appeal to current taste.

224 • *The Great Dominion Myth*

When confronted with an alleged key doctrine that men and women of God have failed to uncover from Scripture in 1900 years of church history, we have good reason to be more than a little cautious. After all, this is the stuff of which cults are made. It takes a certain arrogance to claim to have discovered a vital teaching that the entire church has overlooked for 1900 years.

Dominion Theology—What Is It?

The few verses from which the new dominion teaching is derived are Genesis 1:26-29, where God says to man, "Be fruitful and multiply, and replenish the earth and subdue it; and have dominion over the fish of the sea, and over the fowl of the air, and over every living thing that moveth upon the earth." God is stating in clear language nothing more nor less than the simple fact that man, as a higher order of creation made in His image, has been given dominion over the earth and everything upon it—the trees, herbs, fish, fowls, animals, and all other life-forms. He is to farm and mine the earth and to use the animals for food or pleasure, but he is to be a good steward accountable to his Creator.

Reading into these verses something far beyond that which is so simply stated, Reconstructionists and other dominionists draw four false inferences that in no way follow from the text:

1. That this "dominion mandate" includes ruling over other human beings and setting up governments and institutions, etc.;
2. That "dominion" was lost by Adam at the Fall;
3. That a key purpose of Christ's death, burial, and resurrection was to restore to man the dominion over earth and lower creatures which Adam allegedly lost; and
4. That the Great Commission of Matthew 28 is simply a restatement in New Covenant terms of the original "dominion mandate," and thus involves "fulfilling the same task."

Upon this faulty foundation, the entire Reconstruction movement has been erected. The simple dominion given by God to Adam, and thus to all men as his descendants (dominion over fish, fowls, beasts, and insects), has taken on amazing proportions which even remove it from the capabilities of Adam. It has become a "task" that only born-again Christians can fulfill: "Being born again is a prerequisite to exercising godly dominion."[1] Yet it was given to mankind thousands of years before Christ, and Psalm 8 makes it clear that dominion is common to all men, not only to Christians. Nevertheless, in *The Reduction of Christianity* Gary DeMar and Peter Leithart declare:

> In fact, the Bible teaches that...we are citizens of heaven in order to exercise effective dominion on the earth....*Heaven is the source of dominion, the place from which we begin to exercise dominion....*
> Why was Christ raised to heaven and seated at the right hand of the Father? To exercise *dominion*.
> It is precisely because our *citizenship is in heaven* that we are able to *rule the earth* obediently and effectively.[2]

A new revelation indeed! Why did God even mention dominion to Adam, since it was impossible for him, not being a citizen of heaven, to exercise it? Also, why was it necessary for Christ to have died for our sins, resurrected, and ascended to the Father's right hand in order for Him (and us through Him) to exercise an earthly dominion over fish, fowls, beasts, and insects that all men have clearly been exercising since the beginning?

Some Mysterious Dimensions to "Dominion"

In a similar vein Earl Paulk declares: "Christ in us must take dominion over the earth."[3] He must have in mind something far grander than dominion over plowed fields, forests, and lower creatures—grander, indeed, than anything warranted by the simple statement concerning dominion found in Genesis 1:26-29. There are seemingly some very mysterious dimensions to dominion that are not at all clear to the ordinary reader from what the Scriptures have to say about it.

In fact, dominion theology is the apparent key to everything from eschatology to spiritual warfare. We are told: "The Bible gives us *an eschatology of dominion. . . ."*[4] Even Paul's instructions concerning not warring after the flesh but "bringing into captivity every thought to the obedience of Christ" (2 Corinthians 10:3-5) are interpreted as *"a strategy for worldwide dominion."*[5] What appears to an ordinary reader to be a simple statement that God gave to mankind dominion over lower forms of creation actually contains the secret of Christianizing the world in the last days: "The Dominion Mandate, the task God assigned Adam, will be fulfilled by the triumph of the Gospel throughout the world."[6] Dominion is the alpha and omega, the all-consuming passion and obsession:

> Christians have an obligation, a mandate, a commission, a holy responsibility to reclaim the land for Jesus Christ—to have dominion in civil structures, just as in every other aspect of life and godliness.
> But it is dominion that we are after. Not just a voice.
> It is dominion we are after. Not just influence.
> It is dominion we are after. Not just equal time.
> It is dominion we are after.[7]

Such is the foundation upon which COR's entire agenda has been built, reflecting the Reconstructionist influence in that organization. Along with some of the best-known and most highly-respected Christian leaders in America, COR's steering committee includes Reconstructionists such as North, Rushdoony, and DeMar. It also includes leaders of other dominion-oriented factions: Earl Paulk-type kingdom/dominion advocates such as Maranatha's Robert Weiner, pastors John Giminez and "Bishop" John Meares; and shepherding leaders such as Bob Mumford and Dennis Peacocke. COR has now become the major vehicle giving credibility to Rushdoony's dominion theology and spreading it into mainstream evangelical churches.

Dominion theology takes various other forms, some of them, if possible, even more bizarre than most Reconstructionists would accept, yet growing in popularity among the charismatics with whom they are now working. Some positive confession leaders such as Kenneth Hagin and Kenneth Copeland teach that man's dominion proves he is "in God's class," a little god under God; that we lost our godhood to Satan, but that it has been restored in Christ and we need to reclaim it and exercise our lost dominion once again on that basis. Dominion theology and positive confession are closely related. Advocates of the latter take dominion through speaking it forth, while evangelicals such as those involved in COR recover dominion through activism—but the relationship is clear and most dominionists are working together toward their common goal.

"Restoring" the Vision of the Dominion "Task"

Contrary to this new theology, the dominion God gave Adam was not lost to Satan at the Fall and does not need to be restored. That man never lost but continues to exercise dominion is clearly stated in Psalm 8:6-8 as a given fact—a fact that we all know by experience. We still swat flies, eat chicken, catch fish, and exterminate termites. Recognizing this fact, dominionists nevertheless attempt to argue that we did indeed lose our power of dominion at the Fall and have an ongoing task of restoring it:

> Moreover, is it really true that we have dominion over the animals and the earth? Have we really tapped the potentials of the earth's resources? Have we domesticated bears and lions?
>
> While we do continue to exercise some dominion over the earth, the curse of Genesis 3 implies that the earth is recalcitrant. The curse on the ground has made dominion more difficult.
>
> In principle, the curse has been removed by the resurrection of Christ, but we still have the progressive task of restoring the creation to godly use.[8]

So we didn't *exactly* lose dominion after all, but the curse has made the earth "recalcitrant." It is more difficult for us than for Adam to mine gold and silver and suck oil out of the earth. Yet we must complete the task he left undone of hauling it all up in order to fulfill the dominion mandate. Moreover, this effort has been tied in with the Great Commission, which we must understand does not merely involve preaching the gospel, but also includes domesticating all animals, including bears and lions—and presumably insects and rodents and bacteria as well.

Christ's resurrection has removed the curse of Genesis 3 "in principle," but the reason no one noticed any diminishing of the profusion of weeds or of the ferocity of lions is because it is our task as part of the Great Commission of Matthew 28 to gradually "restore the creation to godly use." What a perversion of the gospel that Paul preached! Are we to assume that the apostles misunderstood the Great Commission and that the Reconstructionists, 1900 years later, have finally understood for the first time in the history of the church that Christ intended His followers to "take dominion" over this present evil world?

Scripture indicates that when Christ returns and personally reigns, "The desert shall rejoice, and blossom as the rose" (Isaiah 35:1) and "The wolf and the lamb shall feed together, and the lion shall eat straw. . . . They shall not hurt nor destroy in all my holy mountain . . ." (Isaiah 65:25). Since the Reconstructionists believe they are already in the millennium, they expect that, through progressively taking greater dominion, these paradisiacal conditions will gradually be manifested without Christ being physically present:

> When a culture departs from God, He surrenders its people to the dominion of wild animals, in order to prevent them from having ungodly dominion over the earth.
>
> But in a godly culture this threat against life and property will progressively disappear; and, ultimately . . . the animals will be tamed, and harnessed again to the service of God's Kingdom.[9]

Presumably we should see the evidence of such a trend in history. One searches in vain, however, around the world and down through history for ungodly cultures, of which there have been and still are many, where the people came under "the dominion of wild animals"—or for godly cultures where "this threat against life and property [has] progressively disappear[ed]." There is no discernible difference in the behavior of wild animals from one country to another or from one period of history to another that could be correlated with the godliness or ungodliness of the nation. Nor did God set a certain goal to be reached in subduing the earth that would serve as a gauge concerning how much or how little dominion was being exercised. Yet North writes:

> The dominion covenant requires men to subdue the earth to the glory of God (Gen. 1:28; 9:1-17). His people still must accomplish this task before He comes again to judge their success.[10]

"What *task*?" we must ask. Is it to build factories in Yosemite Valley and high-rise condominiums on Pike's Peak? Is our task to mine all of the minerals and suck up all of the oil? It does require effort to till the soil, but has God given us the task of putting every acre under the plow or of producing a certain yield per acre? If so, there is no mention of such criteria for measuring "dominion success." And why does North apply dominion only to "His people," when it was given to all men? Its exercise is an innate characteristic of our humanness that results from the very fact that mankind, saved or unsaved, is a higher order of creature than the animals, birds, fish, and insects. To make anything more out of dominion is to be guilty of manipulating the Word of God and doing violence to common sense.

A Mandate to Take Over the World?

Dominion theology, of course, would scarcely be worthy of mention if it simply involved farming and mining and domesticating animals. It only becomes provocative when it includes ruling over other men. Chilton declares: "We must stop acting as if we [Christians] are forever destined to be a subculture. *We are destined for [world] dominion. . . ."*[11] Here is the "task" that stirs the blood of dominionists. North writes:

> God's assignment to man to exercise dominion across
> the face of the earth is still in force. . . . God is in charge,
> waiting for His people to challenge the rulers of the earth
> and take the steering wheel from them. . . . The battle for
> the earth is currently going on.[12]

Certainly the phrase "take the steering wheel from them" in the context of the "battle for the earth" would seem to leave little doubt that everything is not to be left to God's "irresistible grace." In the television interview referred to earlier, Chilton told Moyers, "We believe that institutionally Christianity should be the official religion of the country, that its laws should be specifically Christian." Zealous Christians sincerely believe they are supposed to dominate non-Christians in the process of taking dominion over cultures and nations. It is not surprising, then, that the non-Christians feel threatened by the determination of these dominionists to force their beliefs upon the rest of society.

For those who "understand," the passage in Genesis pertaining to the dominion God gave Adam over the earth and lower creatures has been found to contain within it a secret teaching. It is actually a mandate to take over institutions, set up kingdoms, transform society, Christianize nations, and infiltrate their politics and institutions in order to take dominion over them in the name of Christ. On the contrary, Jesus specifically warned against such ambition:

> Ye know that the princes of the Gentiles exercise
> dominion over them. . . . But it shall not be so among you;
> but whosoever . . . will be chief among you, let him be
> your servant, even as the Son of man came not to be
> ministered unto but to minister and to give his life a
> ransom for many (Matthew 20:25-28).

Christians are not to lord it over one another, nor has the right been given to the church to reign over the world in the present age of

Christ's rejection and God's grace. Not until the resurrected Man, Christ Himself, returns personally to establish His millennial kingdom will Christians reign over this earth—Christians in immortal bodies reigning with Christ in His glory. Mistaking the present for the millennium causes the dominionists to seek, and perhaps most of them very sincerely, a power over human culture that does not belong to mortal man.

Of course, there is a legitimate authority for governing mankind at the present time, but it does not derive from Genesis 1:26-28. It is set forth in Romans 13. And in that passage the governing authority in the present world is clearly not the church, but earthly powers from which the church is distinguished and to which Christians are to submit. And Romans 13 has no more to do with the Great Commission of Matthew 28 than does Genesis 1.

Dominionizing the Great Commission

For those who embrace it, Rushdoony's "dominion theology" has become the new key to understanding the entire Bible. This "lost legacy [of dominion] that must be regained as we move into the 21st century"[13] is even declared, as we have noted, to be the key element in the Great Commission of Matthew 28:18-20. In agreement with that view, COR calls upon the church to exercise dominion as the very heart of the Great Commission. Kenneth L. Gentry, Jr. makes the astonishing statement:

> The Creation (or Cultural) [Dominion] Mandate can be found in Genesis 1:26-30, and the New Creation (or Evangelism) Mandate is the Great Commission. . . . the tasks of both mandates are the same: to subdue the earth.[14]
> The Creation Mandate is consequently undergirded by the restorational activity of God by means of the New Creation [Great Commission] power. Therefore, kingly dominion by man is reflected in evangelistic enterprise. . . .

No Christian should doubt the necessity of soul-win-
ning in a fallen world. But what about culture-winning?
Cultural Christianization.[15]

Most evangelicals, of which Gentry is one, would be appalled by
an interpretation that would turn Christ's command "that repentance and remission of sins should be preached in his name among
all nations" (Luke 24:47) into an assignment to subdue the earth and
domesticate lower creatures! Reconstructionists accuse those who
believe in a pretribulation rapture of a "reduction of Christianity,"
but it is they who have trivialized our high and heavenly calling. Nor
is it honest to suggest that the dominion given to Adam is now
restated in the Great Commission and involves "cultural Christianization." Yet North writes:

This assignment by Christ is simply a recapitulation of
the dominion assignment given to Adam and Noah by
God. It is the same assignment.
Now Christ announces His power over history, for He
has suffered in history: "And Jesus came and spoke unto
them saying, All power is given unto me in heaven and in
earth" (Matt. 28:18).
This is the historical foundation for His recapitulation
of the original dominion assignment.[16]

There is not even a pretense of deriving from the Scripture what is
being asserted above. Without any exegetical basis whatsoever,
dominion theology is simply imposed upon Matthew 28:18. Having
built their entire structure on the false foundation of dominion
theology, Reconstructionists and other kingdom/dominion advocates attempt to make the rest of the Bible fit this view. However, the
dominion mentioned in Genesis 1:26-29 has absolutely nothing to do
with the church, the Great Commission, Christianizing the world,
or taking over institutions or nations. Such theories are pure fabrication, for which those who promote them will have to answer to God.

Dominion Through Technology?

The contradictions in dominion theology are many and glaring. None is more incredible than the attempt to equate modern technology with the Genesis dominion over lower creatures. Amazingly Demar and Leithart, in spite of telling us that only born-again Christians operating from heaven through Christ can exercise the dominion which was lost by Adam and recovered by Christ, nevertheless refer to technological advancements made by non-Christians as "the fruits of dominion." Yet at the same time they try to give Christianity the credit for such inventions. The impression we get is that taking dominion or fulfilling the dominion task, which is now the essence of the Great Commission, also involves technological advancement. They write:

> Some of the most ardent critics of dominion theology are using the fruits of dominion to get their views across. Think where the church would be without the audio cassette, satellite television, and the growing Christian publishing industry.
> How would the spread of the gospel fare if we decided that the airplane and automobile were products of a demonized religion? This is dominion in action, dominion that did not flourish in a religious vacuum. These inventions developed in the Christian West.[17]

That term "Christian West" is a troubling one. They use it often and seemingly with great enthusiasm and approbation, asserting that Reconstructionists "advocate the building of a Christian civilization. . . ."[18] Are they pointing to the Western world as the example of the Christian civilization which they hope to achieve? Then why call it the Christian West if it isn't truly Christian? And if it isn't, then what is the point of sanctifying technological achievements such as audio cassettes and television satellites by crediting them to a Christian West? We can't have it both ways, or "Christian" becomes meaningless, as indeed it did after "Christianity" became the official world religion.

There are other glaring fallacies in their argument. Many of the inventions that laid the foundation for our modern technology, as well as much modern technology itself, are the product of Eastern cultures where paganism is still rampant. Are we not to use them? In fact, we can't avoid them. Japan, which is dominated by such anti-Christian religions as Buddhism and Shintoism, is taking the technological lead from America. Nor can we call America a Christian country. And what about Western Europe, where the Reformation took place but the church today is in such deep apostasy that Christianity has not been a significant factor in the culture for more than a century? Surely Western Germany is hardly a model Christian country, yet its prosperity is becoming the envy of the world. Nevertheless, we are assured:

> An important principle is at work in history. It is this: *God is continually at work to destroy unbelieving cultures and to give the world over to the dominion of His people.*[19]

That statement is simply not demonstrable from history, nor can the fruits of it be seen in the world today. Are Christians more wealthy, healthy, and successful than non-Christians? History for the past 2000 years shows no evidence that unbelieving cultures have been or are in the process of being destroyed. Any which have been destroyed have been replaced with cultures equally ungodly— or more so. For all of the corruption and evil of the Catholic Church during the Middle Ages, one would have to acknowledge that there was more general piety and respect for things spiritual then than there is now.

The more logically we try to apply dominion theology, the more absurd it becomes. Certainly there is no greater example, by their own definition, of what they call "dominion in action," than the atomic bomb. What could be more fundamental than taking dominion over the atom itself! Moreover, it was developed in the "Christian West," which makes it the perfect example. Of course its usage has been anything but Christian. Are we to assume that the hydrogen bomb will one day be given to Christians by God to enable them more effectively to "destroy unbelieving cultures" and thus fulfill the Great Commission by completing the dominion task of taking over the world from the godless?

A Misapplication of the Doctrine of Predestination

In spite of the adverse testimony of history and the fact that neither Christ nor the apostles taught or practiced it, COR and the Reconstructionists and other Kingdom Now advocates persist in their belief that Christianization of the world is the heart of the Great Commission, and that they will accomplish it. The one essential ingredient for this view is Calvinism—the idea that those who either obey or disobey God have no real choice in the matter, but that irresistible grace (or the withholding of it) is the sole determining factor. On that basis, of course, the whole world or any part of it could be converted at any time, thus making possible their optimistic scenario without the need for Christ to intervene personally on this earth. It also would turn what the Bible presents as a genuine conflict between God and Satan for the souls of men into a sham.

The dominionists' dream is based, however, upon a misunderstanding of predestination. The major predestination Scriptures do not teach that God has predestined certain men to be saved and certain ones to be lost. Paul declares that God has predestined believers to certain blessings: "to be conformed to the image of his Son" (Romans 8:29) and also to be adopted as children into His family (Ephesians 1:5). Both Paul in Romans 8 and Peter declare that predestination (or election) is on the basis of "the foreknowledge of God the Father" (1 Peter 1:2). Logically, foreknowledge would not enter into the picture at all if predestination were purely a matter of God's power. As the Romans 8 passage teaches, predestination involves making certain that all those whose response to the gospel, God foreknows will be affirmative, will both have it presented to them and will be preserved unto the blessings it offers.

Christ's declaration to His disciples, "Ye have not chosen me, but I have chosen you" (John 15:16) need not be taken to mean that the disciples had no real choice in the matter. Therefore, it must not be understood in that way because it would render meaningless Christ's call to them to decide whether they would follow Him or not. It would also contradict what many other Scriptures teach about man's responsibility to choose between self and God.

Any employer hiring an employee could declare: "You have not chosen me, but I have chosen you." Such a statement does not deny that the employee's choice was a necessary part of the arrangement, but simply defines the relationship by pointing out that without the employer's decision the would-be employee's desire is of no avail. Such passages as "God hath from the beginning chosen you to salvation" (2 Thessalonians 2:13) can, and therefore must, be interpreted in the same way to maintain consistency in Scripture. While some verses which present predestination could possibly be given a Calvinistic interpretation, to do so would contradict the remainder of Scripture and therefore must not be done.

We have already noted that Scripture testifies that God's love for all men is infinite and that He "desires all men to be saved." Christ came not "to condemn the world, but *that the world through him might be saved*" (John 3:17). God's purpose and desire could not be stated more clearly. Yet in spite of such Scriptures and His command to us to love our enemies and to be Good Samaritans to all who need our help, God Himself, according to Calvinism, has chosen not to save billions from hell even though, through extending His irresistible grace, He could do so. That is both a libel on God's character and such a contradiction of Scripture that it must be rejected vehemently.

It is on the basis of such a misunderstanding, however, that Reconstructionism assures us that things are going to get better and that they will be able gradually to take over the world. It is necessary to pervert their own doctrine of Calvinism in order to make such a statement in face of the many Scriptures which foretell a worsening of conditions in the last days, including apostasy, an increase in wickedness, and the rise of the Antichrist and Armageddon, as we have noted. All of that can be ignored only by postulating their purely hypothetical theory that God has determined (contrary to what His Word says) to extend more and more "common grace" (a lower level of grace that doesn't bring salvation but causes obedient behavior) until eventually the whole world will be Christianized.

Why God has determined to save so few and to take so long to do it no one knows because the Bible doesn't teach this false doctrine. Even if predestination were, as Calvinists believe, a pure determination by God to save some and damn the rest, there is no basis either in Calvinism itself or in Scripture for believing that He has predestined more to be saved toward the end of the world than earlier in time. In fact, the prophets all predict worsening conditions leading to judgment. John Pilkey argues:

> The corruption that exists in the world is characteristic of the ancient Noahic establishment of the *kosmos*; and neither the passage of time nor the presence of the Church can alter that basic fact. God will demonstrate the innocence of the true Church by treating the Rapture as a catalyst for allowing the Gentile *kosmos* to reach its final state of depravity.
>
> In other words, the Church has played a restraining role to be eliminated through the Rapture; but the Reconstructionists have overblown that restraining role into a kind of regenerative role.[20]

The Argument on the Basis of Power/Authority

The confidence that Christians can take over the world in His name is also based upon Christ's statement: "All power [authority] is given unto me in heaven and in earth" (Matthew 28:18). Jesus was thereby, according to the COR *Manifesto*, "declaring that whatever power Satan held over the world was broken by His death on the cross and His victorious resurrection."[21] While that is a biblical statement, its meaning is far different from the implications given by the advocates of Christianization.

Dennis Peacocke, former radical and now shepherding leader along with Bob Mumford, is one of the foremost promoters of this teaching. He declares and the COR *Manifesto* echoes: "When Jesus returns, He will gain no greater authority over this earth and the forces of Satan than He had from the moment He ascended to and sat upon His throne. . . ."[22] Though true, such a declaration is made to promote the false impression that what happens in the world depends only upon God's power. It ignores the fact that God has always been omnipotent, yet His infinite authority and power did not prevent Satan from rebelling nor did it prevent Adam and Eve from joining in that insurrection against their Creator and bringing rampant evil into this world. We cannot escape the fact that God has given men the power to choose whether to love and obey Him or not.

Writing long after Christ "ascended to and sat upon His throne," Paul declared that "the god of this world [Satan] hath blinded the minds of them which believe not . . ." (2 Corinthians 4:4). He warns that an unforgiving spirit could allow Satan to "get an advantage of us" (2 Corinthians 2:10,11); speaks of "the messenger of Satan" that has been buffeting him (2 Corinthians 12:7); declares that Satan hindered him from visiting a church (1 Thessalonians 2:18); and reminds Timothy that some professing Christians have already "turned aside after Satan" (1 Timothy 5:15). James tells us to "resist the devil" (James 4:7) and Peter says that Satan inspired Ananias and Sapphira "to lie to the Holy Ghost . . ." (Acts 5:3). Such Scriptures make no sense if Satan no longer has any power—much less if we are in the millennium and he is locked up, as the Reconstructionists allege.

Moreover, if Calvinism is true, then it matters little whether Satan's power is broken or not because whatever happens is dependent solely upon God's predetermined will and irresistible grace. On the contrary, God never imposed His will absolutely upon men and all angels, or this universe would not be the evil place it is today. Therefore, the fact that Jesus has all authority and power in heaven and earth does not mean that on that basis we, as His servants acting in His Name, can Christianize the world and cause all men everywhere—whether they believe the gospel or not—to obey His laws. Men still have a choice to make—and the overwhelming majority continue to love themselves more than they love God.

To teach that whether men and women believe or not, or rebel or not, is simply a matter of God's power and authority, is a perversion of Scripture. It is not a matter of raw power (God's power has always been infinite), but of how God uses it. In fact COR's *Manifesto* correctly goes on to explain that Christ "will exercise His authority in full power, then ["when Jesus returns"], in a way He is not fully exercising it now." That is exactly what the premillennialist believes: that the establishment of the kingdom upon earth will necessarily involve a physical forcing of peace and lawful behavior upon many who would otherwise not be willing. The Bible makes it clear that God will not establish the earthly manifestation of His kingdom through irresistible grace, but that Christ Himself will return to earth as King and Judge and reign in person for 1000 years on the throne of David, as the Hebrew prophets and the angel Gabriel promised.

Even then, however, after Christ has exercised dominion over the earth for 1000 years, when Satan is loosed and allowed access to mankind again, he will "deceive the nations which are in the four quarters of the earth." The nations will attack Jesus and His saints at Jerusalem and be destroyed. That will be the final proof of the blind pride and incorrigible nature of the human heart. All of the fallacious arguments of the psychologists and sociologists claiming that it is the environment or society or abuse people have suffered in childhood that causes men to err will have been laid to rest.

In the perfect environment of the millennial kingdom with Christ personally upon earth reigning as King, man will have demonstrated the evil of his heart—just as Adam and Eve did in the perfection of the Garden of Eden. No further proof will be needed that without the regenerative work of the Holy Spirit in the human heart there is no hope. The final judgment will be meted out and the real kingdom which is eternal and into which sin can never enter will have begun for those who have repented and received Christ as Savior and Lord.

Further Contradictions

The attempt to tie the Great Commission into what they call the dominion mandate is the foundation of the entire Reconstructionist and COR programs. It has the effect, as we have seen, of confusing the preaching of the gospel with a cultural takeover of the world, and gives more emphasis to Christianization than to conversion. The COR *Manifesto* declares:

> We affirm that the Great Commission is a mandate by our Lord to go forth into all the world and make bible-obeying disciples of all nations. . . . We affirm that God built the universe and man in accordance with the laws of His own Being in such a way that there is a cause and effect relationship between obeying [His] laws . . . and being blessed by God. . . .
>
> It is, therefore, to the great benefit of all mankind, Christian and non-Christian alike, to bring every society's judicial and legal systems into as close an approximation to the laws and commandments of the Bible as its citizens will allow.

There are some obvious problems. The phrase "the laws of His own Being" implies that God is the way He is because of certain *laws* that govern Him—which of course is false. Moreover, if God's blessing flows to man by "cause and effect," then precisely what blessings come from what obedience? We are out of the moral realm and into deism or science. Man's will is not involved, nor is his heart. Technical obedience to the letter alone without the Spirit suffices. But the Bible says that without love obedience is of no value. Moreover, the very first commandment calls us to love God with our whole heart, and he who breaks that is guilty of the whole law (James 2:10). Nor is love in the scientific realm of "cause and effect."

So to hope to get godless people who do not love God and who have never received Christ as Savior and Lord to obey God's laws, and to motivate them with the idea that there is a cause-and-effect relationship that will automatically bring blessing from God upon them, is not biblical. Even worse, it is dangerous. North assures us, however, that when the "Christian reconstruction of society" has produced "a prosperous, safe, strong, wise, and fair America at peace with her neighbors":

[all nations] will stampede to follow suit!...
When they see the blessings of God on a nation run by His principles, the results could dwarf the Reformation.[23] [What happened to his Calvinism?]
We are talking about the transformation of this world.
...Step by step, person by person, nation by nation, Christians are to *disciple* the nations.... the Lord has given us the task of holding "dominion...over all the earth."...How can we disciple the earth if we are not involved in running it?[24]

Biblical discipleship calls for loving care and godly example. Running the lives of disciples—or even worse, running the world—would be the very antithesis of fulfilling Christ's command in Matthew 28. That we are *not* supposed to "disciple the *nations*"[25] ought to be clear from the very nature of discipleship. Only an individual can be a disciple or be discipled. Moreover, those who advocate this error admit that the nations we are to disciple will still contain many non-Christians. Yet the very first step in becoming a true disciple in the intent of Christ's words in Matthew 28 is to receive Christ as Savior and Lord. To say otherwise is to pervert the meaning of the Great Commission and is the very "reduction of Christianity" of which those who believe in the pretribulation rapture have been accused.

The second step in making disciples in obedience to the Great Commission is to baptize them. To be baptized, a person must be a believer in Christ. Consequently the obedience to biblical principles which the Reconstructionists and COR expect to persuade the unsaved to adopt, in the process of discipling nations, cannot be part of the Great Commission as they insist, but is in fact a perversion of it. This is obviously the case, since neither belief in Christ nor baptism would be involved for the large percentage who remain unsaved. Nor could Christianizing worldly institutions qualify as part of the Great Commission, for the same reasons.

So if the Great Commission does not justify the political and social activism which they propose (and in COR there is no room for nonactivists),[26] then what is their biblical basis for it? There is none. The best they can say is that, through individuals coming to Christ, the families, businesses, neighborhoods, institutions, and even cultures will be affected. But that is precisely what evangelicals believe—that the only way to save souls for eternity or to change society is to preach the gospel.

On August 3, 1987, this author wrote the following letter to Jay Grimstead in response to a COR update:

> There is a glaring contradiction, not only between what you stand for and what the Bible teaches, but within your own writings. On the one hand, you rightly emphasize and I appreciate your teaching that a real Christian must be fully submitted to the Lordship of Jesus Christ. After stating that only a true Christian can keep God's moral laws, however, you go on to speak of bringing non-Christians under biblical law by demonstrating to them that this is really the best way to go. In conjunction with this, you imply culpability on the part of those "who fail to labor together toward this common goal while the world is collapsing and hell is filling."[27]
>
> You seem to imply that those who disagree with your position have no concern about hell filling and are doing less to keep it from filling than you. This is unfair. Those who believe in a pretrib rapture have more incentive than anyone to work diligently to win souls to Christ—and that is the only way to slow the flow of souls into hell.
>
> You are not going to prevent hell from filling by getting people to attempt to submit to God's moral laws. You are either going to produce a bunch of hypocrites who claim to submit to God's laws when they really do not, or frustrated people who are attempting to live up to a law when they have neither the power of the Holy Spirit nor the changed hearts to be able to do so.
>
> You can only prevent hell from filling by telling people that salvation does not come through the law but through

receiving Christ as Savior and Lord. I know that you believe this, yet I fear that you have been deceived into an unbiblical emphasis that, in actual fact, will mitigate against the true preaching of the grace of God that you actually believe and will emphasize instead a social/moral reconstruction of the world which will not work—and if it did, would undermine the true gospel of grace.[28]

12

Israel and the Coming Kingdom

Undeniably, an identifying mark of the contemporary Christian scene is an increasing preoccupation with the affairs of this world. And at what a cost! Without the purifying hope of being momentarily caught up to heaven in the rapture, spiritual problems are compounded and the church is laid open both to moral impurity and doctrinal error. We have noted that one of those errors is the growing belief that the church is to establish the kingdom of God on this earth before Christ returns. Inasmuch as Scripture clearly associates Israel with the earthly manifestation of the kingdom of God, the Reconstruction/kingdom/dominion movement leaders have found it necessary to reinterpret the Bible to make it seem that the church has replaced Israel as God's chosen people and heir to her earthly blessings.

Thus the promises which God gave to Israel in the Old Testament are now being applied to the church. The curses still belong to Israel, but the blessings are for the church. National Israel has now been cursed and is denied any place in God's future plans. Earl Paulk, who is one of the leaders in this movement, writes:

> Some of the strongest fundamental churches still preach that Christ will return to gather national Israel unto Himself, and I say that is deception and will keep the Kingdom of God from coming to pass!
>
> In almost any Christian bookstore, about 99% of the books will say that "God's time-clock is Israel" and that

"God's covenant is still with Israel." There is no comprehension . . . [that] whatever has been written concerning
the law and prophecies about Israel as a nation is now
transferred to spiritual Israel, which is the people of God
[i.e. the church]. . . .[1]

In the past, Christians in the West have been the major base of
support for Israel. With the new the-church-is-Israel movement
gaining a wide following among evangelicals who only a few months
or years ago would have rejected outright such a view, a drastic
change is developing in the attitude of Christians toward Israel. This
is especially true among charismatics, and the nation of Israel is
unhappily noticing the difference. While those promoting this belief
deny the charge of anti-Semitism, their increasingly bold use of
sarcasm, ridicule, and openly displayed antagonism toward Israel,
which we noted in chapter three, is ominous. And the trend is
escalating.

The Word of God anticipated this grave error. In fact, it had
already risen in the church in the days of John. He records the severe
judgment of Christ upon this false teaching in His letter to the
church in Smyrna. Those who are tempted to embrace today's
revival of this ancient "we-are-the-true-Jews" heresy need to pay
careful attention to the following harsh words from Christ Himself:

I know the blasphemy of them which say they are
Jews, and are not, but are the synagogue of Satan (Revelation 2:9).

Christian Anti-Semitism on the Rise?

It is quite clear why amillennialism, which has its roots in Catholicism, and its more optimistic Protestant form, postmillennialism,
must both be anti-Israel. The belief that the church is to establish the
earthly kingdom cannot coexist with the biblical teaching that the
coming millennial kingdom will have its headquarters in Jerusalem
with the Messiah ruling the world from the throne of David and with
national Israel restored to its place of supremacy over the nations.

Thus it is not surprising that with the growing popularity of the kingdom/dominion/Reconstruction movement we are also witnessing a revival among Protestants of the traditional anti-Semitism of the Catholic Church, which was never thoroughly purged by the Reformation. Anti-Semitism was one of the most grievous offenses that had flourished under the uncontested power of Roman Catholicism. The church that claimed as its first pope a Jewish fisherman and whose founder, Christ Himself, had been a Jew—as had been the apostles and the entire church in its infancy—very early became a persecutor of Jews.

Of course *anyone* who disagreed theologically with Rome was subject to persecution, if not death. The "heresy" of Judaism, however, was especially odious to the leaders of the "one true church," causing anti-Semitism to be made official. It was therefore not unexpected that the Vatican should remain silent as the smoke of extermination camp furnaces blackened the skies of Europe. Durant reminds us that Hitler had good precedent for his sanctions against the Jews:

> The Council of Vienne (1311) forbade all intercourse between Christians and Jews. The Council of Zamora (1313) ruled that they must be kept in strict subjection and servitude. The Council of Basel (1431-33) renewed canonical decrees forbidding Christians to associate with Jews . . . and instructed secular authorities to confine the Jews in separate quarters, compel them to wear a distinguishing badge, and ensure their attendance at sermons aimed to convert them.
>
> Pope Eugenius IV . . . added that Jews should be ineligible for any public office, could not inherit property from Christians, must build no more synagogues, and must stay in their homes, behind closed doors and windows, in Passion Week (a wise provision against Christian violence). . . .
>
> In a later bull Eugenius ordered that any Italian Jew found reading Talmudic literature should suffer confiscation of his property. Pope Nicholas V commissioned

St. John of Capistrano (1447) to see to it that every clause
of this repressive legislation should be enforced, and
authorized him to seize the property of any Jewish physician who treated a Christian.[2]

In later life Luther's anti-Semitism even exceeded that of his
former mentors. His pamphlet *Concerning the Jews and Their Lies*
(1542) was filled with lies about Jews. Its fulminations were many:
that God hated Jews, that the Talmud encouraged lying, robbery,
and even the killing of Christians; that Jews poisoned springs and
wells in order to accomplish their evil intentions; and that they used
the blood of murdered Christian children in their rituals. Providing
Protestant confirmation to match Catholicism's justification of
much that Hitler would do to the Jews, Luther:

> ... advised the Germans to burn down the homes of
> Jews, to close their synagogues and schools, to confiscate
> their wealth, to conscript their men and women to forced
> labor, and to give all Jews a choice between Christianity
> and having their tongues torn out.[3]

At present the charge of anti-Semitism is technically being
avoided by venting animosity only against the *nation* of Israel, while
professing a love for Jewish people as individuals. Leaders in this
movement are as insistent upon the total defeat of national Israel as
they are upon the total victory of the church, in spite of the many
biblical promises that Israel will be restored to her land, with
Messiah reigning. Instead of "God is dead," we are now told that
"Israel is dead." A declaration of the latter, however, is tantamount
to affirming the former, since He is so often identified as "the God
of Israel."

Denying History's Greatest Witness to God

David Chilton's *Days of Vengeance* attempts to justify the astonishing thesis that "[With] Israel's final excommunication in A.D. 70,

when Jerusalem was destroyed...the Kingdom had been transferred to His new people, the Church (Matt. 21:43; 1 Pet. 2:9; Rev.
11:19; 15:5; 21:3). The Kingdom ... will never again be possessed
by national Israel."[4] The Reconstructionists would have us believe
that Christ's promise to His disciples, "I will come again and
receive you unto myself," was the comforting assurance to the
Christians of that generation that He would soon return in the form
of the Roman armies to destroy Jerusalem, instead of rescuing it, as
Zechariah 12–14 indicated He would do:

> Our study of the New Testament is drastically off-
> course if we fail to take into account the apostolic expec-
> tation of an imminent Coming of Christ...[to] fully
> establish the New Covenant Church.
> The coming of the Roman armies [in A.D. 70] will be,
> in reality, Christ's Coming in terrible wrath against His
> enemies [Israel], those who have betrayed Him and slain
> His witnesses....[5]

Chilton does not explain what he means by the vague term "fully
establish the New Covenant Church." The concept is a Reconstructionist invention with no biblical basis. In fact, it is blasphemous to
suggest that the church which was founded at Pentecost was not
"fully establish[ed]" upon Christ and His Word but *needed* the
additional cornerstone of Jerusalem's destruction. Such an incredible proposal is only part of the confusion caused by the necessity for
postmillennialists, as we have already noted, to insist that Christ's
prophecies in Matthew 24–25 and Revelation 1:1–20:3 were all
fulfilled in A.D. 70.

The contradictions are so blatant that it is difficult to see how
anyone could seriously believe such a proposal. First of all, the Book
of Revelation was written at least 20 years after A.D. 70, most likely
about A.D. 96. That one fact destroys this entire theory. For those
interested in a scholarly discussion of the verification for this date,
the new book by House and Ice is recommended once again.[6]

House and Ice also include documentation of the well-known fact
that this A.D. 70 theory did not arise until the 1600s. It was invented

early in that century by a Spanish Jesuit named Alcasar specifically to counter the claims made by the reformers that the Roman Catholic Church was the whore on the beast in Revelation 17—claims that we have seen are fully justified. Alcasar's ingenious method of disassociating the Catholic Church with Revelation 17 was to show that Revelation was simply a prophecy concerning the destruction of Jerusalem. Had all of Revelation been fulfilled in A.D. 70, its prophecies could not possibly apply to the Catholic Church.

Zechariah 12, to which we have already referred, depicts Christ intervening at Armageddon (Revelation 19) from heaven to rescue Israel and to destroy the many nations from the entire world that were attempting to destroy her. In A.D. 70 it was only one nation, Rome, through her legions, that destroyed Jerusalem—with no rescue by her Messiah. In fact, the language Christ used to describe His return to earth in Matthew 24, which correlates with Zechariah 12, is so explicit that there can be no doubt that it did not occur in A.D. 70. Certainly no one saw or recorded the following:

> For as the lightning cometh out of the east and shineth even unto the west, so shall also the coming of the Son of man be.
> And then shall appear the sign of the Son of man in heaven; and then shall all the tribes of the earth mourn, and they shall see the Son of man coming in the clouds of heaven with power and great glory.
> And he shall send his angels with a great sound of a trumpet, and they shall gather together his elect from the four winds, from one end of heaven to the other (Matthew 24:27,30,31).

There are other serious difficulties. If we are to believe that Israel was cut off by God in A.D. 70, then one of the greatest events in the history of the world—the return of the Jewish people to their own land and the rebirth of Israel in 1948—is a freak accident with no significance. On the other hand, if this astonishing occurrence is in fact the fulfillment of biblical prophecies, as the church has so long believed it to be, then here is a modern miracle known to the entire world—an event to which Christians can point as giving irrefutable evidence for the validity of God's Word.

The-church-is-Israel advocates would rob the church of the most convincing available witness to God's existence, righteous judgment, and faithfulness: the remarkable history of the Jewish people, their prophecy-fulfilling odyssey and return to their historic homeland, and the prophesied climactic future events yet to occur there. Under the title "The Church Is Israel—A Vital Teaching," James McKeever has written:

> We love the Hebrews who live . . . in the nation of Israel. We support them and thank God for such an ally in the Mideast. However, the Lord has shown us clearly that in no way are they Israel. Israel is composed of all believers in Jesus Christ. . . .
>
> It is vitally important for the body of Christ to realize that they *are* Israel and that the unfulfilled prophecies concerning Israel are theirs to participate in. The unfulfilled promises to Israel are for the church to receive.[7]

The Abundant Testimony of Scripture

While there are no doubt spiritual applications that can be made to the church from God's dealings with Israel and His promises to her, there is much that simply cannot be spiritualized without doing violence to the meaning of language and the consistency of Scripture. National Israel is associated with the land of Palestine, and many biblical prophecies specifically involve that land. We need only recall part of that list: the removal of Israel to be scattered around the world because of her sin; the gathering of Israel back to her own land in the last days; the subsequent attack by the armies of the world against Israel in their attempt to destroy her at Armageddon; the intervention of Christ to rescue Israel and to execute judgment upon those who sought to destroy His people, including such details as His descent upon the Mount of Olives, which then splits in half.

When was there a worldwide dispersion of the church from its promised land and then a regathering? It never happened and never will. The church is associated with the "New Jerusalem" that comes down out of heaven in the new universe, but it is not associated with the old Jerusalem in a literal land called Palestine.

The last days events prophesied in Zechariah 12–14 simply cannot be applied to the church by any stretch of the imagination. It is equally clear that they did not occur in A.D. 70. Zechariah tells us that at the time of Christ's miraculous intervention to rescue His people, He will be recognized by Israel as the One whom they pierced (i.e. crucified), and the whole nation will believe on Him. Clearly this cannot apply to the church, which is composed of those who already know Him and have believed that He died for their sins.

The Old Testament contains scores of such definite prophecies involving specific details related to God's historic chosen people, Israel, and their promised land. There is no way that an interpretation which is honest and consistent with the remainder of Scripture could apply these to the church. They could only relate to the ethnic nation Israel, the descendants in the flesh of Abraham, Isaac, and Jacob, and to the land which they inhabited—until their worldwide dispersion and to which they have now returned. The following is a brief excerpt of the common phrases found in many such Scriptures—promises which could only apply to the 1948 rebirth of Israel and subsequent events, not to anything that happened to Israel previously or could ever happen to the church:

> Then the Lord thy God will turn thy captivity, and have compassion upon thee, and will return and gather thee from all the nations whither the Lord thy God hath scattered thee . . . from the four corners of the earth. . . .
>
> Rejoice ye with Jerusalem, and be glad with her, all ye that love her . . . For thus saith the Lord, "Behold, I will extend peace to her like a river . . . and ye shall be comforted in Jerusalem. . . . Israel shall dwell safely . . . in their own land . . . in the land that I gave to your fathers; and ye shall be my people, and I will be your God.

Thus saith the Lord, which giveth the sun for a light by day, and the ordinances of the moon and of the stars for a light by night, which divideth the sea when the waves thereof roar . . . "If those ordinances depart from before me," saith the Lord, "then the seed of Israel also shall cease from being a nation before me forever."

Thus saith the Lord: "If ye can break my covenant of the day, and my covenant of the night, and that there should not be day and night in their season, then may also my covenant be broken with David my servant, that he should not have a son to reign upon his throne, and with the Levites the priests, my ministers. . . .

"If my covenant be not with day and night, and if I have not appointed the ordinances of heaven and earth, then will I cast away the seed of Jacob. . . ."[8]

Did the sun rise this morning and cross the sky? Did the moon and stars still shine last night? Will the sun rise again tomorrow? If so, then Israel has not ceased from being that special nation to whom God has given specific promises (which pertain alone to her and to her promised land and not to the church)—definite promises concerning the future which have not yet been fulfilled but which surely will. If this is not the case, then the God of the Bible has lost all credibility.

While some Old Testament prophecies refer primarily to the return from Babylon, many others clearly indicate a later regathering of Israel from *all nations*. And even the return from Babylon is presented as a picture of a greater and final gathering: when the lion will lie down with the lamb, the Messiah will reign from Jerusalem, all of Israel's enemies will be destroyed, and "peace will cover the earth as the waters cover the sea." There can be no doubt that such prophecies have not yet been fulfilled but refer to the millennium, as do the following. They foretell the conversion of individuals and of Israel as a nation:

"Behold, the days come," saith the Lord, "that I will make a new covenant with the house of Israel, and with the house of Judah. . . . I will put my law in their inward parts, and write it in their hearts; and will be their God, and they shall be my people.

"And they shall teach no more every man his neighbor, and every man his brother, saying, 'Know the Lord': for they shall all know me, from the least of them unto the greatest of them," saith the Lord, "for I will forgive their iniquity, and I will remember their sin no more.

"And I will give them one heart, and one way, that they may fear me forever . . . that they shall not depart from me. . . . I will rejoice over them to do them good, and I will plant them in this land assuredly with my whole heart and with my whole soul. . . .

"And I will pour upon the house of David, and upon the inhabitants of Jerusalem, the spirit of grace and of supplications; and they shall look upon me whom they have pierced, and they shall mourn for him, as one mourneth for his only son. . . ."

And his feet shall stand in that day upon the mount of Olives, which is before Jerusalem on the east, and the mount of Olives shall cleave in the midst thereof. . . .

In that day there shall be a fountain opened to the house of David and to the inhabitants of Jerusalem for sin and for uncleanness . . . and the Lord shall be king over all the earth. . . .[9]

The New Testament, as well, associates the future kingdom with national Israel. Matthew goes to great pains to show that Jesus, in keeping with the Messianic prophecies, was of the seed of Israel and of the tribe of Judah. That fact would not be of any importance if the nation of Israel were going to be destroyed and the promises to Israel concerning the kingdom being restored and the Messiah sitting on David's throne were no longer in effect. The importance God places upon national Israel and the Messiah's relationship to her in the coming climax of history is shown in the fact that the angel Gabriel, who did not say a great deal to the virgin Mary, made it a point to tell her specifically that her son Jesus would rule from the throne of His father David.

Three Basic Facts About the Kingdom

Central to our concern over the loss of a heavenly perspective and the growing preoccupation with building a kingdom on this earth must be a basic understanding of the kingdom itself. Some Bible teachers have attempted to distinguish between the "kingdom of heaven," the phrase which is used only in Matthew, and the "kingdom of God," which is used in the other gospels. It is obvious, however, that these two terms are used interchangeably. It would be absurd to suggest that in their frequent references to the kingdom the other three gospels never once refer to the kingdom Matthew wrote about. That this is not the case is quite clear from the fact that the other gospels sometimes repeat the same story as Matthew tells, using almost identical words, except that they refer to Matthew's "kingdom of heaven" as the "kingdom of God."

Both words, "God" and "heaven," make it clear that, as Jesus said: "My kingdom is not of this world: if my kingdom were of this world, then would my servants fight . . ." (John 18:36). The kingdom of heaven stands in the fullest contrast to the kingdoms of this earth. Nevertheless, Gary North declares:

> Now His kingdom is of this world. Now His followers do fight for His honor, for they serve a risen Lord who has demonstrated His power over death. His kingdom is now visible in this world through His people.[10]

While it does have an earthly manifestation during the millennium, the kingdom will not be realized in its eternal fullness— which "flesh and blood cannot inherit" (1 Corinthians 15:50)— except in the new indestructible and incorruptible universe that will be created after the present one is destroyed. Nor can earthly beings rule with the glorified Christ over even the temporary millennial kingdom. One of the basic errors of Reconstructionism, as we have noted, is to imagine that mortals can in their flesh-and-blood bodies participate in the kingdom that Scripture plainly says can only be inherited by those in transformed bodies. S. J. Andrews puts it succinctly:

> To affirm that mortal and sinful men are already admitted to have part in His functions of universal rule, and are empowered by Him to govern the nations, is a proud and presumptuous antedating of the Kingdom.
> His kings must be first made like Him, immortal and incorruptible. When the earthly in them is changed into the heavenly, then can they exercise His heavenly authority.[11]

So we see two related errors. The Reconstructionists hope to achieve in mortal bodies what only the immortalized can accomplish. Manifested Sons of God adherents recognize the need for immortal bodies in order to function in the kingdom, but they will not wait until God's time for this to occur. And both groups share the common error of imagining that the kingdom can be established by the church in Christ's absence. To deal with the kingdom fully is far beyond the scope of this book. However, there are certain simple but important concepts which we must understand.

In Acts 1 the disciples asked Jesus if He would at that time restore the kingdom to Israel. That would have been the perfect time for Him to state (if it were the case) that Israel was finished or was shortly to be finished and that the kingdom never would be restored to her, but that the church had become Israel. It would have also been the perfect time to state that the kingdom was *now*, having already been inaugurated through His resurrection, and that the church would gradually fully establish it. In contrast to such teaching, Christ's reply—"It is not for you to know the times or the seasons, which the Father hath put in his own power"—implied three major points that provide a necessary foundation for any understanding of Israel and the coming kingdom:

> 1) that the kingdom of God, contrary to the Reconstructionists, had not yet come but would be inaugurated

at some future undisclosed time "which the Father hath put in his own power" (Acts 1:7);

2) that the kingdom would primarily involve national Israel, and would be restored to her specifically (verse 6); and

3) that it would not be manifested on this earth until King Jesus Himself returned personally to reign ("wilt *thou . . . restore*").

The very wording of the disciples' question demonstrates that they had never been told by Christ that His earthly ministry or His resurrection, as some are teaching today, had marked the inauguration of His kingdom. On the contrary, it is quite clear that they knew that the kingdom had been deferred to a future time. John the Baptist, Christ Himself, and His disciples had repeatedly declared, "The kingdom of heaven is at hand" (Matthew 3:2; 4:17; 10:7; etc.). The Jews, however, had rejected and crucified the One who had been "born King of the Jews" (Matthew 2:2), just as their prophets had foretold. As a consequence, the establishment of the promised kingdom would have to await the prophesied Second Coming of the Messiah that would turn Israel back to God.

The establishment of the kingdom that had been foreseen and described by the Hebrew prophets and that Israel had looked forward to for hundreds of years could only occur when the resurrected Messiah would be recognized and accepted by His people. The first time, meekly as the Lamb of God to bear away their sins, "He came unto his own and his own received him not" (John 1:11). The second time He would come in the awesome majesty and power of His resurrection to "fight against those nations [the armies of Antichrist]. . . . And his feet shall stand in that day upon the mount of Olives" (Zechariah 14:3,4). Then His people would "look upon me whom they have pierced [to death on the cross] . . . [and] there shall be a fountain opened to the house of David and to the inhabitants of Jerusalem for sin and for uncleanness" (Zechariah 12:8–13:1).

The very words "Wilt thou at this time" conveyed the disciples' understanding that the kingdom had not yet been established and that only Christ Himself could accomplish it. The fact that Christ did not correct them on this but said that the time for the restoration was "in the Father's hands" (i.e. future) is evidence enough that those, no matter how sincere, who claim we are now in the millennium are deceived themselves and are deceiving others. Certainly the events prophesied in Zechariah 12–14 and elsewhere that bring about the inauguration of the kingdom through Christ's return to this earth to personally reign have not yet occurred.

Both their expectation that the kingdom was in the future and their conviction that Christ Himself would establish it were consistent with what Jesus had so often taught His disciples. Peter, James, and John were present on the mount when Christ was "transfigured" (glorified) and Moses and Elijah came to speak with Him. Telling His disciples beforehand of this special event, Christ had stated that they would "see the Son of man coming in his kingdom" (Matthew 16:28). Of course what they saw wasn't the kingdom itself, but a powerful preview thereof. The message, once again, however, was that the kingdom was yet to come and that it involved the personal presence of Christ. What was previewed on the Mount of Transfiguration has certainly not come to pass as yet.

At the "last supper," Christ said that He would not eat of the Passover again "until it be fulfilled in the kingdom of God"; and that He would not drink "of the fruit of the vine, until the kingdom of God shall come" (Luke 22:14-20). This double message tells us again that the kingdom has not yet come and that when it does, Christ Himself will be present eating and drinking and even partaking of the Jewish Passover. Clearly that hasn't happened.

A Kingdom Without Its King?

Many other examples could be given, but one more must suffice. Many of the parables Christ taught contain this same dual message: that the kingdom is yet in the future and that He will personally inaugurate it. On one occasion He told a particular parable "because they thought that the kingdom of God should immediately appear" (Luke 19:11-27). Surely this tells us that the kingdom had not yet appeared. It also tells us that it was not going to be manifested very soon. This story provides insights into most aspects of the kingdom, of which we can only note a few:

A certain nobleman went into a far country to receive for himself a kingdom, and to return.

And he called his ten servants . . . and said unto them, "Occupy till I come."

But his citizens hated him, and sent a message after him, saying, "We will not have this man to reign over us."

And it came to pass that when he was returned, having received the kingdom, then he commanded these servants to be called unto him. . . .

[He rewards his servants for their faithfulness or lack of it, then deals with those who were in rebellion.]

"But those mine enemies which would not that I should reign over them, bring hither and slay them before me."

Representing the church, the faithful servants were a small minority. The prince (Christ), who had not yet received the right to reign over the kingdom, was rejected by the vast majority of those who could otherwise have been citizens in the realm over which he was eventually to rule. The kingdom was still in rebellion when he received title to it and returned to destroy his enemies and establish his reign. So it is with our Lord, who is now rejected by the vast majority on planet earth, but who is coming again to set up His kingdom and mete out judgment upon those who have rejected Him. Such is the consistent message of Scripture.

There can be no kingdom without the king being present, as eminent radio Bible teacher J. Vernon McGee has been expounding for many years. All Christians admit this to be the case when it comes to the spiritual kingdom in their hearts. Christ must reign there. And the same is equally true of the outward manifestation of

260 · *Israel and the Coming Kingdom*

His kingdom upon earth during the millennium. He must personally reign there as well.

It is quite clear from Luke 24:47,48 and other passages that the disciples were not expected to inaugurate the kingdom but to be witnesses concerning the King and His future coming. McGee points out what should be indisputable: In order for the conditions which the Bible predicts (peace and harmony among men and nations and the lion lying down with the lamb, etc.) to prevail during the millennium, Satan must be removed from the earth. The curse pronounced by God upon the earth must also be removed. Certainly the church is in no position to accomplish either of these preconditions. Thus the presence of our Lord is an imperative.[12]

Prophetic Scriptures that have long been understood to promise that Christ Himself would return to physically reign on this earth are increasingly being interpreted as prophesying a triumphant church reigning in His absence. Writing to promote the Kingdom Now teaching in Britain's *Restoration Magazine*, which claims to be "A Prophetic Voice to the People of God," internationally known author and conference speaker Arthur Wallis cites Psalm 2 as predictive of "the promised end-time outpouring of the Holy Spirit" upon a "triumphant church." Wallis even quotes verse six—"Yet have I set my king upon my holy hill of Zion"—as evidence of "a mighty triumph [by the church] over the enemies of Christ" before Christ returns.

Here we have the roots of another popular but very serious error: the teaching that the church is Christ. Not only are Scriptures that pertain to Israel being applied to the church, but the same is being done with prophecies concerning the Messiah. We are reminded of John's solemn warning about the spirit of Antichrist, which he identifies with the denial that Christ has come in the flesh. This new teaching involves a similar but no less serious error. It denies that Christ will come in the flesh to reign over the kingdom, and instead grants to the church and individual Christians the prerogatives and powers that belong only to Christ Himself. Nor can these powers be displayed in mortal man, but only in those who have been resurrected or been given immortal bodies.

Who Will Stop Armageddon?

The Scripture Wallis quotes, particularly in the context of ruling the nations "with a rod of iron," could only refer to Christ personally reigning from Jerusalem, which is specifically identified throughout Scripture as God's "holy hill of Zion." Without any biblical exegesis to explain how he interprets the *king* ruling from Zion to mean the last-days *church*, Wallis goes on to declare:

> The church has been given authority to bring in the kingdom by saving the lost, delivering the captives, healing the sick and building up the body of Christ.
>
> The growing response is only the firstfruits. Along with it has come a new emphasis on a kingdom lifestyle in marriage and family life, in social and moral issues and in business and work ethic.
>
> The church is limbering up, not to splutter out like a spent candle but to exit to the coming age in a blaze of glory.[13]

One can only marvel at the deep prejudice required to liken being taken to heaven in the rapture to "splutter[ing] out like a spent candle"! Being caught up to be forever with her bridegroom in the Father's house in glory has somehow lost its appeal to a large portion of His bride. Never mind the world to come. Taking over this present world seems much more challenging and, frankly, enjoyable. As C. Peter Wagner reminds us, however:

> God has not made us responsible for bringing in the Kingdom of God in its fullness. Only God will do that at the end of this age.[14]

There is good reason for what McGee and Wagner state, if we take Scripture seriously. Who else but Christ could put an end to the Great Tribulation that culminates in Armageddon? Who else could intervene to stop the armies of the world just as they are about to destroy Israel? One of the most awesome insights into the horror of that incredible world conflict is found in the following statement by Christ:

> And except those days should be shortened, there should no flesh be saved; but for the elect's sake those days shall be shortened (Matthew 24:22).

Christ is clearly stating that the destructive forces at work in that day will have the capability of destroying all life on planet earth and would do so if they were not forestalled in some way. Neither the threatened destruction of all life on earth nor Christ's intervention to prevent it was fulfilled in A.D. 70. Great as the loss of life was at the destruction of Jerusalem, by no means did it threaten all life on the planet—a holocaust obviously beyond the capability of swords, spears, and arrows. That prophecy only made sense with the advent of modern nuclear, chemical, and biological warfare, and thus it could well be fulfilled in our time.

Who would be powerful enough to intervene to "shorten those days" and stop the annihilation of all life on this earth? Certainly not the church, which could hardly be in control of a Christianized world at the time to which Christ refers, or such a horrible tribulation would not be in process. Surely only the miraculous intervention of Christ Himself in the full display of His power could play the necessary role. In fact, this is exactly what numerous Scriptures to which we have already referred indicate will happen.

Strange Rules of the Dominionist's Game

As the new key to understanding all Scripture, however, dominion theology rejects the clear prophecies that the Messiah Himself will restore and reign over Israel in a coming millennium. The King is not allowed to have any personal part in His kingdom. Instead, dominion theology makes it *our* responsibility to take dominion and establish the kingdom *without His personal presence*. Christ is not allowed to reign in glory and honor and power in the world where He once suffered humiliation, scorn, shame, and rejection. DeMar and Leithart declare:

Dominion Theology teaches that we can, do, and will have a kingdom of God on earth without Jesus' physical presence in Jerusalem.[15]

In Manifested Sons of God tradition, Earl Paulk goes so far as to say: "Death will not be conquered by Jesus returning to the earth. It will be conquered when the church stands up boldly and says, 'We have dominion over the earth!' "[16] Conquering death is also part of the so-called dominion mandate. Paulk writes:

The fifth function of the church is to conquer the last enemy, which is death, and to bring redemption to the Body of Christ. . . .

When the church becomes so conformed to His image that those who die do not pass through the grave, but become instead gloriously changed in the twinkling of an eye, it will be that church which will bring the Kingdom of God to pass on the earth.[17]

Scripture, however, specifically declares that the change into immortality "in the twinkling of an eye" will occur when Christ returns to raise the bodies of dead Christians from the grave and transform the bodies of the living. He will take these now immortal saints all to heaven for that glorious marriage, then return with His bride at His side to intervene personally to rescue Israel, destroy His enemies, and establish His millennial kingdom. One would think that such a victorious scenario would bring joyful anticipation to Christians. Strangely enough, however, those who espouse such beliefs are denigrated for adopting an "eschatology of defeat."

Dominion theology so twists Scripture that it is only "victory" if the church takes over the world and establishes the kingdom in Christ's absence. It would be defeat for Him to intervene to do it personally. Why? Because the original dominion mandate which Adam failed to fulfill has been reassigned to us through the Great Commission. Thus it is our responsibility to take over the world without any interference from Christ. Earl Paulk explains:

> We must move from servant to son to the likeness
> of Jesus and become God's literal incarnation in the
> world. . . .
> The whole earth groans, waiting for the manifestation
> of the sons of God, and you and I, as the church, must
> begin to function in a dimension that the church has
> heretofore not known. . . .
> At this point in the life of the church and in the process
> of bringing the Kingdom of God into reality, God has
> done everything that He can possibly do. There is abso-
> lutely nothing else He can do. God, in His sovereignty,
> limited Himself when He said, "Man, this is your estate,
> and now you must live it out."[18]

A thorough search of the Scriptures fails to discover where God
intimated that the return of Christ was dependent upon our efforts
and exactly what those efforts were to be. Nevertheless, this teaching is being increasingly accepted, thanks to the efforts of men like
Royal Cronquist, who has a growing following among charismatics.
At last count, Cronquist, a one-time apostle in the now almost-
defunct cult known as The Walk, founded by the recently deceased
John Robert Stevens, claimed that "Christ" had appeared to him 92
times to update his instructions. Like Paulk, he declares:

> Jesus cannot and He will not return until there is a
> remnant of believers called sons of God that have appeared
> and become manifested.
> Don't assume that the way of qualification [for full
> sonship] is through death and resurrection. . . . you put it
> [immortality] on while you are alive today.[19]

On the contrary, Scripture is very clear that immortality will
come both to the living believers and to those who have previously
died only at the resurrection, an event that will be initiated by God
Himself, not by men who have attained to some special spiritual
state. This false teaching should be finally laid to rest by the

following Scripture, which clearly states when bodily immortality will be received:

> Now this I say, brethren, that flesh and blood cannot inherit the kingdom of God; neither doth corruption inherit incorruption.
>
> Behold, I show you a mystery: We shall not all sleep [die], but we shall all be changed, in a moment, in the twinkling of an eye, at the last trump; for the trumpet shall sound, and the dead shall be raised incorruptible, and we [the living at the time] shall be changed.
>
> For this corruptible [body] must put on incorruption [in order to be in the millennial kingdom], and this mortal must put on immortality (1 Corinthians 15:50-53).

Christ or Antichrist?

The kingdom/dominion/Reconstructionists have misunderstood both history and prophecy. Their vision of the kingdom is too small. They have lost, along with the hope of an imminent rapture to heaven, the vision of immortal, glorified man returning from heaven to reign with Christ in His kingdom. Instead, they imagine that God's plan for human history can be fulfilled by those still in flesh-and-blood bodies. On the contrary, as we have noted, to enter the kingdom requires a transformation into glorified bodies like Christ's.

The requirement of being "born again," which Christ explained to Nicodemus, is not a catchy slogan or a vague theological term, but an absolute necessity and reality. God has to do something radical and remarkable in order to fit us for His presence. The rapture, Great Tribulation, and the millennial kingdom ruled by Christ in person, assisted by His resurrected bride, are all part of God's progressive dealings with man and must be taken for what Scripture states, not twisted to fit our ambitions.

We have noted the dangers inherent in the growing belief that a Christian elite has a mandate to set up the kingdom without Christ's personal presence. Yet nothing less than an absolutist theocracy will hold in check the evil and bring about the radical solution that the world's ills require. Moreover, international developments point inexorably to the establishment of such a regime. It will either be under the false world religion of Satan and his personal incarnation, or under the truth of God and through the personal intervention of His Son, our Lord Jesus Christ.

Whether men are ready to admit it or not, the only viable choice is between Christ and Antichrist. No mere man or group of men could qualify to rule this world, all of the good intentions of COR and the Reconstructionists and assorted other dominionists notwithstanding.

"Yet have I set my king upon my holy hill of Zion" (Psalm 2:6) is clearly a prophecy concerning the future. It pertains to that day when, *not the church,* but the One of whom the Father said, "Thou art my Son; this day have I begotten thee" shall be given by the Father "the heathen for [His] inheritance, and the uttermost parts of the earth for [His] possession." He will rule them "with a rod of iron" (verses 7-9) from Jerusalem.

Clearly this day has not yet come, nor can it until the Son of God Himself personally returns to this earth in power and glory. That He will do so we can have no doubt. Jesus Himself told His disciples that "all things must be fulfilled, which were written in the law of Moses, and in the prophets, and in the psalms, concerning me" (Luke 24:44). Among those things is this prophecy that is repeated so often at Christmastime:

> But thou, Bethlehem Ephratah, though thou be little among the thousands of Judah, yet out of thee shall he come forth unto me that is to be ruler in Israel; whose goings forth have been from of old, from everlasting (Micah 5:2).

The church was not born in Bethlehem, nor has its "goings forth been . . . from everlasting." Clearly the One referred to is none other than Christ Himself, the One whom the Father has said: "shall rule my people Israel" (Matthew 2:6). Jesus Christ did not fulfill that Scripture when He was here the first time. To do so He must come again personally to this earth—and He will very soon. Then and not until then shall His earthly kingdom be established.

13

True Victory in Christ

Those who believe that the church must Christianize the world and establish the kingdom before Christ can return often rely more upon rhetoric than upon careful exegesis of Scripture in defending their theories. Appealing to the natural desire to be a winner rather than a loser, Gary North asks: "Does God's Word teach that Satan will be victorious over God's people in history? Do you really believe that the Lord Jesus Christ, the Lord of glory, plans to be a loser in history?"[1] The COR *Mandate* places a similar emphasis upon the church being victorious.

Of course, what is meant by "victorious" and "loser" is extremely important. The dominionists' view of victory turns out to be a strange one indeed—so strange that the cross of Christ itself wouldn't qualify. North writes:

> [Hunt is] a no-nonsense defender of the earthly defeat of the Church. . . . *Dave Hunt denies the progressive maturation of Christianity and Christian-operated social institutions in history* (meaning pre-Second Coming history). . . . Hunt argues [that] the plan of God points only to the defeat of His Church in history. . . .
>
> I have said that pessimists . . . in their attempt to refute Christian optimism regarding the Church's earthly future . . . [deny] the long-term social transformation of society at large.

... wouldn't our defeat by Satan's forces in history
make Jesus a loser in history?[2]

The Reconstructionists have set their own rules and definitions,
among which is the arbitrary decision that although Christ came to
earth once *in* history, His return would be *outside* history. History
now belongs exclusively to us. Jesus Christ is outside of it and cannot
get back in under the new rules. Thus Christ's intervention to
destroy His enemies at the end of Armageddon and His reign during
the millennium would somehow not qualify as a victory in history.
This is a fanciful distinction invented by the dominionists for their
own peculiar purpose.

An Obsession with Earthly Mortal Existence

Not only may Christ not return, but the Reconstructionists are not
willing to be taken from this earth into heaven, to return with Christ
and reign with Him in immortal bodies. That would disconnect
them also from what they call "history" and thus from their earthly
plans. They have lost the heavenly vision in their obsession with
what they call "the Church's *earthly* future"—a future that does not
include Christ reigning on this earth at all. He would get in the way
of their personal project: the "long-term social transformation of
society at large," which it has been decided must take place before
the Second Coming of Christ so that the transformation can be
accomplished by mortal men.

Like Dostoevsky's Grand Inquisitor, the Reconstructionists would
seem to look upon the return of Christ to this earth as unwelcome
interference in their plans for establishing the millennial kingdom.
It seems strange, indeed, that the King Himself is not allowed to set
up His own kingdom, nor even to be present to reign over it. He has
gone to heaven—a place which increasing numbers of His blood-
bought people seem only willing to enter when forced by death to do
so. And He must remain there, out of their way, because they have a
long-range program for improving this world in His absence. They
mistakenly believe that the church is in this world to eliminate evil,

when in fact it is only here as God's instrument of restraint. It is not our job to transform this world but to call out of it those who will respond to the gospel.

When the church is raptured, its Holy Spirit-empowered restraining influence upon evil will be removed (2 Thessalonians 2:6-10). Satan will thus be left unhindered by the church in his attempt to establish his utopian kingdom. The rapture is no mere escape for the church. It is not the cop-out which its critics try to characterize it as being. On the contrary, it is a vital part of God's plan for dealing with mankind, an integral and important working out in history of God's purposes.

Having forgotten that "flesh and blood cannot inherit the kingdom of God," the Reconstructionists imagine, as we have already noted, that they can accomplish in these mortal bodies what is only possible for immortal man. One marvels at the reluctance to accept the glorious bodies God desires to give us in exchange for the bodies of weakness and sin in which we are now confined—and at the overblown confidence in "Christian-operated social institutions." Why is there such an unwillingness to admit that it will take a heavenly visitation, an invasion of this earth by heavenly beings led by the Lord of glory Himself, to right the grievous wrongs on this earth and establish the millennial kingdom? The Reconstructionist view of that kingdom, and thus of the needed "long-term social transformation of society," is far too small. Might we not also say it is a "reduction" of His glorious plan?

The Great Tribulation and Armageddon leading up to Christ's justified and necessary intervention on planet earth to stop the destruction and set up His kingdom are also part of God's outworking of His will in human history. These events are clearly prophesied in Scripture, and to present them as a warning to the world is not "gloom and doom" but simply faithfulness to the truth. Yet critics, in attempting to take a more "positive" approach to history than God Himself has taken in His Word, arbitrarily attach the label "pessimistic" to the pretribulation rapture belief and label their own scenario "optimistic"—certainly an insufficient reason for clinging to a theory.

270 · *True Victory in Christ*

The Irrelevance of Pessimism/Optimism Rhetoric

Jeremiah was a pessimist in the eyes of his contemporaries, prophesying defeat for Israel against Nebuchadnezzar's armies when all of the other prophets were united in predicting victory. The same accusation of negativism was leveled against Micaiah (1 Kings 22) when he courageously pronounced defeat upon King Ahab in the proposed battle against the Syrians, and did so in the face of the repeated assurances of victory by the king's entire school of 400 false but optimistic prophets. The defeatist pessimism of Jeremiah and Micaiah proved to be correct, while the victorious optimism of their opponents brought disaster. We ought to turn a deaf ear to emotional labels of pessimism or optimism and give our attention to what God has to say in His Word, be it reproof or encouragement.

Some of those to whom Noah preached the destruction of their world may have complained about his pessimism, but we can all be thankful that he did not reject what God said because it sounded so negative. In contrast we have Gary DeMar's appealingly optimistic "positive agenda for Christians to influence their world."[3] What bearing does positive or negative have on this issue? Supposing Noah had opted for changing the world and, instead of building an ark, had spent his 120 years building Christian-operated institutions for effecting long-term social transformation—and a large estate with house and barn and stables as well. He would, by that optimistic program, have assured the total destruction of life on this earth.

Unfortunately, Lot had made that very mistake and had invested everything he had in Sodom, building for the long-term there—and losing it all. Nor was the issue pessimism versus optimism at Sodom any more than at the flood. It makes no better sense to reject as pessimistic the clear prophecies concerning the Great Tribulation or the rise of Antichrist and Armageddon in favor of an optimistic eschatology of victory that is denied by both history and Scripture.

Those who oppose the pretribulational rapture betray the weakness of their position by their frequent appeal to emotion rather than Scripture and reason. Instead of demonstrating exegetically why pretribulationalists are wrong, North falsely accuses them of harboring a "needless fear of the antichrist [which] is paralyzing Christians' required fear of God. . . ."⁴ He quotes no example of any credible source telling Christians to fear the Antichrist. Gary DeMar, likewise without documentation, refers to a "misguided belief in the power of the Antichrist," which he claims "puts a damper on any long-term program that expects success in turning back the tide of evil in our society."⁵

Such emotionalism is a poor substitute for responsible exegetical treatment of such Scriptures as: "And it was given unto him ["the beast," or Antichrist] to make war with the saints, and to overcome them: and power was given him over all kindreds, and tongues, and nations. And all [of the unsaved] that dwell upon the earth shall worship him . . ." (Revelation 13:7). The COR *Manifesto* reflects a similar emotionalism when it depicts Christians as "trembling in fear of the secular culture or of the anti-Christ."⁶ In response, this author wrote to Jay Grimstead:

> I am not trembling in fear of the secular culture, nor of the Antichrist. But I do seek to warn Christians and non-Christians alike that the world is being prepared to accept the Antichrist.
>
> And I seek to call all to become citizens of heaven and to set their affection upon and to lay up treasure in heaven.⁷

Is God a Defeatist?

Furthermore, the charge of pessimism made against those who reject dominion theology is like the pot calling the kettle black. As Calvinists, these "optimists" believe that God deliberately chooses to damn the vast majority of mankind. Is that victory? And if it is defeat, then who takes the blame? How can it be an "eschatology of victory" to predict that the majority will finally be Christians at the end, when far more people—in fact, multiplied billions—during the many thousands of years of a Reconstructionist "millennium" yet to come will have followed Satan? History is more than the last few years.

Since God is perfect, victory for Him must be 100 percent. It is not enough to say that God "won" during the last few years of world history, or even that He won most of the time. He must win all of the time or He is not God. Therefore it must not be defeat for God when men, no matter how many, reject His love and offer of salvation. If it is defeat for God for a soul to go to hell, then God has already been defeated many times. It cannot be defeat for God even if all men end up in hell. Was God defeated because Israel rebelled against Him in the wilderness and only two out of the several million who left Egypt entered the Promised Land? Then why does it make Christ a loser in history to declare what He Himself said—that few will be saved?

God mourned over Israel for its rejection of Him, and the Holy Spirit foretold that even when God would come as a man to His own people, as their promised Messiah, they would hate, reject, and crucify Him. Was that prophecy defeatism or pessimism on the part of Isaiah and the Holy Spirit who inspired him? Jesus had very few disciples to show for His gracious ministry of healing the sick, feeding the hungry, raising the dead, and powerful preaching of the gospel of the kingdom throughout Palestine. In fact, in all of Scripture and history there have always been very few who believed, just as there were at the flood and at Sodom. Strangely enough, however, contradicting his own definition, North cites Sodom as an example of victory:

> We must fight theological hellfire with theological heavenfire, just as God fought it at the destruction of Sodom. The Sodomites lost that confrontation, not Lot, and certainly not Abraham. Pessimists forget this.[8]

No, the "pessimists" haven't forgotten that. In fact, Sodom is a perfect example of the very kind of victory they predict. One wonders, therefore, how the destruction of the vast majority and the rescue of only a very few at Sodom qualifies for victory by North's standards. It doesn't. Instead, it offers a picture of the very pretribulational rapture that he opposes, with the church being taken out of a wicked world just before God's judgment falls upon it.

We dare not major on those portions of the Bible that appeal to us as positive and victorious and ignore the oft-repeated warnings in the Bible that few will be saved (Luke 13:23-30) and that "evil men and seducers shall wax worse and worse, deceiving, and being deceived" (2 Timothy 3:13). A dislike for anything negative is hardly good reason to reject the clear teaching of Scripture that the last days will be a time of great religious deception led by false prophets, will involve counterfeit miracles, and will be supported by false doctrine.

Was the Cross Victory or Defeat?

Through His death, burial, and resurrection Christ triumphed over sin, Satan, death, and hell. Nor is that victory dependent at all upon mankind's evaluation or response to His cross. The infinite victory He won there was not at all dimmed by the fact that just before Christ went to the cross "all the disciples forsook him and fled" (Matthew 26:56). North, however, requires that anything less than the conversion of the vast majority of the world and the Christianization of the remainder would be "our defeat by Satan's forces" and "make Jesus a loser in history." By that definition, Christ died a loser in history and His death upon the cross was a defeat, for when He returned to heaven He left only a small handful of followers upon earth in spite of all He had wrought.

Yet the cross is the Christian's example and represents the kind of victory we must win. The Christian's battle is not against people or kingdoms or institutions but against the deceitful wickedness of his own heart and against the evil world system and the devil. In that fight of faith, denying self and taking up the cross to follow Christ in His submission to the Father's will and being rejected by the world is the only means of victory. And that victory has nothing to do with taking over worldly institutions or governments or with how many people respond to the gospel.

Having accomplished the Father's will by our redemption, it is thereafter not a defeat for Christ if all mankind does not believe in

274 • *True Victory in Christ*

Him and receive the benefits of the salvation He has procured for them upon the cross. This is true both from the Calvinist and non-Calvinist point of view. If, as Calvinism teaches, the Father withholds saving faith and grace from man, it can hardly be defeat for Christ if the vast majority are lost. And if, as most of today's evangelicals believe, a choice is involved on the part of those who hear the gospel, and the vast majority choose to reject Christ, it is still not a defeat for Him. Yet the dominionists insist that if the majority of people are not converted and the world is not Christianized *prior to the Second Coming*, then it has been a defeat for Christ and for the gospel.

On the contrary, all those—whether few or many—who put their trust in Christ, share in His victory. God's people are victorious because the One who defeated Satan at the cross has come to live in their hearts as their Lord and Savior. They have placed themselves under His protection. The ungodly have not done so. One could, therefore, scarcely fault either God or His people if the ungodly are seduced by Satan. And if a person does not wish to give mankind credit for being able to make a genuine choice in the matter, then instead of blaming God's people, should not the blame be placed upon God Himself for withholding the irresistible grace that could convert the entire world?

Human Responsibility and God's Glory

North charges the "pessimists" with having "called into question the power of the Holy Spirit to bring people to the foot of the cross."[9] He seems to ignore the fact that billions of people in history have already died and gone to hell without being drawn to the foot of the cross by the Holy Spirit. How does it call into question the Holy Spirit's power to suggest that the vast majority of people will continue to reject Christ in the future just as they have in the past? It is not a reflection upon the Holy Spirit or the gospel if men, by their own willful choice, refuse to be drawn to Christ. And if Calvinism is true, then men do not have that choice, but God has decided to allow billions to perish even though the Holy Spirit could draw all men to the foot of the cross. So it is not a lack of power after all. Is it a lack of love? But God *is* love!

North admits that his theory is based upon his confidence in Calvinism's teaching that "God's predestinating irresistible grace [will] force conversions."[10] Even if that were the case, God has apparently, to this moment in history at least, chosen to *force* only a very small minority to believe and has withheld the requisite irresistible grace from the vast majority. According to the Reconstructionists' own Calvinism, it is God Himself and not the "pessimists" who has made Jesus "a loser in history." And wouldn't the victory have a rather hollow ring if men were forced by God's irresistible power to do what they otherwise wouldn't do? Where then would love come into the picture?

Calvinism's doctrine of irresistible grace turns the great conflicts between God and man—God's love, patience, and mercy and the preaching of the gospel and the warnings to those who reject it— into empty charades. It makes no sense for God (for example, in Isaiah 1) to bemoan the fact that He has raised children and they have rebelled against Him if it is impossible for human beings to do otherwise because God is deliberately withholding from them the power to love and obey Him. If nothing prevents God from dispensing His requisite grace except His willingness to do so, then why does He plead with mankind and mourn its waywardness?

We must interpret Scripture consistently and without putting the blame for evil upon God's unwillingness to make men good. The only conclusion we can come to is that God has given man the power of choice in order for him to respond to His love. Thus to influence man to do something against his will would destroy man as God made him. There would then exist no human beings capable of loving God and He would thus be robbed of the love for which He created man. True victory, then, must be the triumph of God's love. To win hearts is far more meaningful than to coerce with power.

There is an inconsistency, as we have already pointed out, in the way North's Calvinism is being applied. Although those espousing dominion theology teach the total depravity of man, they are optimistic about even non-Christians seeing the advantages of following God's law. And in spite of the statements of Jesus about few being saved, they arbitrarily decide, contrary to what the Bible says, that God has determined to gradually force more and more people either to believe in Christ or to obey biblical law, until the world is eventually Christianized. Calvinism turns history into a meaning-less game of puppetry with God pulling the strings behind the scenes. Even so, there is no basis in Scripture or in Calvinism itself for believing that God is going to pull more strings in the future than He has in the past.

It would be a libel upon God's character (as well as a denial of the clear teaching of many Scriptures), to say that He is able, but unwilling, to save all. It is not, however, a slur upon either God's love or power to say that, having given man the power of choice, and having done all He could to *persuade* man to choose aright, He is unable to *force* him to do so. That inability to violate love, which is the essence of His own character, no more diminishes God's omnip-otence than to say that He is unable to commit sin in violation of His holiness.

Calvinists argue that it detracts from God's glory and gives credit to man if he has the power to say "yes" or "no" in response to the gospel. On the contrary, it is no credit to man that Christ, in loving response to our helpless and hopeless condition, has provided a full and free salvation. Nor is it any credit to those who, in recognition of their own inability to save themselves, accept such an offer, for only a fool would refuse.

God has all the glory when we say "yes" to His grace and love, because He has both provided the salvation and drawn us by His Spirit. And man has all the blame when he rejects Christ, for God has done all that He can to persuade him to believe. Calvinism diminishes God's glory in both respects.

Who Runs the World?

Jay Grimstead is traveling the country, successfully taking the Reconstructionist message to mainstream churches. In persuading pastors and their congregations to sign the COR *Mandate*, he explains that the key issue is always "whether Satan owns the world or God owns the world." The inference is that if we only believe that

God owns and runs the world, then we will be victorious. If we only realize that God, not Satan, is the legitimate master of the world, we will move out in victory and take dominion over institutions and Christianize cities and counties and nations.

In a typical talk to a group of pastors, where he was unveiling a new strategy for taking over California's Santa Clara and Orange counties through getting secular society to obey God's laws, Grimstead explained:

> Let me now turn to the Great Commission in Matthew 28. ... the discipleship we're talking about is getting people to live in obedience to this book. ... And when we go to nations in missionary tasks, we are to get that nation to try to conduct itself through individuals to live in obedience to the Bible.
>
> ... the Lord's prayer and the Great Commission are identical in their major message. ... He says, "Thy kingdom come, thy will be done, on earth as it is in heaven." ...
>
> Most of my friends and I ... had thought there is no way that we can get God's will done on this earth, because Satan's in control ... so let's just expect His will to be done in the millennium ... [but] when Jesus died on the cross and rose and ascended to the right hand of the Father, all authority in heaven and on earth was given Him. ... Jesus when He returns will have no more power or authority then than He ... had the moment He ascended to the right hand of the Father.[11]

Of course, the entire universe is God's, but that does not mean that everything that has ever happened is according to His will. He allows evil because He has given man the right of choice. Nor is it either biblical or rational to suggest that because Jesus now has all power on earth—and we as His disciples exercise that power in His name—that we can therefore cause even one person to believe the gospel, much less influence entire nations to obey biblical principles. Yet that seems to be the implication. Christianizing the world would then have nothing to do with whether men's hearts had been won to Christ, but only with God's irresistible power with which we could overwhelm sinners, if only we would believe it was available to us.

A major weapon that COR expects to use in Christianizing the world is the imposition of biblical law upon society. This is set forth in *The Christian World View of Law*, of which Jay Grimstead is the general editor. Certainly the committee that worked to bring this thesis into print is made up of distinguished Christian legal experts, theologians, and scholars. However, they have set themselves the impossible task of the worldwide reestablishment of a legalistic relationship to God that the history of Israel and the rest of mankind has proved doesn't work and which the cross of Christ has rendered obsolete and even condemned.

Like Dennis Peacocke's *Winning the Battle for the Minds of Men*, COR's treatise on law is based upon the false premise that God's blessing comes as a cause-and-effect response to obedience to His laws,[12] and that "when individuals and societies conform their outward actions to God's Law and civil law based on it, conditions ensue that promote societal revival and individual conversion to Jesus Christ."[13] This thesis is an illogical and unbiblical attempt to apply to all nations the blessings of obedience promised only to Israel. Clearly, some of those promises could not possibly apply to all other nations (for example, Israel was to be the head of all nations, to loan and not borrow, blessings which could not apply to all nations at once). Moreover, the letter of the law ("outward actions") is honored at the expense of attitudes of the heart. Thus a technical obedience is promoted for earthly benefits without the love that is declared to be absolutely essential.

Jesus certainly has no more authority now by virtue of His ascension than God always had. Yet that authority and power did not prevent Satan and many angels and mankind from rebelling, nor has it stopped the continuing growth of evil upon planet earth to this day. Moreover, even before conquering death, sin, and Satan upon the cross, Christ exercised the authority of His Father over storms, demons, and disease. He was not lacking power or authority over this world and its inhabitants, yet He was crucified in apparent weakness. And because they thought He had been defeated, His disciples fled, and the overwhelming majority of His own people rejected Him just as the prophets had foretold. Neither Scripture nor logic would attribute the small number of disciples nor the unfaithfulness of those few to any lack of power on the part of Christ that was remedied by the bestowal of additional power or authority after His resurrection. The difference was made at Pentecost as Christ Himself indwelt His disciples through the Holy Spirit. Yet Grimstead goes on to say:

> This is the amazing thing. Many of us have just found out after 25 years of ministry, we do not have to let Satan control the world, we do not have to let Satan and his forces control this valley or any of our cities. . . .
> We had no concept that . . . when Jesus came and said, "The kingdom of God is at hand," that . . . from this point on God's kingdom like a wedge is plowing through the earth and it's going to grow and grow . . . like the yeast and take over more and more.[14]

History certainly presents no evidence that "God's kingdom like a wedge is plowing through the earth." If this had indeed been the case for the past 1900 years, we should see some evidence of increasing righteousness. A simple comparison between the biblical promises of the perfect peace and righteousness that will characterize the millennium and the rampant godlessness and innumerable wars that now prevail should make it quite clear that God's kingdom has not come to this earth except in the hearts of individual Christians. Statements such as the above by Grimstead can only be made by those who are out of touch with God's Word, history, and present reality—and who hope to create conditions on earth that the Bible clearly says will only be realized at the Second Coming.

God's Power and Authority—And Man's Rebellion

What Grimstead presents is very similar to the "name-it-and-claim-it" charismatic variety of Christian Science known as positive confession and popularized by Kenneth Hagin and Kenneth Copeland. The only difference is that Grimstead is claiming healing for *society* rather than for *individuals*. Of course there is work to be done, too. But the key to the success of the COR goal is this new insight: God and not Satan is actually in control, Christ has all power, and if we will only begin to confess this truth and use this power and authority in His name nothing can prevent us from taking over the world for God.

To understand the folly of such a belief, we need only remember what happened in the Garden of Eden (to which the dominionists, oddly enough, wish us to return). In spite of His infinite power, God's authority did not prevent Satan from persuading mankind to rebel and go its own way. In that perfect environment Adam and Eve, fresh from God's creative hand and free from the corrupting influences of civilization and the sophisticated temptations we face today, nevertheless turned their backs upon the Creator who had graciously placed them in that paradise.

Wasn't God sovereign then? Did He not have all power? Of course He did. We surely have no more authority today over the nations in the name of Christ than God had over Adam and Eve, and we can expect to fare no better. Nor did the imposition of law from Mount Sinai solve the problem of sin and rebellion. Each person must exercise his individual choice, and that choice cannot be forced even by God Himself.

Of course, Satan was defeated at the cross. That only means, however, that those who now belong to Christ do not have to allow Satan any place in *their* lives. It does not mean that we can choose for the rest of the world not to continue in his kingdom and thereby take over cities and nations. We cannot extend to others who are in rebellion against God the personal victory that is ours because of our submission to His will. They must be willing to obey Him also. There is an eternity of difference between the robotic response under the insistence of the irresistible grace of Calvinism, and the warm and loving response from the heart by those who have been genuinely wooed and won by God's love. It is the latter which God desires and for which He made man capable.

A Distorted View of History and the World

In his promotional talks, Grimstead enthusiastically declares: "The amazing thing is what happened the first 300 years. The little band of disciples armed with the Holy Spirit and the Word of God and love for each other marched out there and took over the Roman Empire. Not particularly by design." Why was it not by design? He is admitting that the early church did not have the vision of world conquest which he has lately come to embrace. Then why insist that adopting a takeover view which the early church did not have is the key to accomplishing what he believes they achieved without it?

The alleged takeover of the Roman Empire is the one great event in history that Reconstructionists point to as an example of the Christianization of the world they say we must unite to effect. Peacocke refers to it ("It took barely 300 years for Christ to triumph over Caesar through his Church"),[15] as do DeMar and Leithart. The latter attempt to prove their point by quoting Tertullian expatiating on how "the world as a whole . . . has grown progressively more cultivated and populated . . . the number of cities today exceeds the number of isolated huts in former times . . . etc."[16] But Tertullian was writing in the second century, and the progress he praised was attributable to the *pagan* empire. Furthermore, shortly after its takeover by Christianity, the empire began a steady slide into the Dark Ages, in which the progress Tertullian lauded was reversed— hardly the blessing that is supposed to follow Christianization.

It is not true that the early church "marched out there and took over the Roman Empire." As we have already seen, the church was still small, despised, and under terrible persecution when Constantine was converted and began to favor Christianity. Far from taking over the empire, as Grimstead inaccurately suggests, the church received it as a gift from Constantine and his successors. It is therefore extremely misleading to present what happened in the fourth century as a laudable example of the fulfillment of the Great Commission to which we should aspire. Moreover, Grimstead declares:

> And by God's grace they created in Western culture a Christian world view, a Christian view of man and life

and reality and morals. And this Christian world view, coming right out of the Bible, permeated Western culture up through the 16th century.

And though the Catholic Church, the Roman church that our early church developed into in the middle ages, though it was corrupt and it made some doctrinal mistakes . . . and there needed to be a Reformation, yet one of the great things Christianity did even during the middle ages was to establish upon culture in the field of law and in all governments and in economics and business and education—every area of life had to submit to the view of life and man that was in the Scripture.[17]

It is astonishing that the Roman Catholic Church of the Middle Ages is credited with having accomplished, prior to the Reformation, COR's present goal of once again getting godless society " . . . to submit to the view of life and man that was in the Scripture." To another group of pastors, the same speaker declared: "By 1500, the Christian church had taken the view of truth and the view of reality in the Bible and had gotten it into every field. . . . We have let it slip . . . and so we're trying to recover it."[18] Have the members of COR's steering committee forgotten the evils that permeated society, and the fact that the vast majority, though church members, were bound for hell during the time of the Christian consensus that Grimstead lauds and says we must recover?

Such was the world, as Grimstead himself points out, that spawned the enlightenment, with its resultant socialism, humanism, higher criticism, and hedonism. Surely history gives no basis for believing that the touted Christianization of the world will ever create the benefits which COR holds out as the carrot for getting involved in its unbiblical goals. That agenda will more likely produce the same corruption that was bred under Constantine.

"Even though they did it poorly," Grimstead adds, "they imprinted the Scriptures on the minds of even non-Christians so that non-Christians conducted law, government, economics, business . . . according to a Biblical worldview. It doesn't mean the whole world was Christian, but it does mean that they succeeded in imprinting the Scripture on the minds of men." To whatever extent that may have been so, that world knew less of the Scripture than Nicodemus, who needed desperately to be born again—and had he missed the new birth, he would have been lost for eternity.

The most troubling feature of the COR and Reconstructionist agendas is that they are designed to create a world not only of Nicodemuses but of Pharisees of the worst sort. In their zeal to bring both the world and the church back under the Law, they do violence to grace and pervert the Great Commission. Our fears that the gospel of salvation of individuals will take second place to the desire to impose a superficial morality upon society would seem to be justified.

Victory with a Hollow, Worldly Ring

On the one hand, we welcome the call of COR to pledge ourselves to obey the Bible in every area of life. On the other hand, however, there is a macho, worldly ring to the victory they expect—a victory which not only lacks Christian humility but disdains as defeatist the biblical call to take up the cross and follow Christ in His rejection by the world. The humble and despised way of the cross cannot be reconciled with COR's optimistic eschatology of Christianizing the world.

A call to obedience to Old Testament moral law is 1900 years behind the times. We live in an age of superficiality, of tinsel, where we are impressed with the wrong values, admire the wrong attitudes. Unfortunately, the world's standard of success rather than Christ's has inspired this call to a victory that none of the men and women of faith referred to in Hebrews 11 and throughout the entire Bible ever expected, much less achieved—a takeover of worldly culture and its institutions.

Paul warned of those who wanted the church to conform to Jewish customs in order to avoid "persecution for the cross of Christ" (Galatians 6:12). Today many Christians reject the biblical teaching that the truth will never be popular. There is a reproach in the cross, a reproach in being identified with Christ, but we are determined to make Christianity the majority religion, the prestigious practice, to somehow present it in such a way that it will become the prevailing worldview. The honorable cause of raising moral standards and living ethical lives in order to bring ecological wholeness, social justice, and international peace and prosperity has an appeal to all mankind. Should the whole world, however, be persuaded to join such a cause, it would only be a delusion and lead them further from the truth.

In a chapter titled "Peace and Power in the End Times," James McKeever suggests that even during the Great Tribulation the Christian will be able to defeat all enemies and escape suffering and death through exercising God's power as Elijah did in calling fire from heaven to destroy those who would have killed him. In the midst of his talk about victory, he quotes Romans 8:35-37, commenting only upon the last verse which reads: "Nay, in all these things we are more than conquerors through him that loved us."

In his enthusiasm to be optimistic, McKeever forgets that "all these things" refers to suffering and death, not to calling fire from heaven upon our enemies. He writes: "We are not just barely victors and conquerors in Jesus Christ...we are far 'more than conquerors'...."[19] These verses, however, are not referring to the kind of victory he promises, but to the reality of true victory in Christ—a victory which shines brightest on a martyr's brow. Consider the context, which McKeever quotes but promptly ignores:

> Who shall separate us from the love of God? Shall tribulation, or distress, or persecution, or famine, or nakedness, or peril, or sword?
> As it is written, "For thy sake we are killed all the day long; we are accounted as sheep for the slaughter."[20]

"Except a Grain of Wheat Fall into the Ground..."

Such self-sacrifice in obedience to God's will was perfectly displayed in Christ upon the cross. It was, in fact, the secret of His victory over Satan—and it is the missing ingredient in the victory that many find so much more appealing today. The church still retains too much of the quality of the caesars' Roman legions and too little of the humility and submission to God's will that Christ exemplified. The meaning of "Onward Christian soldiers, marching as to war" has been perverted by the standards of this world to the detriment of the church's vision of heaven.

Christ was led as a lamb to the slaughter, and He told His disciples that they (and that would include us today) should not expect to be treated any better than He was. It was in obedience to His Father that He allowed Himself to be slain, because it was through death that He would "destroy him that had the power of death, that is the devil" (Hebrews 2:14). So Paul in the Roman epistle is declaring that the same fate will befall many Christians, but that just as our Lord triumphed in death and suffering, so we shall also. This Scripture does not teach that the Christian will be able through the power of God to escape suffering and death, but that we will conquer *through* suffering and death. This was Paul's own experience. To Timothy he wrote:

> But thou has fully known my doctrine [note the first thing he mentions, the foundation of all that follows], manner of life, purpose, faith, longsuffering, charity, patience, persecutions, afflictions, which came upon me at Antioch, at Iconium, at Lystra [and many other places]; what persecutions I endured; but out of them all the Lord delivered me.
>
> Yea, and all that will live godly in Christ Jesus shall suffer persecution (2 Timothy 3:10-12).

The deliverance of which Paul speaks has enabled him to endure trial, not to escape it. And this deliverance out of the many persecutions of the past, for which Paul has praised God, is about to culminate in his martyrdom. Nor does he offer any better future to Timothy or to the rest of us. Indeed, the suffering Christians in the Soviet Union, in China, and in other places where the blood of the martyrs has flowed have wondered what ails the church in the West.

They have difficulty understanding that we are not persecuted as they are since the Bible declares so plainly that this is to be the fate of all who "live godly in Christ Jesus."

Alva J. McLain declares, "The theory that Christ and the saints are now reigning in a present kingdom of God on earth is specifically refuted by the Apostle Paul." He reminds us:

> For the Church, this interim [between Pentecost and the Second Coming] is a time of humiliation (Phil. 3:21, ASV), testing (Jas. 1:12), trouble and persecution (II Cor. 4:8-9), suffering and groaning (Rom. 8:18-23), patient endurance (Jas. 5:7-11), refining and perfecting (Jas. 1:2-4), unceasing labor (I Cor. 3:8-15), agonizing conflict (I Tim. 6:12; II Tim 4:7, Grk.), and unrelenting struggle toward a goal which lies beyond this age and world (Phil. 3:12-14).
>
> For the present, therefore, the members of the Church must in a peculiar sense walk by faith (II Cor. 5:7), live in hope (Rom. 8:24-25), endure hardship as good soldiers of Christ (II Tim. 2:3), not looking at the things which are seen but at the things not seen (II Cor. 4:18).[21]

True Victory in Christ

This is the way of life that Paul lived and which he held out as the example for Christians of his day—and it must be the example for us as well. Because of his faithful life he was able to write Timothy in confidence just before his martyrdom: "For I am now ready to be offered, and the time of my departure is at hand. I have fought a good fight, I have finished my course . . ." (2 Timothy 4:6,7). Can it be that the fruitful life of this greatest apostle through whom Christ raised the dead and did so many miracles will be snuffed out at the command of a pagan emperor? Indeed, it will. How could that be victory? Certainly it is not the kind of victory that COR and the Reconstructionists and other kingdom/dominion advocates present as appropriate today.

Yes, Paul has won many converts and has even been accused of "turning the world upside down." The number of true believers, however, represents only a fraction of the population in his day. He has established churches in many cities, but the growing company of Christians represents a small minority despised by the general populace. He has even won converts in caesar's household, but that happened when he was first in Rome, under house arrest and able to receive visitors and speak freely. Now he is in prison, and Rome is demanding his head. All of the apostles except John will be martyred and the church will be driven into the catacombs.

Writing at this time to Timothy, Paul knows that he is going to heaven without seeing the victory that we are now being told is the responsibility of the church to effect. Indeed, the church is already departing from the truth and he has confessed with sorrow, "All they which are in Asia be turned away from me" (2 Timothy 1:15). Moreover, Paul knows that the situation for the entire church will become much worse. In his last words to the Ephesian elders when he called them to meet him at Miletum, Paul warned:

> For I know this, that after my departure shall grievous wolves enter in among you, not sparing the flock.
> Also of your own selves shall men arise, speaking perverse things, to draw away disciples after them (Acts 20:29,30).

Far from holding out the promise of some future Reconstructionist victory for the church, everything Paul says and writes indicates the opposite. Does he then feel defeated that he has failed to transform society as the Coalition on Revival insists is the responsibility of the church under the Great Commission? On the contrary, to the Ephesian elders Paul declares:

> But none of these things [trials and persecutions and threat of death] move me, neither count I my life dear unto myself, that I might finish my course with joy and the ministry, which I have received of the Lord Jesus, to testify the gospel of the grace of God (Acts 20:24).

So without achieving a takeover of the world or even working toward it, Paul triumphantly completes the ministry Christ has given him. Despising this biblical path to glory, Chilton caricatures the Christian who follows Christ in the victorious way of the cross:

He has one main duty in life: Get stepped on for Jesus.
The "spiritual" man, in this view, is a wimp. A Loser.
But at least he's a *Good* Loser.[22]

The Christian "optimists" are like those mockers who said to Christ as He hung on the cross, "If thou be the Son of God, come down, save thyself." That is the kind of victory they are calling for—a victory that appeals to the worldly mind but which, thank God, Christ rejected. As His bride and witnesses, we are to follow in His steps. As the chorus says: "The world behind me, the cross before me; no turning back, no turning back!"

Stephen was not defeated in boldly standing for the truth, though it cost him his life. Such has been the example of true discipleship down through history and such it will continue to be. The early church, as we have seen, was victorious when it was hated, tortured, thrown to the lions—but it went down to defeat without knowing it when the Roman world was Christianized. Although Revelation 13 indicates that the Antichrist has power to physically overcome the saints and to slay them, yet they are the victors spiritually through their martyrdom:

And they overcame him ["that old serpent called the devil and Satan"—verse 9] by the blood of the Lamb [Christ], and by the word of their testimony; and they loved not their lives unto death (Revelation 12:11).

The victory that overcomes the world is our faith—a faith that does not waver even unto death. Far from indicating that they were to take over the world, the letters to the seven churches in Asia emphasized remaining faithful unto death. Those who pray for true revival should remember that it will almost certainly be accompanied by fierce opposition and persecution.

Were the martyrs defeated? Was Paul defeated? Were those who died in the arenas or at the stake defeated? No, a thousand times no! They demonstrated genuine victory—the same victory that Christ manifested over hatred, abuse, ridicule, suffering, death, and Satan. The call to a victory that appeals to self and wins earthly kingdoms is really the deceitful call to present defeat (no matter what the outward appearance), and future loss in the world to come.

The nature of Christ's victory is continually held out to the church as its example. To the Laodiceans Christ writes: "To him that overcometh will I grant to sit with me in my throne, even as I also overcame, and am set down with my Father in his throne" (Revelation 3:21). Clearly they were to overcome in the same way that Christ did—by being obedient unto death, even the death of the cross. The challenge and the promise are for us today, as they were to the church at Smyrna: "Be thou faithful unto death, and I will give thee a crown of life" (Revelation 2:10).

Nor does death apply only to the physical body. Essential to the path that Christ asks us to follow is the denial of self as part of the process of the cross in our lives. It is no less victorious to remain alive as a witness for Christ—a living witness to whom the success, pleasure, and prosperity of worldly victory have no appeal. Such is the triumph of those whose affection has been set on things above, where Christ is and from whence He will soon return to take His own to His Father's house.

14

The Spirit and the Bride Say Come!

The Bible is one book, even though it is divided into two distinct parts. The New Testament is the fulfillment of what was prophesied in the Old, and in the Old Testament we can find many types or pictures that are intended to provide deeper insight into what is revealed in the New. This understanding is firmly grounded in Scripture itself. The writer of the epistle to the Hebrews, for example, explains that the law, the religious ordinances, and the tabernacle and its sacrificial offerings, were "figure[s] for the time then present" (9:9,10,24) that are fulfilled in Christ and which pictured heaven itself. Some of the individuals in the Old Testament are clearly types of Christ, presenting in their own lives, though imperfectly, remarkable portraits of the promised Messiah.

Of all of the characters in the Old Testament, none so fully typified Christ as did King David. Much of what he wrote in the first person was fulfilled in the life, death, and resurrection of Jesus. In Psalm 22, for example, the crucifixion of Christ is clearly portrayed even to the soldiers gambling for His clothing, plus some of the very words Jesus would speak from the cross. In many ways David's kingdom was a picture of the millennial kingdom yet to come. It is upon David's throne as His descendant and successor-king ruling over the restored kingdom of Israel, with Jerusalem as the headquarters for the millennial kingdom, that Christ will yet reign. We have already referred to the announcement of the angel Gabriel to the virgin Mary:

And, behold, thou shalt conceive in thy womb, and bring forth a son, and shalt call his name Jesus.

He shall be great, and shall be called the Son of the Highest; and the Lord God shall give unto him the throne of his father David;

And he shall reign over the house of Jacob forever, and of his kingdom there shall be no end (Luke 1:31-33).

Why Not Invite the King Back?

Even the rejection of Christ by His own people is portrayed in David in many ways. Limited space permits us to deal with only one example. David was not only rejected by his father and brothers and by Israel before he became king, but he was rejected by Israel again toward the end of his life and had to flee from Jerusalem in the face of an uprising led by his son Absalom. There was no doubt that David and his elite corps of 600 incredible warriors could defeat all of Israel. Jerusalem was not the place to fight, however, and Israel no longer wanted him, so he left in humiliation.

Even though his men were outnumbered perhaps one thousand to one, David ordered his commanders to "Deal gently, for my sake, with . . . Absalom" (2 Samuel 18:5), knowing that Israel would quickly be routed. His men made short work of Israel's huge army when it attacked, chasing it back across the Jordan in a stunning defeat. Contrary to orders, however, they killed Absalom as well, a blow which broke David's tender heart. With their leader dead, Israel fled, every man to his home in shame. David could have marched back into Jerusalem and ascended the throne immediately, but he did not. Israel had rejected him and now must ask him to return.

Waiting for that summons, David sat in the gate of the city where he had set up his headquarters on the eastern side of Jordan. His informants had told him that Israel was wondering why he did not come back—but he had no official invitation, which he particularly wanted to come from Judah, his own tribe. Calling the two head priests, Zadok and Abiathar, he sent them to Judah with this message: "Ye are my brethren, ye are my bones and my flesh; wherefore then are ye the last to bring back the king?" (2 Samuel 19:12). The scriptural account continues:

> And he bowed the heart of all the men of Judah, even as the heart of one man, so that they sent this word unto the king: "Return thou, and all thy servants." So the king returned . . . (2 Samuel 19:14,15).

Could we not say that the seductive Absaloms of earth, with their false but appealing promises, have all been found wanting? Even the secular world is desperate to find a ruler capable of establishing a new world kingdom that will bring order out of chaos. And could it be that our "David," having been rejected and hounded off this planet, is sitting in the gate of heaven, grieved that His bride, His body, "bone of [His] bones and flesh of [His] flesh" (Genesis 2:23) is not calling upon Him to return to rule a world that so desperately needs Him? Could it be, that the message of the hour for faithful Christian leaders, today's Zadoks and Abiathars, is to call upon the church to lift its voice to heaven and say, "Come, Lord Jesus!"? Rather than waiting for His bride to become united and mature or to take over the world for Him, might it not be that our Bridegroom is waiting and longing instead for just one thing: for love's simple cry from sincere hearts: "Come back, Lord!"?

What Is Your Excuse?

Many books could be written based solely upon the parables of our Lord that provide various pictures of the Second Coming. One of the most fascinating and yet misunderstood stories concerns the rich man who had difficulty persuading his invitees to come to the magnificent banquet he had prepared. The story is known for the ridiculous excuses made by those he had expected to be his guests:

> The first said unto him, "I have bought a piece of ground, and I must needs go and see it; I pray thee have me excused."

And another said, "I have bought five yoke of oxen,
and I go to prove them; I pray thee have me excused."
And another said, "I have married a wife, and therefore I cannot come" (Luke 14:18-20).

This parable has been a favorite with evangelists, who consistently portray those excusing themselves as sinners rejecting the
offer of salvation. Clearly, however, such is not the message of the
parable. The invitation to the feast had been sent out R.S.V.P.
earlier and a full complement of guests had eagerly responded with
promises to be there. It was when the feast had been prepared, the
time announced had arrived, and no one had appeared, that the host
sent his servants around "at supper time . . . to them that were [had
been previously] bidden" (verse 17). It was at this time, after having
initially accepted the invitation, that each went back on his promise
to come and made his absurd excuse.

Rather than being gospel rejecters, the guests who were expected
but failed to come to the feast clearly represent professing "Christians" who have seemingly accepted Christ as their Savior and are
probably churchgoers. When it comes time to rapture them to
heaven for the marriage supper of the Lamb, however, the Lord
looks into their hearts and sees that their true affection is not on
things above as it should be, but on the things of this world. They
would rather not even think of going to heaven until, in old age, with
death imminent, the only other choice would be hell. Until then they
are too involved in earthly matters even to think of leaving this
planet. Perhaps a trip to Hawaii has been planned, or there is a big
promotion with a large salary increase, or a new home to build.
Their hearts are really not with Christ in heaven at all, but are held
captive by this world's prospects.

The inappropriate excuses which betray the hypocrisy in the
original acceptance of the invitation anger the host. That is when he
tells his servants: "Go out quickly into the streets and lanes of the
city, and bring in hither the poor, and the maimed, and the halt, and
the blind. . . . Go out into the highways and hedges, and compel
them to come in, that my house may be filled."

We must be careful not to build too much on a single parable. This story, however, is quite consistent with others the Lord told and also with His teachings. It seems to indicate a last-days apostasy in the church. It portrays, at the same time, a great harvest of souls with multitudes coming to Christ who appear to be unlikely candidates for heaven. Those in the "streets and lanes of the city . . . the highways and hedges" could represent the drug addicts, criminals, New Agers, citizens of Communist countries (at least 50 million have become Christians in the last few years in China), and others of our day who would seem to be the most unlikely candidates for the gospel.

The parable presents a solemn challenge to each Christian to examine his own heart with the utmost honesty. Do I really love Christ so much that no other love, no earthly involvement or ambition prevents me from saying with sincerity and with passion, "Come, Lord Jesus, come!"? Is it possible that the many arguments against the any-moment rapture of the church could provide just the excuse some may be looking for to justify a professed faith in Christ that lacks the real love for Him which He says is the essential ingredient? While those Christian leaders who oppose the rapture may not lack that love, is there not a danger that they are fostering such a lack in others? As C.S. Lewis put it:

> Most of us find it very difficult to want "Heaven" at all—except in so far as "Heaven" means meeting again our friends who have died.
>
> One reason for this difficulty is that we have not been trained: our whole education tends to fix our minds on this world. . . .
>
> I must keep alive in myself the desire for my true country . . . I must make it the main object of life to press on to that other country and to help others to do the same.[1]

Exchanging Heaven for This Earth

Like Pascal and Augustine and many other great thinkers, Lewis referred to a God-given desire that is common to all mankind—"a desire which no experience in this world can satisfy." He argued that such a universal, though often misunderstood longing is in itself evidence "that I was made for another world."[2] The new vision of earthly victory, however, that seems to be sweeping the church requires that the innate longing for heaven, to which Lewis referred, must be stifled and even rejected as somehow harmful to the church's real goals.

Gary Greenwald is a southern California pastor with a growing church and a popular tape-and-television ministry. Apparently convinced that the Father's house of many mansions is hidden away somewhere on this earth, he told his congregation:

> I used to sing all those unscriptural songs . . .: "This world is not my home, I'm just a passing through; my treasures are laid up away beyond the blue. . . ." Did you ever sing that one?
> I've got news for you. This world is your home. Forever, according to the Word [of God]. . . . Our final home is right here on earth.[3]

Yet the heroes and heroines of the faith mentioned in Hebrews 11, in perfect harmony with the song that Greenwald used to love but now maligns, are described as "strangers and pilgrims on the earth" who "seek a [heavenly] country" (Hebrews 11:13-16). Greenwald's attitude, however, is becoming increasingly typical, prompting us to ask again: Whatever happened to heaven? Why has sentiment turned so against it, when the Bible is full of heaven? Paul assures us that "we have a building of God, a house not made with hands, *eternal in the heavens*" (2 Corinthians 5:1). And Peter writes:

> Blessed be the God and Father of our Lord Jesus Christ, which according to his abundant mercy hath begotten us again unto a living hope by the resurrection

of Jesus Christ from the dead, to an inheritance incorruptible, and undefiled, and that fadeth not away, *reserved in
heaven for you*, who are kept by the power of God
through faith unto salvation ready to be revealed in the
last time (1 Peter 1:3-5).

As we have noted, the Coalition on Revival indicts the church
with having been too much oriented toward "heaven, the future, and
escaping this world at Christ's Second Coming. . . ."[4] Other than
that, heaven is scarcely mentioned in the COR documents except in
the oft-repeated but misapplied phrase: ". . . to get God's will done
on earth as it is in heaven." In clear conflict with what Lewis
considered to be a basic Christian attitude, Grimstead explains that
COR has a "massive task" of reeducating the church from heavenly
mindedness to a new earthly involvement.[5] Such reeducation is
necessary because the church has too long put great importance
upon what Paul referred to as "the hope which is laid up for you *in
heaven*" (Colossians 1:5). David Chilton explains the earthly benefits of building one's future in this world rather than in heaven:

> Having tasted victory, Christians today are talking
> much less about escaping in the Rapture, and much more
> about God's requirements in this life. They are even
> thinking about the kind of world they are preparing for
> their grandchildren, and the heritage of godliness which
> they will leave behind them.[6]

Snubbing the Rapture

COR's prestigious influence is massive and growing, and its
Manifesto purports to set the future standard for Christianity
worldwide. Before accepting such a basic change in attitude, however, we ought to go back and see what respected Christian authors
have had to say on the subject of heaven. We ought also to recognize
that the historic view which they represent will have to be abandoned in order to adopt the new view. C.S. Lewis considered the

heavenly minded attitude to be essential. In his classic *Mere Christianity* he wrote:

> Hope is one of the Theological virtues. This means that a continual looking forward to the eternal world is not (as some modern people think) a form of escapism or wishful thinking, but one of the things a Christian is meant to do.
>
> It does not mean that we are to leave the present world as it is. If you read history you will find that the Christians who did most for the present world were just those who thought most of the next.
>
> The Apostles themselves, who set on foot the conversion of the Roman Empire, the great men who built up the Middle Ages, the English Evangelicals who abolished the Slave Trade, all left their mark on Earth, precisely because their minds were occupied with Heaven.[7]

While Lewis was not referring specifically to a belief in the rapture, certainly nothing turns our thoughts more seriously to heaven than the conviction that we could be taken there by our Lord at any moment. Yet Arthur Wallis describes the church of those who are expecting the rapture as "forlorn and beleaguered . . . with its back to the wall, waiting for evacuation . . . ."[8] In a similar vein the COR *Manifesto* caricatures those of us who earnestly look for His appearing as "gazing up into the sky with our mouths open and our hands idle, waiting to be 'rescued.' "[9]

The same *ad hominem* language is found in Don Paulk's criticism of those who "sit back and await cataclysmic events that will *rescue* us from this planet and transport us to other worlds."[10] Explaining that Christ is imprisoned in heaven and waiting helplessly for us to liberate Him so that He can rejoin us on planet earth, Earl Paulk declares:

> Likewise, those who are waiting for Christ to catch a few people away so God can judge the world are waiting in vain!

Jesus Christ has now done all that He can do, and He
waits at the right hand of His Father, until you and I, as
sons of God, become manifest and make this world His
footstool. He is waiting for us to say, "Jesus, we have
made the kingdoms of this world the Kingdom of our
God, and we are ruling and reigning in Your world. Even
so, come, Lord Jesus."[11]

Paulk's call to the Lord to "come" is not so that He will take us to
heaven, but for the Lord to settle down on this earth and reign over
the kingdom we have established in His absence. For some the
question of whether there will be a rapture or not, or when it might
occur, is meaningless. In a recent Trinity Broadcasting Network
(TBN) newsletter, Paul Crouch says: "You know, Hal Lindsey [pre-
trib rapture] may be right—and you know, Bishop Earl Paulk [no
rapture—Christ returns to rule the nations after Christians have
taken over the world in His name] may be right." He goes on to argue
that it doesn't matter who is right. Crouch is only representative of
many who wrongly assume that the rapture is a mere appendage to
history with no real purpose. As we have pointed out, however, it is
one of the culminating acts essential in the unfolding of God's plan,
which allows those who remain, with the help of Satan's unhindered
power, to build their paradise on earth if they can.

If we take the Bible seriously then we will long for our Lord to
catch us away from this earth into His eternal presence. Among the
many reasons why we ought to be eagerly looking for the rapture,
the most compelling is neither theological nor eschatological, but is
our love for Christ. If the church is indeed His bride, then surely we
ought to be eagerly anticipating His return to take us to His Father's
house for our marriage to Him. Here we have the most basic and yet
most neglected aspect of heaven—that it is to be the scene of a great
wedding that our Savior has long anticipated. How can His bride not
share that joyful hope?

There's a Wedding Day Coming!

While some Christians argue the point, there can be little doubt that the church is likened in Scripture to the bride of Christ and finally is called His "wife." In expressing his concern that the Corinthian believers not be deceived by Satan, Paul said: "I have espoused you to one husband, that I may present you as a chaste virgin to Christ" (2 Corinthians 11:2). Israel had already been called God's wife in the Old Testament, an adulterous wife to whom He will yet be reconciled, thus she could scarcely be the virgin referred to above. To the Ephesians Paul used the relationship between Christ and the church to express how husbands and wives were to relate in love to each other:

> For the husband is the head of the wife, even as Christ is the head of the church. . . .
> Therefore as the church is subject unto Christ, so let the wives be to their own husbands in every thing.
> Husbands, love your wives, even as Christ also loved the church, and gave himself for it. . . .
> For this cause shall a man leave his father and mother, and shall be joined unto his wife, and they two shall be one flesh.
> This is a great mystery; but I speak concerning Christ and the church (Ephesians 5:22-33).

In picturing His Second Coming, Christ told a number of parables involving weddings. Much of the terminology He used was right out of Jewish marriage traditions known to His listeners. In *A Christian Love Story*, Zola Levitt relates that tradition and explains how beautifully it fits the promises that Jesus gave His disciples. Presenting the results of his research of rabbinical sources, Levitt writes:

> When that matter [of the marriage contract and price to be paid for the bride] was settled the groom would depart. He would make a little speech to his [espoused] bride, saying, "I go to prepare a place for you," and he would return to his father's house.
> Back at his father's house, he would build her a bridal chamber, a little mansion, in which they would have

their future honeymoon . . . remain[ing] inside for seven days. . . . At the end of the week, the bride and groom would make their long awaited appearance . . . [and] there would be . . . a marriage supper, which we might refer to as the wedding reception. . . .

This construction project would take the better part of a year . . . and the father of the groom would be the judge of when it was finished. . . .

The bride, for her part, was obliged to do a lot of waiting . . . [and] she had to have an oil lamp ready in case he came late at night . . . she had to be ready to travel at a moment's notice. . . .

[The groom] and his young men would set out in the night, making every attempt to completely surprise the bride. . . .

The church is called "the bride of Christ" in the New Testament for good reason.[12]

One can readily see that Christ expected His disciples to understand what He said in reference to such a tradition. His statement, "In my Father's house are many mansions. . . . I go to prepare a place for you . . . and will come again to receive you unto myself," clearly depicted Him as the groom and those who believed on Him as His espoused bride. His statement, "But of that day and that hour knoweth no man . . . neither the Son, but the Father" (Mark 13:32) was not a denial of His deity and omniscience. It pointed again to the wedding tradition with which His listeners were familiar. The bridegroom couldn't just throw a lean-to together and rush off and claim his bride. It was up to the father to decide when the honeymoon cottage was suitable; then he would tell the groom that he could bring his bride there.

A clear picture is provided of the pretribulation rapture. The seven days of honeymoon at the father's house are like the seven years of the Great Tribulation during which the raptured church will be with Christ. At the end of the seven years comes the wedding supper or reception mentioned in Revelation 19. Of course the bride must already be in heaven for the wedding to take place. She couldn't still be upon earth going through the Great Tribulation. We have earlier referred to her cleansing and being clothed in white, the righteousness of the saints. After the marriage supper she is then able to return with Christ from heaven when He comes to rescue Israel and to stop the destruction at Armageddon.

In spite of Revelation 19, the Reconstructionists deny that there will be such a marriage supper in heaven. North favorably quotes James B. Jordan's declaration that "the act of marriage between God and His Church is nothing more and nothing less than the Holy Eucharist."[13] Likewise, in his exposition of Revelation, David Chilton declares that even this event also took place at A.D. 70. What John seems to present as a future marriage supper in heaven involving Christ and the church was really the destruction of Jerusalem on this earth, after which the eucharist took on a new meaning. He writes:

> With the final divorce and destruction of the unfaithful wife [Israel] in A.D. 70, the marriage of the Church to her Lord was firmly established; the Eucharistic celebration of the Church was fully revealed in its true nature as "the marriage supper of the Lamb" (v. 9).[14]

The Reconstructionists have robbed the church again, this time of a vital hope, and have perverted the eucharist in the process. The partaking of the bread and wine is specifically stated to be in remembrance of Christ's death, burial, and resurrection, not the repeated reenactment of our marriage to Him—a poor substitute for that marriage yet to take place in heaven. Much less does it have anything to do with Jerusalem being destroyed. DeMar and Leithart declare: "In destroying Israel, Christ transferred the blessings of the kingdom from Israel to . . . the church."[15] Chilton adds, ". . . and this was her [the church's] wedding day."[16] To suggest that the relationship of the church to Christ is somehow dependent upon the destruction of Jerusalem, or takes on a new meaning relative to that event, does violence both to reason and Scripture.

Of course, the Calvinists insist that reason cannot be appealed to because it is totally perverted and cannot be trusted at all. That is not only a cop-out but the very strategy used by numerous cults. How better to delude one's followers than to persuade them that they dare not think for themselves because their reason is *ipso facto* false? Yet God Himself says, "Come now and let us *reason* together..." (Isaiah 1:18). Faith is not the surrender of reason, but the highest act of this vital capacity which God has given man and expects him to use to His glory.

What About the Contradictions?

When one studies the Scriptures pertaining to the Second Coming, it is obvious that there are a number of contradictions which cannot be reconciled—except in one way. For example, the rapture as expressed in 1 Thessalonians 4 seems to be a private event involving the church only, and unseen and unknown to the world. Of course the world will suddenly be aware that millions of people have vanished from this planet but will not have a clue as to what happened to them. The actual event seems to be a secret experienced only by the church. The world only learns about it after the fact.

Yet other passages to which we have already referred make it equally clear that His coming will be as visible as lightning flashing across the sky and that "every eye shall see him, and they also which pierced him [an obvious reference to Zechariah 12:10]; and all the kindreds of the earth shall wail because of him" (Revelation 1:7). Both Peter and Paul tell us that the Day of the Lord (which is ushered in with the Second Coming) will suddenly intrude upon this earth without warning as a thief during a time of peace and safety (2 Peter 3:10; 1 Thessalonians 5:2,3) when disaster or judgment seems too remote even to imagine. Christ presented a similar picture stating that His coming would be during a time like "the days of Noah," a time of business as usual when judgment would be the last thing one would expect (Matthew 24:37-42). Yet other Scriptures just as clearly depict Christ coming in the midst of worldwide war and destruction; surely a time when His people would look to His appearing with utmost hope and expectation (Zechariah 12, Revelation 19).

Some Scriptures make it sound as though He will come *before* the Great Tribulation; while others could only be referring to a Second Coming *at the end* of that horrible time, when destruction is at its worst. There is only one way to reconcile all of the seemingly contradictory statements, and that is to accept the fact that He comes at both times, *before* and *after* the Great Tribulation. First He comes secretly to rapture away His bride. Then later He comes with her to rescue Israel, destroy His enemies, and set up His kingdom in its earthly manifestation in fulfillment of the promises to Israel.

Immediately those who object to this scenario cry, "Foul! Nowhere does the New Testament state that there will be two phases to the Second Coming!" Their objection has a familiar ring to it: in fact, the religious leaders in Christ's day rejected Him on this very basis. Nowhere does the Old Testament say that there are two comings of the Messiah. That should have been clear, however, because of the contradictory statements that could be reconciled in no other way. And that there must be two phases to the Second Coming is demanded on the same basis.

Some of the Old Testament prophecies depicted the Messiah as coming in power and glory to destroy His enemies, rescue Israel, and set up His kingdom. Such was the great hope of the Jewish people when Jesus came upon the scene. Yet their prophets had also pictured the Messiah as coming in weakness, meek as a lamb. According to some Messianic Scriptures He was to be hailed and honored and worshiped; yet other prophecies, just as clearly Messianic, said He would be despised and rejected. His kingdom was never to end, and yet He was also to be killed.

The distinct contradictions could not be denied. What did the rabbis do with them? They justified their rejection of Christ by simply blanking out the suffering-servant prophecies as not fitting into their scenario and accepting only the triumphant ones. Here was the major reason why they did not recognize Jesus for who He really was and, in rejecting and crucifying Him, fulfilled the prophecies they could not fit into their scheme.

Those who reject the pretribulation rapture today are falling into a similar error. They refuse to recognize that the seeming contradictions require two distinct phases to the Second Coming, just as there had to be two distinct comings of the Messiah. And as in the Old, so in the New Testament, the contradictions can be reconciled in no other way.

Jesus repeatedly emphasized the surprise element to the point of saying, "Therefore be ye also ready; for in such an hour as ye think not the Son of man cometh" (Matthew 24:44). That could hardly be referring to either a posttribulation or postmillennium coming. Surely in the midst of Armageddon, with the Great Tribulation events having occurred as stated in Revelation, it is preposterous to suggest that, if the church were still upon earth, at such a time she would not be expecting her Lord to return. There can be no doubt that He comes unexpectedly before the Great Tribulation, obviously not in power and judgment because that would be inappropriate at that time and would end the Great Tribulation before it began. He could only come at that time to catch His bride away to heaven to be with Him at that great wedding feast, before coming back to earth with her to reign in power and glory.

The Millennium Is Not the Final Kingdom

There are many reasons why the millennium, great as it will be, is not the ultimate hope of the church. As we have noted frequently, Christians are a *heavenly* people. Our destiny lies in heaven, not here upon this earth. The kingdom of God or of heaven encompasses the entire universe, not just this small part of it. A misunderstanding of this basic fact causes the focus of Christians to remain upon this earth when they ought to have their sights set much higher.

We do want Christ to return to stop the evil and to rule over this planet. But most of all we want to be with Him, at His side wherever He may be, forever—our great Lord of the universe! The hope of the kingdom/dominion/Reconstruction advocates is far too small. In putting the focus entirely upon this earth (at least for the next several hundred thousand years), they—rather than those whose hope is in heaven—are guilty of a gross "reduction of Christianity."

It is very clear from Scripture that the millennium is not the final kingdom of God, but only the temporary earthly manifestation of it. Paul reveals a mystery that was not at all clear from the Old Testament prophecies, and to which we have already referred: "flesh and blood cannot inherit the kingdom of God" (1 Corinthians 15:50). Yet there will be many flesh-and-blood people in the millennium. We are also told repeatedly that God's Kingdom "is *everlasting*" (Psalm 145:13; Daniel 4:3; 7:27; 2 Peter 1:11). Yet the millennium ends. The prophecy of Isaiah, so familiar a reading at Christmas, makes it very clear:

> Of the increase of his government and peace there shall be no end, upon the throne of David, and upon his kingdom, to order it, and to establish it with judgment and with justice from henceforth even forever. The zeal of the Lord of hosts [not the church] will perform this (Isaiah 9:7).

In contrast to the eternal kingdom, the millennium not only ends, but it does so with a tremendous battle (Revelation 20:7-9). Its 1000 years of peace being thus terminated, the millennium is disqualified on that count also from being the kingdom Isaiah refers to, with peace that never ends. As soon as Satan is loosed at the end of his 1000-year confinement, he deceives the nations living in the millennial paradise just as he did Eve in the Garden. They march against Jerusalem and are destroyed. Then comes the final judgment of Revelation 20:11-15, with the destruction by fire of this present universe and the creation of a new one in its place (Revelation 21:1).

Beyond Restoration to a New Creation

Adam's sin cost the entire human race its place in the Garden of Eden. Unlike the dominionists, however, the heavenly minded Christian has no desire to return to that earthly paradise. It was in that perfect environment that sin entered into the world, so it is quite obvious that a return to that idyllic state would be of no lasting benefit. Nevertheless, the COR *Mandate* declares that through His death and resurrection for us: "As Son of God and representative man, Jesus regained authority over the earth which Adam, as representative man, lost. This is the meaning of His being seated at the right hand of God."[17] Grimstead further explains:

> Jesus, the Second Adam . . . regained the position we had originally in the Garden before the Fall. [He] essentially re-established man in the person of Himself as God's chosen ruler on the planet earth.[18]

Man's unbiblical invention, dominion theology, blinds those who embrace its earthly orientation to the much greater truth of Scripture. As "new creations in Christ Jesus," we have been promised something far better than "the restoration of Eden," which Chilton declares "is an essential aspect of the salvation that Christ provides."[19] In contrast to Adam who died, we have the assurance of endless life in a new universe of absolute perfection. Adam was not born of the Spirit and redeemed by the blood of the Lamb with the penalty paid for all sin, past, present, or future—but such is our happy condition before God.

Instead of an earthly garden which God visited on occasion in the cool of the evening, we have the promise of being in the very presence of God in the Father's house of many mansions. Adam lost the indwelling presence of God's Spirit, which he surely must have enjoyed before the fall; but we have the promise that we are sealed with His own Holy Spirit who will never leave nor forsake us. We are indwelt not only by the Spirit of God, but by the Spirit of Christ. This One, who is both God and man joined in one person, effects that union and reconciliation between us and God within our hearts— a union that will never be broken.

Thus it is a terrible reduction of Christianity to say that the salvation Christ procured merely puts us back in the position of Adam. The church looks beyond the earthly restoration of Eden's paradise in the millennium to the everlasting state of the new creation, the ultimate eternal kingdom into which sin can never enter. None but those who have been born from above as new creations and have received transformed, immortal bodies can inhabit the new universe of bliss.

"Wilt Thou Go with This Man?"

The Lord presented the gospel as involving not so much a choice between heaven and hell as between heaven and this earth. And those who opt for this earth, which is slated for destruction, end up in hell: "For what is a man profited if he shall gain the whole world and lose his own soul? Or what shall a man give in exchange for his soul?" (Matthew 16:26). The desires and ambitions of this life all too often lure us away from the eternal home Christ offers.

We cannot live both for this world and the next. What we do in this world must primarily have heaven in view or it could cost us heaven. This world is temporary. We are warned not to look upon the visible and temporal things with desire (2 Corinthians 4:8-18), but to set our affection on things above where Christ sits at the right hand of God.

The great seduction is to turn us from heaven to earth, from the true God to ourselves, from the denial of self to the acceptance, love, and esteem of oneself, from God's truth to Satan's lie. At the heart of this seduction are beliefs that have a deceptively spiritual appeal, but which actually turn us from loving Christ and His appearing to the earthly ambition of taking over society and remaking this world into the paradise that Adam and Eve lost.

In all honesty, however, the longing to be raptured home to heaven imminently does not come easily. There should be a great conflict in the heart of every true Christian. On the one hand there ought to be a genuine longing for Christ to return so that we can see Him at last, fall at His feet, and enjoy the bliss of His presence forevermore. On the other hand, however, there ought to be a passion to win the lost to Christ before it is too late—and that would cause us to want more time in which to fulfill the Great Commission. He, in fact, has delayed His coming for that very reason (2 Peter 3:9). For many people today, however, there is no conflict at all because they no longer believe that departing to be with Christ at any moment in the rapture is even possible, much less something to be desired.

How could we genuinely long for His imminent return if we still had loved ones who were not believers and who would therefore be left behind to be separated from God and from us forever? Christ confronted those who wanted to be His disciples with this very dilemma. "He that loveth father or mother more than me is not worthy of me," He told them. "And he that loveth son or daughter more than me is not worthy of me" (Matthew 10:37). A difficult choice, perhaps, but once made there must be no regrets. In fact, He said we must hate our own lives and abandon everything—nothing must stand in the way of our devotion to Him. Is that too much for the Lord of glory, who gave Himself for us, to ask?

One of the most beautiful Old Testament pictures of the church as the bride of Christ is found in Genesis 24. Abraham's servant, a type of the Holy Spirit, had claimed Rebecca as Isaac's bride. As it is with us, however, she had to choose for herself between the husband waiting for her in a far country, and the family she would have to leave in order to join him. "Wilt thou go with this man?" her family asked her. And she said, "I will go."

Such is the choice that confronts us. It is a choice that countless earthly brides have made and not regretted. No less is demanded by our Lord of His heavenly bride.

In contrast to the attitude of the early church, however, heaven has become for today's church that place that everyone wants to go to—but not yet. Surely the Bridegroom must grieve over a bride that is so reluctant to join Him in that great heavenly marriage.

Is it not time that the bride of Christ, laying all else aside, became excited about the prospect of seeing and being with her Bridegroom forever? Oh, that a great cry would arise from the church: "We love you, Lord Jesus! Please come and take us home! The Spirit and the bride say, Come! Come, Lord Jesus, come!"

15

Restoring Our First Love

It has been suggested that the unique ability to form conceptual ideas and to express them in speech separates mankind from all lower creatures by a chasm that no evolutionary process could ever span.[1] While that is true, there is another capacity which separates man even further from animals. Paul explained it thus: "Though I speak with the tongues of men and of angels, and have not charity [love], I am become as sounding brass, or a tinkling cymbal" (1 Corinthians 13:1). To put it in a contemporary context, without love man is a robot, a computer programmed to meaningless reactions. In a word, it is *love* that makes a human being.

God has given mankind marvelous abilities. Think of the great scientists and philosophers who have probed the mysteries of life; and the poets, novelists, and musicians who have expressed the depth of human experience in compelling ways. We don't need to argue the absurdity of evolution to be convinced that the ability to look into the mysteries of the atom or to compose or appreciate an opera involves qualities that no animal could acquire by developing a larger brain and a more advanced nervous system. Marvelous as these capacities are, however, they are not primarily what differentiates between human and animal life. It is *love*.

What do we mean by love? Certainly not the popular notion portrayed in today's media. The bumper stickers, "Make love, not war," reflect an all-too-common trivialization of man's highest capacity. Love is far more than sex. Animals can enjoy that. And if real love is missing, then sex becomes a mere gratification of animal instincts which cannot satisfy the spirit of man.

Yes, there are similarities between human beings and animals as long as we live in bodies of flesh and blood on this planet. We have certain basic needs for food, warmth, and water. We know hunger and thirst as do animals. We also experience powerful sexual desires and other fleshly cravings, but God intended these passions to be controlled by love. The will is no match for lust, but God's love working in man can conquer evil with pure desires.

A failure to be motivated by God's love brings defeat into our personal lives. There are those who can, for selfish motives such as the praise of others, seemingly conquer physical desires and remain faithful to God. True victory, however, is not necessarily won by those who seem from outward appearances to be victorious. If love—which Paul reminds us is the essential ingredient—is missing, then even a fiery death at the stake would be of no value in God's sight.

God Has Said "I Love You!"

Without love, Paul reminds us, we are nothing. That "nothing" doesn't mean that we don't exist, but that we are not what we were intended to be by our Creator. We are not fully human without love, no matter how much knowledge we have or how clever we are. It should be clear why this is the case. We are made in the image of God, who, speaking of Himself, has said "God is love." Thus the very essence of the Creator who made man in His image must be the essence of man the creature. And it is in the perversion of that essence that we have ample proof that something went horribly wrong.

We do not need to know Greek and the difference between the types of love (for which Greek has separate words) to realize that the love which Paul goes on to describe in 1 Corinthians 13 is beyond anything mankind usually experiences or expresses. There is a divine quality that shines through, a quality which rings true to conscience and condemns us. We cannot quarrel with the standard Paul sets. We know that true love ought to be precisely what he depicts, but at the same time we hang our heads in shameful admission that such love is beyond us. Nevertheless, we also know that somehow we were made for that very kind of love and that our failure to experience it is a defect for which we are responsible and for lack of which we feel a deep loss.

Paul is depicting a love that is not of this world. It is additional evidence, as C.S. Lewis points out, that we were made for another world. We recognize it for what real love ought to be, and it strikes a chord in us like the description of a land we have never seen but to which we somehow feel we belong. We need read no other part of the Bible than this "love chapter" to know that man is a fallen creature. We can say "I love you!" and perhaps not even realize that deep inside we really mean "I love me and I want you!" Such is the tragedy of present human experience.

Nevertheless, those words, "I love you," have the power to wonderfully transform both the person who speaks them and the one to whom they are spoken. They are the highest expression of which man is capable as a creature made in the image of God. Some people find these words difficult to speak, and other people find them embarrassing to hear. What we all find nearly impossible to believe is that the God who created the universe has spoken these wonderful words personally and intimately to each of us. And He has done it in a way that no one else could: by entering into our humanity and dying for our sins upon the cross. He has thus so fully proved His love that there is no excuse for ever doubting it.

The Uniqueness of Christianity

It is this unparalleled manifestation of God's love that makes Christianity what it is. There are many facets of our life in Christ which make it totally unique. Among the most wonderful distinctives is the relationship that each Christian is intended to enjoy with Christ Himself—an intimate *personal* relationship that is not only unmatched by any other faith but is absolutely essential if someone is to be a Christian.

In contrast, for a Buddhist to have a personal relationship with Buddha is neither possible nor necessary. Neither is the practice of

Islam impaired because Mohammed is in the grave. It is no hindrance at all to any of the world's historic religions that their founders are dead and gone. Not so with Christianity. If Jesus Christ were not alive today there would be no Christian faith because He *is* all that it offers. Christianity is not a mass *religion* but a personal *relationship*.

At the heart of this relationship is a fact so astonishing that most Christians, including those who have known the Lord for many years, seldom live in its full enjoyment. It is not that we do not believe it intellectually, but that we find it too wonderful to accept its full implications into our moment-by-moment experience of daily life.

We are like a homely, small-town girl from a very poor family who is being wooed by the most handsome, wealthiest, most powerful, most intelligent and in every way most desirable man who ever lived. She enjoys the *things* he gives her, but is not able fully to give herself to him and really get to know him because she finds it too much to believe that *he*, with all the far more attractive women in the world, really loves *her*. And to leave the familiar surroundings of her childhood—the friends and family that have been all she has known and loved—to go off with this one who seems to love her so much and to become a part of another world so foreign and even inconceivable to her, it is all too overwhelming.

Some of us grew up as children singing "Jesus loves me, this I know, for the Bible tells me so," and found a certain amount of childish comfort in its simple assurance at the time. We never matured in that love, however, because we were not taught to do so. Meanwhile, other loves entered our lives and were given priority over the love of God. In his classic, Augustine declares that man has become earthly minded and lost his heavenly vision of *The City of God* because of a "wrong order of loves"—self has replaced God:

> These two cities were made by two loves: the earthly city by the love of self unto the contempt of God, and the heavenly city by the love of God unto the contempt of self.[2]

To be sure, we still read the love chapter (1 Corinthians 13) now and then and sing lustily (and at times even with great feeling) such classics as "The love of God is greater far than tongue or pen can ever tell. . . ." But we are no longer children, and the simple fact that "Jesus loves *me*" has somehow lost its power for us. Not because it is intellectually too shallow, but because its deeper implications, which we now begin dimly to perceive, are spiritually and emotionally too wonderful.

Like the small-town girl, each of us finds it very difficult to believe that Jesus really loves us. While we appreciate His blessings, we find it difficult to become intimate with our heavenly Suitor, because it seems so inappropriate that the Lord of the universe should be wooing *us*. That He loves everyone and that we are included in that great love is intellectually accepted, but that He has singled *me* out personally as an object of that love is too marvelous. My response falls far short of the joy that He intends for me.

Thus the essence of the Christian life—its true source of joy and confidence and power—is missing in so much that calls itself Christian. We can be very fundamental, evangelical, and biblical, yet not realize that the heart of our faith is missing. This sad fact is then reflected in the way we present Christ to the world.

Love—The Heart of the Gospel

Unfortunately, as we have seen, the church early in its history departed so far from the fundamentals of the faith that the essential personal relationship with Christ lost its importance and meaning. Eventually it was even denied to those who needed it by those who claimed to represent Him. Christ says, "Come unto *me* . . . *I am* the door . . . the way, the truth, the life." The church, however, began to claim that *it* was the means of salvation and called the world to itself instead of to the One of whom Peter had said, "Neither is there salvation in any other" (Acts 4:12).

Not only for Catholics, but for many Protestants today as well, joining the church has become a substitute for an essential saving relationship with Christ. While the Reformation repudiated a host of heresies, it left intact a great deal of "churchianity." From that base, forms and formulas and attitudes have grown until, within much of Protestantism today, the affection and honor that Christ Himself deserves is directed toward pastors and denominational loyalties. The passionate love which the bride ought to have for the Bridegroom is all too often deficient, if not lacking.

The love of God creates love for others whom He loves, thus providing the only true motivation for fulfilling the Great Commission. In preaching the gospel we are to be messengers of God's love, expressing and sharing it with the world. In making disciples, we are bringing others into a love relationship with Him. We are not calling them back under the law, but into the freedom of God's grace. It is love that motivates us to obey in a way that legal obligation and fear of judgment could never do. As Jesus told His disciples:

> He that hath my commandments and keepeth them, he it is that loveth me; and he that loveth me shall be loved of my Father, and I will love him, and will manifest myself to him. . . .
>
> If a man love me, he will keep my words, and my Father will love him, and we will come unto him, and make our abode with him.
>
> He that loveth me not keepeth not my sayings . . . (John 14:21,23,24).

It is a tragedy that we so easily forget the glory and wonder of God's love, not only as the joy of our lives and the motivation for obedience, but in its relationship to the gospel as well. We can present the truth of John 3:16, for example, as a judicial act on the part of God and forget that the verse begins, "For God so *loved* the world. . . ." The work of salvation was conceived and executed by divine *love*. We can present the gospel correctly and remain true to its basics concerning the death, burial, and resurrection of Christ in our place for our sins, and forget—and thus not convey to others—

the heart of God, which is the very heart of the message.

Some of the classic old hymns expressed it so well: "Son of God, 'twas *love* that made Thee, die our ruined souls to save. ...." Another exults, "O love that will not let me go, I rest my weary soul on Thee. ...." "O, the wonder of it all!" exclaims yet another. Charles Wesley put it so powerfully:

And can it be that I should gain
An interest in the Savior's blood?
Died He for me, who caused His pain?
For me, who Him to death pursued?
Amazing love, how can it be,
That Thou, my God, shouldst die for me!

Many preachers attempt to entice the world to "come to Christ" with the popular offer of lesser rewards: health, prosperity, an improved society, and long life upon earth, when the real essence of salvation is to know God and to be partakers of His love and life. A rejection of the gospel, therefore, is the rejection of God Himself and His love.

Man's problem is not that he was driven from an earthly paradise, but that he was separated from God's presence. That is the great tragedy. Those who seek to recover the physical benefits of Eden, to restore paradise without the missing Presence, to establish a kingdom without the King Himself reigning in power and glory, have misunderstood both problem and solution. The distinctions we have attempted to make in previous chapters are more than moot theological points. Our purpose has been to reawaken a hunger for God Himself and to stimulate the wonder, worship, and love we ought to have for Him.

What God lovingly offers is Himself, a restoration to His presence; no longer in an earthly garden, but in His heavenly home. "Ye shall seek *me* and find *me* when ye shall search for *me* with all your heart" (Jeremiah 29:13) is His promise. Instead, techniques are being sought and taught in the church for getting *things* from Him. The gift rather than the Giver is the sought-after prize.

The Secret of Obedience and Joy

I remember well as a young Christian thinking that Hebrews 11:6 (". . . he that cometh to God must believe that he is, and that he is a rewarder of them that diligently seek him") revealed the key to getting rewards from God. I had missed the clear message: Instead of the things and success I sought, I was supposed to seek *Him*. Yet there it was, so very plain—He rewards those "who diligently seek *Him*."

The man who is really seeking Him will not settle for any lesser reward. He who has a passion for God Himself would consider it a bad bargain indeed if he were given a worldly fortune instead. God may give earthly blessings, and does, to be used for His glory—but such are the lesser rewards, as Jesus said, added on for those who seek *first* "the kingdom of God and his righteousness" (Matthew 6:33).

Getting to know God and His love is the great vision that should have captured our hearts, but which is missed so early and easily in the Christian life. One reason is fairly obvious. The immediate reaction to our first realization of God's love is that He loves us because we are lovable and desirable, because something in us draws Him. Thus we fail to appreciate the wonder of a love that loves us not because of, but in spite of, who and what we are. C.S. Lewis expressed this struggle of our proud hearts so well:

> As Bunyan says, describing his first illusory conversion, "I thought there was no man in England that pleased God better than I."
> Beaten out of this, we next offer our own humility to God's admiration. Surely He'll like *that*? Or if not that, our clear-sighted and humble recognition that we still lack humility.
> Thus, depth beneath depth and subtlety within subtlety, there remains some lingering idea of our own, our very own, attractiveness.
> It is easy to acknowledge, but almost impossible to realise for long, that we are mirrors whose brightness, if

we are bright, is wholly derived from the sun that shines
upon us.
   Surely we must have a little—however little—native
luminosity? Surely we can't be *quite* creatures?[3]

Far from being a negative put-down, the factual realization that
we have nothing to commend us to God forms a wonderful basis for
solid confidence in our relationship with Him for eternity. As Lewis
says, "this pretence that we have anything of our own . . . has kept us
from being happy."[4] The reasons should be quite clear. If God loves
us because we somehow deserve His love, then we could change and
lose that appeal and thus lose His love. But if He loves us, as is the
glorious truth, because He *is* love—because of Who He is in Himself—then, knowing that He never changes, we are secure for
eternity and need never fear that we could lose His love by anything
we might do or neglect to do.
   Do we not, then, have license to defy Him, to do evil, to take our
own way? Yes, the possibility is left open, for love does not force
itself upon those who are loved. Love that tries to possess is not true
love and will lose what it hordes for itself. Love that gives itself
away, asking nothing in response, inspires a return of that same love.
Thus the Scripture says that "We love him, because he first loved
us" (1 John 4:19). We have no love in and of ourselves, but are only
able to love Him with the love He gives to us and the capacity He
gives for appreciating His love. And it is that appreciation which
awakens in us a love for Him that grows ever more precious.

The Impartiality of God's Love

   Knowing that He loves us not because of anything in us but
because He is love tells us something else that is very important:
God loves all mankind with the same love. There is no special
reason why He should love one of us more than another. He is no
respecter of persons; there is no favoritism with God. And here we
see another reason for rejecting the view that God does not love all
mankind enough to want everyone to be in heaven. There is no basis
in man (all have sinned and the hearts of all are the same) for God to

love some and not others—but neither is there any basis in God for His loving one but not another. Thus we are told that He "so loved the *world*" that He sent His Son into the *world* "that the *world* through him might be saved."

So we understand that God's love for each one is the same and that His love for all of mankind is personal. God's love is not some lofty principle, some immutable cosmic power that envelopes the masses of humanity in its inexorable process. God loves each person as an individual and calls all who will respond to His love. He longs to bestow not just blessings, but Himself upon all who genuinely seek *Him*. And He weeps with deep sorrow over those who reject Him and His love. At the same time He is allowing Satan to gather disciples and to set up his false kingdom, while giving to men the freedom to choose whom they will serve.

It would be wrong, however, for us to imagine that because God weeps and longs for our love, that in any way He has *need* of us. Here again we have a difference between the God of the Bible and the false gods of the world's religions. Islam's Allah is a single entity, who was therefore alone and could not know love or fellowship or communion until he had created other beings. Hinduism's Brahman, who is the All, cannot love or fellowship because it is impersonal and all-encompassing. Thus there can be no I-thou relationship. In contrast, the God of Israel consistently reveals Himself throughout the entire Bible, from Genesis to Revelation, as one God comprising a unity of three persons. Father, Son, and Holy Spirit have always fellowshipped, loved, and communed with one another in perfect completeness, and thus had no need to bring any creatures into existence.

We are the ones who have need—and our problem, as Augustine pointed out, comes in giving priority to lesser or even false needs. If we love God because we need His protection and care, then we have missed the joy of loving Him for Himself. Indeed, our great need is for God alone. All else is added blessing. Even Christian leaders have been deceived by accepting the "hierarchy of needs" invented by Abraham Maslow, a godless humanist and one of the fathers of today's New Age movement. He declared that man's lesser needs for food, clothing, shelter, etc. had to be met first, and only then could there be any appreciation of the higher ethical and spiritual values. This claim contradicts Scripture ("Seek ye *first* the kingdom of God. . . .") and interferes with the love relationship we ought to have with Christ. Yet Maslow's teaching has infected the church, along with much more of psychology's poison.

The Joy and Satisfaction of Heaven

What do we want from the person whom we love? Not things, not gifts, but closer communion, more love, more intimate fellowship. Thus it is that we are moved to give *ourselves* in our desire to please the One whom we now love with a passion. We are told that God will give us crowns and rewards in heaven. It is not possible for us to understand what that means because we have such a dim perception of what heaven will be like. Whatever the rewards may be, however, we know that each is an expression of His approval, a declaration that we have in some small way, as He has given the grace, pleased Him. Knowing that fact alone is all the reward we could ever desire and will give us joy for eternity. Its anticipation should give us great joy here and now.

It is not unusual for Christians to feel discouraged and even depressed. At such times it seems impossible to believe (knowing there is no reason in us for Him to love us) that He could ever be pleased with us. Surely eternity will bring sorrow rather than reward for our miserable failure. We long to hear His "Well done, good and faithful servant . . . enter thou into the joy of thy lord" (Matthew 25:23), but fear that it could never be so. Such humility of soul, because it reflects the simple truth of our situation except for His grace, is becoming of a Christian—but at such times we do well to remember the amazing and comforting statement of Scripture:

Therefore judge nothing before the time, until the Lord come, who both will bring to light the hidden things of darkness and will make manifest the counsels of the hearts; *and then shall every man have praise of God* (1 Corinthians 4:5).

Would not such praise give us cause to be pleased with ourselves and thus to imagine that there was something of value in us after all? If so, that attitude would dim the glory of God and rob us of the real joy of heaven. What is that joy? It is not to become something in and of ourselves so that we deserve praise. It is ever to be in a state of wonder and amazement and gratitude that He would take us and make of us a joy to His heart.

We will never be worthy of heaven or of His love. A sense of self-worth would ruin everything by turning some of the attention and glory to ourselves. We will always be creatures and He the Creator; we will always be sinners saved by grace and bought with His blood, and He will ever be our glorious Savior. Because He has filled us with His love, our passion for eternity will ever be to see Him exalted and praised and to love Him with all the capacity He supplies. His eternal joy will be to bless us with Himself.

Such will be the wonder of heaven. That He should be pleased with us will bring joy beyond the possibility of present comprehension. That every man will receive praise of God does not mean that each will be praised in the same way or to the same degree. Every cup will overflow with joy, but some cups will no doubt be deeper than others. There will be no need for us to recognize such differences, however, were they even apparent, for such comparisons would be meaningless in heaven's bliss. All that He is, the full infinitude of His person, will be equally available to all.

David, who knew the Lord very well, tells us the secret of that intimate relationship which he enjoyed: "One thing have I desired of the Lord, that will I seek after; that I may dwell in the house of the Lord all the days of my life, to behold the beauty of the Lord, and to enquire in his temple" (Psalm 27:4). There can be no doubt that knowing God and experiencing the wonder of His love was the continual and intense longing of David's heart, as so many of his psalms attest: "O God, thou art my God; early will I seek thee: my soul thirsteth for thee..." is the way Psalm 63 begins, and this same passion is expressed in so many others.

In spite of the rejection he experienced by family and friends during so much of his life, David's heart was filled with the joy of the Lord—a joy that strengthened him for the many trials he endured.

He also had a deep understanding of heaven and knew that the joy he experienced in part during this brief life of faith would be realized in its fullness there. It is the anticipation of the heavenly joy and, yes, intense *pleasure* of God's presence, that raises our hopes from this earth to heaven. In his meditation on Psalm 48 Augustine suggested that "in heaven hath been promised that which on earth we are seeking. . . ."[5] In another psalm, David had written:

> Thou wilt show me the path of life; in thy presence is fullness of joy; at thy right hand there are pleasures forevermore (Psalm 16:11).

A Challenge to Our Hearts

Paul indicated that in the last days men would be "lovers of pleasures more than lovers of God" (2 Timothy 3:4). What an indictment! How it challenges us to reexamine our priorities. How ashamed we will be one day that the pitiful pleasures of this world could ever have blinded us to the infinite and eternal pleasures God has "prepared for them that love him" (1 Corinthians 2:9). What a bad bargain to exchange the heavenly for the earthly. Writing more than 200 years ago, William Law put it in powerful perspective:

> And when the lusts of the flesh have had their last day, and the pride of life has only a dead body to inhabit, the soul of man which remains will know at last that it has nothing of its own, nothing that can say, "I do this," or "I possess that."
>
> Then all that man has or does, will either be the glory of God manifested in him, or the power of hell in full possession of his soul.
>
> The time of man's playing with words and intellect, of grasping after positions among men or of amusing himself with the foolish toys of this vain world, can last no longer than he is able to eat and drink with the creatures of this world.

When the time comes that he must take his leave of earthly treasure and honors, then all the stately structures which genius, learning, and proud imagination have painted before his own eyes or those of others must bear full witness to Solomon's "vanity of vanities, all is vanity."[6]

We have noted John's promise that the hope of Christ's return has a purifying effect upon those who enjoy it. There is a purity of heart that is required if we are to see God (Matthew 5:8). Jesus seemed to drive that point home when He warned, "But and if that evil servant shall say in his heart, 'My lord delayeth his coming . . .' " (Matthew 24:48). It is significant that our Lord associates wickedness with rejoicing in the thought that His return will be delayed—while righteousness is produced by loving His appearing.

Surely He is showing us the importance of holding the hope of His imminent return, the reward for which, Paul tells us, will be "a crown of righteousness" (2 Timothy 4:8). Again the implication is that not to love His appearing leaves an opening for evil to invade our lives. It shows a lack of love for our Lord and a love of our own selfish ambitions which would be interfered with by His return. We must ask the Lord to examine our hearts on this point.

Are there things we want to accomplish, places we want to go, even victories we want to "win for God" that are more important to us than being caught up by our Lord into His eternal presence? It is the attitude of our hearts that counts. "If in this life only we have hope in Christ," declared Paul, "we are of all men most miserable" (1 Corinthians 15:19). The joyful Christian has put his hope in heaven. He is not living for this world and makes sacrifices in this life to please his Lord and to be assured of hearing His "well done" in heaven. The Bible is full of examples of those who, in order to please God, turned their backs on earthly rewards and honors. They will rejoice through eternity for that decision.

Such is the message of Hebrews 11, where we are given a list of some of the heroes and heroines of the faith and are told of their exploits. The outstanding characteristic of everyone on that roll of honor was the fact that their ultimate hope was in heaven. Confronted by a choice between this world and the one to come, they chose the latter.

God is no man's debtor. The idea that many people have of suffering for Christ and missing out on so much in order to please God is a caricature concocted by Satan. It is certain that no one, when it comes time to die, regrets having missed out on worldly pleasures or treasure or honors as a result of serving God. And how can even those who have lost position and possessions, have been tortured, imprisoned, or killed because of their faith hold any regret that as a result an eternal reward awaits them? Paul reminds us:

> For I reckon that the sufferings of this present time are not worthy to be compared with the glory which shall be revealed in us.
>
> For our light affliction, which is but for a moment, worketh for us a far more exceeding and eternal weight of glory. [7]

Moses, because of the eternal and heavenly perspective with which he viewed all of life, "refused to be called the son of Pharaoh's daughter" and chose rather to suffer—not prosperity and dominion, but *affliction*—with the people of God than to partake in the rewards of this world. He didn't decide that it would be best for him to hang in there until he took over the throne of Egypt one day and that this would be the best path to follow in order to reconstruct Egyptian society and culture along godly lines. We are told that he esteemed "the reproach of Christ greater riches than all the treasures of Egypt: for he had respect unto the recompense of the reward [not upon earth but in heaven]" (Hebrews 11:26).

Love—An Eternal Commitment

We know that as His bride we ought to long to be with Christ and we are sorry that we don't love His appearing as we should. How can we reawaken our love for Him? First of all, we need to remember that love is not merely a sentiment that sweeps over us and which is beyond our control. Marriages are breaking up among Christians because husband or wife claims no longer to love the other and often has "fallen in love" with someone else. This is not love at all, but a Hollywood-inspired counterfeit.

Love involves unshakable *commitment* of oneself to another—thus it involves not just emotions but an act of the *will*—which Calvinism again, denies is possible. Christ is our example, and husbands are to love their wives as He loved the church. A Christ-like marriage, as C.S. Lewis points out,[8] would not be all peaches and cream, but may well involve suffering hatred and abuse and misunderstanding and giving love in return. That is what Christ did, and that is the kind of love husbands are to have for their wives.

Not only does love require a faithful commitment, but it is a commitment in response to God's command: "Thou shalt love the Lord thy God with all thy heart, and with all thy soul, and with all thy strength, and with all thy mind; and thy neighbour as thyself" (Luke 10:27). Love does indeed involve deep emotion, but it is first of all obedience to God's command. We can love our husband or wife or parent or mother-in-law and even our enemy, no matter how much evil we think they have done to us. It simply takes the willingness to let God pour out His love through us.

Christ has committed Himself to us for eternity, and He expects us to make the same commitment to Him. And that commitment involves loving others if we truly love Him—for a lack of love for our brother is, according to Scripture, proof that we do not really love God (1 John 4:20,21). How much more is the insistence that we cannot love wife or husband or parent a betrayal of the fact that our love for God, no matter how loudly we profess it, is not genuine at all.

There is another motive for loving Christ's appearing. It is not only that we long to see Him for ourselves, but we also want to see Him glorified on this earth where He has been rejected for so long. What a tragedy that "He was in the world, and the world was made by him, and the world knew him not" (John 1:10). The hearts of those who love Christ are grieved that this world, blinded by pride, goes about its business building its plastic utopia in complete disregard for the One who longs to rescue it from an eternity of horror which it is bringing upon itself.

If we love our Lord, then we will want to see Him revealed to the world and made known for who He is. We want to see Him honored and praised where He was rejected. We long to see Him rule, whose right it is to rule, and we want to be at His side, singing His praises, pointing men to Him who is the Lover of our souls.

Our relationship with Christ and with God through Him will forever be one of perfect love. When we see Him, faith and hope will have given place to sight. But love, the greatest gift of all, will endure forever.

He desires to have us in His presence even more than we could ever desire to be there. He loves us with a love that will never let us go. And because He has captured our affection, we will be eternally bound by love to Him—a love that not only flows to us from God, but which our redeemed hearts will return to Him with a purity and joy that will be His eternal gift.

The signs that His return is near are in the world today as never before. The sleeping church may soon be shaken with that cry of which Christ spoke in a parable that is difficult to understand, but which could well be fulfilled in our day:

> While the bridegroom tarried, they all slumbered and slept.
>
> And at midnight there was a cry made, "Behold, the bridegroom cometh; go ye out to meet him!" (Matthew 25:5,6).

Notes

CHAPTER ONE—Life, Death, and Immortality

1. Senator Claiborne Pell, from his Welcoming Address at the November 1987 "The Greater Self: New Frontiers in Exceptional Abilities Research" Conference held in Washington, D.C., quoted in *Noetic Sciences Review*, Number 6, Spring 1988, opening page.
2. *Characters and Characteristics of William Law*, Selected and Arranged with an Introduction by Alexander Whyte (London: Hodder & Stoughton, 1893), pp. 237-41, selection taken from Law's *A Serious Call to a Devout and Holy Life*.
3. Isaiah 65:17-25; 2 Peter 3:10-14; Revelation 21:1-8, etc.
4. Malcolm Muggeridge, *Jesus Rediscovered* (Doubleday, 1969), pp. 234, 117.
5. Muggeridge, *Jesus*, p. 28.
6. John Pilkey, unpublished "Commentary on Rough Draft of *Whatever Happened to Heaven?*", July 1988, p. 2.

CHAPTER TWO—The Hope of the Early Church

1. Paul David Dunn, "John Marks Templeton: The Humble Approach," in *Possibilities*, Summer 1986, pp. 8, 12.
2. "The Graying of a Church: Christian Science's Ills," in *Newsweek*, August 3, 1987, p. 60.
3. From the tape of a talk by Jay Grimstead in February, 1987.
4. C.S. Lewis, "A Reply to Professor Haldane," in *Of Other Worlds* (Harcourt, Brace, World, 1967), p. 81.
5. Gary DeMar and Peter Leithart, *The Reduction of Christianity* (Dominion Press, 1988), p. 26, quoting David Chilton, *Productive Christians in an Age of Guilt-Manipulators* (3rd rev. ed.; Institute for Christian Economics, 1985), pp. 94-95.
6. Luke 12:35-40, Matthew 25:13.
7. David Chilton, *Paradise Restored* (Reconstruction Press, 1985), pp. 221-22.
8. Pilkey, "Commentary," July 1988, p. 4.

CHAPTER THREE—The Late Great Rapture Theory?

1. Garry Friesen, "A Return Visit: Hal Lindsey was premature. The earth is great, but it's too early to call it late," in *Moody*, May 1988, p. 30.
2. Gary North, "1988: Dispensationalism's Year of Crisis," in *Dispensationalism in Transition*, Vol. 1, No. 1, January 1988, the first issue of a new Institute of Christian Economics newsletter, p. 2.
3. Michael R. Gilstrap, "The Late Great Theologian Lewis Sperry Chafer," in *Dispensationalism in Transition*, Vol. 1, No. 3, March 1988 (Institute of Christian Economics), p. 2.
4. John F. Walvoord, *Israel in Prophecy* (Zondervan Publishing, 1962).
5. Dominion Press brochure advertising "The Biblical Blueprint Series" of four books, one each by George Grant, Gary North, Dennis T. Peacocke, and Ray Sutton, released by Thomas Nelson in the fall of 1986. That series has since been expanded to include ten books.
6. Gary North in a letter to Peter Lalonde dated April 30, 1987.
7. George Grant, "Dominion Theology," an interview by Eric Pement and Jon Trott in *Cornerstone*, Vol. 16, Issue 83, p. 32.
8. Kenneth J. Gentry, Jr., "The Greatness of the Great Commission," in *The Journal of Christian Reconstruction*, Winter 1981, p. 34, quoting Gary North.
9. David Ebaugh in *Monarch*, Oct./Nov. 1986, p. 3.
10. Cited in *Report From Concerned Christians*, March/April 1988, P.O. Box 22920, Denver, CO 80222, p. 4.
11. Rick Godwin, Sunday evening sermon at Metro Church; Edmond, Oklahoma; April 11, 1988; "Rick Godwin No. 2" audio tape.
12. Earl Paulk, *The Handwriting on the Wall* (booklet self-published by Paulk's Chapel Hill Harvester Church, Decatur, GA 30034), pp. 17, 19-20.
13. Fyodor Mikhailovich Dostoevsky, Translated by Constance Garnett, *The Brothers Karamazov* (University of Chicago, Great Books edition, 1952), pp. 129-30.

CHAPTER FOUR—What Holds Christ in the Heavens?

1. Robert G. Grant, *American Freedom Coalition*, January 1988, p. 2.
2. From the brochure for "Southern California Regional Seminar of the Coalition on Revival, April 25, 1987, Speaker Jay Grimstead," which ended with "Signing of The Manifesto Covenant and Prayer of Dedication."
3. *A Manifesto for the Christian Church, Declaration and Covenant*, July 4, 1986 (Coalition on Revival, Inc., 89 Pioneer Way, Mountain View, CA 94041), p. 4. See also Appendix A, p. 3.
4. George Grant, *The Changing of the Guard: Biblical Principles for Political Action* (Dominion Press, 1987), p. 15.
5. From the rough draft to H. Wayne House and Thomas D. Ice, *Dominion Theology: Blessing or Curse? An Analysis of Reconstructionism* (Multnomah Press, 1988).
6. Charles Colson, *Kingdoms in Conflict* (William Morrow/Zondervan, 1987), p. 88.
7. Ibid., p. 93.
8. *Thy Kingdom Come*, November 1987, p. 3.
9. Earl Paulk, *That the World May Know* (K Dimension Publishers, 1987), p. 72.
10. Earl Paulk, *Held In the Heavens Until . . .: God's Strategy for Planet Earth* (K Dimension Publishers, 1985), pp. 100, 228, 233-34.
11. *Thy Kingdom Come*, November 1987, p. 3.

12. Richard M. Riss, *Latter Rain: The Latter Rain Movement of 1948 and the Mid-Twentieth Century Evangelical Awakening* (Honeycomb Visual Productions Ltd., 1987), pp. 117-21.
13. George R. Hawtin, an editorial in *The Sharon Star*, April 1, 1949, p. 2. See also Cornelius John Jaenen, *The Pentecostal Movement*, an M.A. Thesis, University of Manitoba, 1950.
14. Kenneth L. Gentry, Jr., "The Greatness of the Great Commission," in *The Journal of Christian Reconstruction*, Winter 1981, p. 39.
15. Gary North, *Christian Reconstruction*, May/June 1988.
16. Gary North, "The Three Legs of Christian Reconstruction's Stool," in *Christian Reconstruction*, January/February 1984, p. 2.
17. Gary North, "Reconstructionist Renewal and Charismatic Renewal," in *Christian Reconstruction*, May/June 1988, p. 2.
18. Paulk, *Held*, p. 231.
19. *Thy Kingdom Come*, November 1987, p. 3.
20. Maxwell Whyte, "Search for the New Testament Church," in *Christian Life*, January 1984, pp. 36-39.
21. Earl Paulk, *Thrust in the Sickle and Reap* (K Dimension Publishers, 1986), p. 141.
22. Paulk, *Held*, p. 230.
23. Whyte, *Christian Life*, p. 39.

CHAPTER FIVE—Bringing Heaven Down to Earth

1. Tertullian, *Apology*, 40.2.
2. Tacitus, *The Annals and the Histories*, XV, 44, 3-5.
3. W.H.C. Frend, *The Rise of Christianity* (Fortress Press, 1984), pp. 109-10.
4. Colman J. Barry, O.S.B., (ed.), *Readings In Church History*, Vol. 1, *From Pentecost to the Protestant Revolt* (The Newman Press, 1960), p. 75.
5. Tertullian, *To The Nations*, 1.14.
6. *Epistle of Diognetus*, V, 4-11.
7. H. Chadwick, *The Early Church* (Wm. B. Eerdmans, 1967), p. 91.
8. Chadwick, *Early*, p. 69.
9. Walter A. Elwell, (ed.), *Evangelical Dictionary of Theology* (Baker Book House, 1984), R.G. Clouse, "Millennium, Views of the," p. 716. See also Philip Schaff, *The History of the Christian Church: Nicene and Post-Nicene Christianity*, Vol. 3 (Eerdmans Publishing Company, 1910); and J.N.D. Kelly, *Early Christian Doctrines* (Harper & Row, 1978), pp. 460-70, etc.
10. Kelly, *Doctrines*, p. 465.
11. David Chilton, *Days of Vengeance: An Exposition of the Book of Revelation* (Dominion Press, 1987), p. 494; Thomas Ice and H. Wayne House, *Dominion Theology: Blessing or Curse?* (Multnomah Press, 1988), p. 196, citing a personal letter from Chilton to Ice dated December 17, 1986, p. 4.
12. R.J. Rushdoony, *Thy Kingdom Come: Studies in Daniel and Revelation* (Thoburn Press, 1970), p. 134; R.J. Rushdoony, *God's Plan for Victory: The Meaning of Post Millennianism* (Thoburn Press, 1977), p. 5.
13. Ice and House, *Dominion*, pp. 208-9.
14. *The Epistle of Barnabas*, 4, 21.
15. *Epistle to the Ephesians*, 11.
16. *Life of St. Anthony*, IV, 16.
17. Frend, *Christianity*, pp. 253-56.
18. Quoted in Thomas D. Ice, "A Critical Analysis of Theonomic Post-millennialism," in *Bibliotheca Sacra*, Vol. 145, No. 579, July-September 1988.
19. Clement, *Miscellanies*, II.20.125.
20. Philip Hughes, *A History of the Church, Volume 1: The World in which the Church was Founded* (London: Sheed & Ward, 1983), p. 6.
21. Ibid., p. 165.
22. William Byron Forbush, (ed.), *Fox's Book of Martyrs* (Zondervan, 1962), p. 14.
23. Ibid., p. 17.
24. Hughes, *History*, Vol. 1, p. 165.
25. Chadwick, *Early*, p. 118.
26. Hughes, *History*, Vol. 1, p. 172.
27. Ibid., p. 166.
28. Ibid., p. 175.
29. Ibid., p. 176.
30. Frend, *Christianity*, p. 124.
31. Ibid., p. 125.
32. Will Durant, *The Story of Civilization*, Vol. IV, *The Age of Faith* (Simon and Schuster, 1950), p. 75.
33. Chilton, *Paradise*, p. 5.
34. Eusebius, *Oration on the Tricennalia of Constantine*, 2.4, 3.5-6, 5.4.
35. Hughes, *History*, p. 198.
36. Frend, *Christianity*, pp. 727-28.
37. Eusebius, *Life of Constantine*, IV, 24.
38. Hughes, *History*, p. 195.
39. Ibid., pp. 190-91.
40. Eusebius, *Life*, IV, 60.

41. Chadwick, *Early*, p. 128.
42. Frend, *Christianity*, p. 773.
43. Chadwick, *Early*, p. 243.
44. Frend, *Christianity*, p. 707.
45. Ibid., pp. 710-11.
46. Chadwick, *Early*, p. 175.

CHAPTER SIX—Power Corrupts

1. Frend, *Christianity*, p. 704.
2. Chadwick, *Early*, p. 132.
3. Ibid., p. 245.
4. Ibid., p. 143.
5. Ibid., p. 132.
6. Constantine to Domitius Celsus, *Vicarius Africae* in Optatus *De Schismate Donatistarum*, App. VII, pp. 211-12.
7. Frend, *Christianity*, p. 492.
8. Rev. Peter Geiermann, C.SS.R., *The Convert's Catechism of Catholic Doctrine* (Tan Books and Publishers, Inc., 1977), Imprimatur Joseph E. Ritter, S.T.D., Archbishop of St. Louis, pp. 25-27.
9. Ibid., pp. 14, 19, 27, 34, 36.
10. Ibid., p. VI.
11. Karl Keating, *Catholicism and Fundamentalism: The Attack on "Romanism" by "Bible Christians"* (Ignatius Press, 1988), pp. 124-27.
12. Ibid., p. 127.
13. Henry Clarence Thiessen, *Introduction to the New Testament* (Wm. B. Eerdmans Publishing, 1943), p. 25.
14. Geiermann, *Catechism*, pp. 101-3.
15. Frend, *Christianity*, p. 704.
16. Chadwick, *Early*, p. 174.
17. Ibid., p. 161.
18. Origen, *Contra Celsum*, III.9.
19. Frend, *Christianity*, p. 411.
20. Hughes, *History*, p. 149.
21. Leviticus 19:31; 20:6; Deuteronomy 18:11; 1 Samuel 28:3,7; 1 Chronicles 10:13,14; Isaiah 8:19,20, etc.
22. Chadwick, *Early*, p. 174.
23. Charles MacKay, *Memoirs of Extraordinary Popular Delusions* (London: Richard Bentley, 1841), Vol. 1, pp. 695-702.
24. Frend, *Christianity*, p. 710.
25. Ibid., p. 726.
26. Ibid., p. 728.
27. R.W. Southern, *Western Society and the Church in the Middle Ages* (Penguin Books, Vol. 2 of Pelican History of the Church Series, 1970), pp. 24-25.
28. Geiermann, *Catechism*, p. 24.
29. Walter James, *The Christian In Politics* (Oxford University Press, 1962), p. 47.
30. Frend, *Christianity*, pp. 624-25.
31. Barry, *Readings*, p. 108.
32. *Los Angeles Herald Examiner*, December 21, 1987, p. A4.
33. *The Catholic Encyclopedia* (Thomas Nelson, 1976), under the heading, "Rome."

CHAPTER SEVEN—Babylon the Great

1. Frend, *Christianity*, pp. 728-29.
2. Maurice Keen, *The Pelican History of Medieval Europe* (Pelican, 1969), pp. 14-15.
3. Barry, *Readings*, p. 223.
4. *Collier's Encyclopedia* (P.F. Collier & Son, 1959), Vol. 5, p. 32.
5. Barry, *Readings*, p. 233.
6. Southern, *Western*, pp. 18-19.
7. Barry, *Readings*, pp. 438-39.
8. Southern, *Western*, p. 144.
9. Henry Paolucci, (ed.), *The Political Writings of St. Augustine* (Henry Regnery Co., 1962), pp. XVII-XVIII.
10. Barry, *Readings*, p. 457.
11. Ibid., p. 466.
12. Will Durant, *The Reformation: A History of European Civilization from Wyclif to Calvin: 1300-1564* (Simon and Schuster, 1957), p. 6.
13. Machiavelli, *The Prince*, chapter 18.
14. Harry J. Margoulias, *Byzantine Christianity: Emperor, Church and the West* (Rand McNally, 1982), pp. 103-4.
15. G.G. Coulton, *Five Centuries of Religion*, Vol. 2, (Cambridge, England, 1923), p. 400.
16. Southern, *Western*, p. 200.
17. Frederic Seebohm, *The Oxford Reformers* (London, 1869), pp. 70-71, 74-76, 110.
18. Barry, *Readings*, p. 542.
19. Ibid., pp. 470-71.
20. *Cambridge Modern History*, 12 Volumes (New York, 1907), Vol. 1, p. 670.
21. Barry, *Readings*, p. 471.

22. David A. Yallop, *In God's Name: An Investigation Into the Murder of Pope John Paul I* (Bantam Books, 1984).
23. Ibid.
24. Geiermann, *Catechism*, p. 45.
25. Ibid., p. 45.
26. Keating, *Catholicism*, p. 194.
27. Geiermann, *Catechism*, available from the publisher or at Catholic bookstores.
28. William Canton, *The Bible and the Anglo-Saxon People* (London: J.M. Dent & Sons, Ltd., 1914), pp. 27-28.
29. From the Decretal of Pope Clement VI.
30. Earle E. Cairns, *Christianity Through the Centuries: A History of the Christian Church* (Zondervan Publishing House, 1981), p. 282.

CHAPTER EIGHT—The Reformation

1. Cairns, *Christianity*, pp. 251-52.
2. E.H. Broadbent, *The Pilgrim Church* (Pickering & Inglis, Ltd., 1955), pp. 124-25.
3. G.G. Coulton, *Five Centuries of Religion* (Cambridge, England, 1923), Vol. 2, p. 411.
4. Roland H. Bainton, *Here I Stand: A Life of Martin Luther* (The New American Library, 1950), p. 90.
5. Ibid., p. 92.
6. Durant, *Reformation*, p. 348.
7. Bainton, *Here*, p. 144.
8. Durant, *Reformation*, p. 377.
9. Ibid., p. 619.
10. Ibid., p. 448.
11. Philip Schaff, *History of the Christian Church: The Swiss Reformation* (Edinburgh, 1893), p. 739.
12. E.H. Broadbent, *The Pilgrim Church* (London: Pickering & Inglis, Ltd., 1955), p. 149.
13. John T. McNeill, (ed.), John Calvin's *The Institutes of the Christian Religion* (The Westminster Press, 1960), Volume XX, Chapter VI,19, p. 340.
14. Calvin, *Institutes*, Vol. XXI, Ch. XXI,7, p. 931.
15. Schaff, *History*, p. 519.
16. Durant, *Reformation*, p. 473.
17. Pasquale Villari, *Life and Times of Girolamo Savonarola* (New York, 1896), p. 491; Schaff, *History*, pp. 491-92; Charles Beard, *The Reformation of the Sixteenth Century in Relation to Modern Thought and Knowledge* (University of Michigan Press, 1962), p. 250, etc.
18. Edwin Muir, *John Knox: Portrait of a Calvinist* (The Viking Press, 1929), pp. 106-8.
19. Cairns, *Christianity*, p. 311.
20. Schaff, *History*, p. 491.
21. Durant, *Reformation*, pp. 472-73.
22. R. Tudor Jones, *The Great Reformation* (Inter-Varsity Press), p. 140.
23. Beard, *Reformation*, p. 255.
24. Bainton, *Luther*, p. 184.
25. *Manifesto Covenant* of the Coalition on Revival, quoted in a brochure advertising the "Southern California Regional Seminar of the *Coalition on Revival*, April 25, 1987 . . . speaker Dr. Jay Grimstead, founder and director."
26. Bainton, *Luther*, pp. 184-85.

CHAPTER NINE—Dare We Forget?

1. E.H. Broadbent, *The Pilgrim Church* (London: Pickering & Inglis, Ltd., 1955), p. 164.
2. *The Canons and Decrees of the Council of Trent*, Translated and Introduced by Rev. H.J. Schroeder, O.P. (Tan Books, 1978), p. 75.
3. Ibid., p. 46.
4. Ibid., p. 214.
5. Ibid., pp. 17-19, 22-23, 33, 35-36, 46, 52-53, 90, 144-46, 149-50, etc.
6. Geiermann, *Catechism*, p. 103.
7. Geiermann, *Catechism*, pp. 101-4.
8. *Christianity Today*, July 15, 1988, p. 46.
9. James B. Jordon, "No Longer Strangers, But Still Heretics," in *Christian Reconstruction*, July/Aug. 1988.
10. Paulk, *Unity of Faith*, an undated booklet self-published by Paulk's Chapel Hill Harvester Church, Decatur, GA 30034), p. 4.
11. Maxwell Whyte, "Search for the New Testament Church," in *Christian Life*, January 1984, p. 39.
12. *Christianity Today*, September 4, 1987, p. 44.
13. Wilson Ewin, *Evangelism: The Trojan Horse of the 1990's* (Bible Baptist Church, P.O. Box 1348, Nashua, NH 03061), pp. 12-16.
14. "Fact Sheet: Lutheran World Federation," undated, offered to visitors by the Lutheran World Federation at WCC headquarters in Geneva during September 1988.
15. Colson, *Kingdoms*, p. 173-74.
16. Paulk, *Unity*, p. 4.
17. *Valley Daily News*, October 2, 1987, p. C3.
18. *Christian News*, June 13, 1988, p. 18.
19. Robert Schuller, *Self-Esteem: The New Reformation* (Word, 1982), p. 19.
20. Rodney Clapp, "Remonking the Church," an editorial in *Christianity Today*, August 12, 1988, p. 20.

21. Geiermann, *Catechism*, pp. 23-26, 66-67, 74-80, 102-3.
22. Jonathan H. Wilson, *Los Angeles Herald Examiner*, September 19, 1987, Religion page.
23. Geiermann, *Catechism*, p. 27.
24. Don A. Schanche, "Pope Offers Olive Branch to Lutherans," in the *Los Angeles Times*, Part I, p. 5, May 4, 1987.
25. Don A. Schanche, "Pope Calls for Unity for All Europeans," in the *Los Angeles Times*, Part I, p. 6, May 5, 1987.
26. Rev. David J. Engelsma, *The Church Today And The Reformation Church: A Comparison* (Protestant Reformed Church, 16511 South Park Ave., South Holland, IL 60473), pp. 20, 22.
27. Durant, *Reformation*, p. 598, cited from John Foxe, *Acts and Monuments (Book of Martyrs)* (London, 1841), Vol. 8, pp. 82-83; see also Jones, *Reformation*, p. 165.
28. Bishop J.C. Ryle, *Why Were Our Reformers Burned?* (Leeds, England: Maranatha Revival Crusade, 1982), p. 17.
29. Dostoevsky, *The Brothers Karamazov*, p. 129.
30. Ryle, *Why?*, pp. 33-35.
31. Ibid., p. 18.
32. Jones, *Reformation*, p. 165.

CHAPTER TEN—The Reconstruction Delusion

1. Hugh T. Kerr, (ed.), *Compendium of Luther's Theology* (Westminster Press, 1966), p. 218.
2. Chadwick, *Early*, p. 221.
3. Peter Brown, *Augustine of Hippo* (University of California Press, 1967), p. 213.
4. Augustine, *de cat. rud.*, XXV, 48.
5. From the preliminary manuscript for the book by House and Ice. Compare House and Ice, *Dominion*, pp. 158-59, 163-65.
6. North, *Liberating Planet Earth*, Vol. 1 of Biblical Blueprint Series (Dominion Press, 1987), p. 25.
7. House and Ice, citing James D. Bratt, *Dutch Calvinism in Modern America: A History of a Conservative Subculture* (William B. Eerdmans Publishing Company, 1984), p. 14.
8. Raymond P. Joseph, *The Counsel of Chalcedon*, Aug. 1982, "Kingdom Victory."
9. Tom Rose, "Christ's Kingdom: How Shall We Build?" in *Journal of Christian Reconstruction*, Summer 1981.
10. Francis Nigel Lee, "From Atheist to Christian Minister," in *The Counsel of Chalcedon*, June 1984.
11. David Chilton, *Days of Vengeance* (Dominion Press, 1987), p. 587.
12. North, *Liberating*, pp. 24, 178.
13. George Grant, *Bringing in the Sheaves* (American Vision Press, 1985), p. 98.
14. David Chilton, *Paradise Restored: An Eschatology of Dominion* (Reconstruction Press, 1985), pp. 214-19.
15. *C.O.R. National Newsletter*, December 1987.
16. Gary North, *Dominion and Common Grace: The Biblical Basis of Progress* (I.C.E., 1987), p. 153.
17. Gary North, *Is The World Running Down? Crisis in the Christian Worldview* (Dominion Press, 1988), p. 225.
18. *A Manifesto for the Christian Church: Declaration and Covenant, July 4, 1986—An Act of Contrition and Humble Repentance, A Solemn Covenant, A Statement of Essential Truths and A Call to Action* (The Coalition on Revival, 89 Pioneer Way, Mountain View, CA 94041), p 12.
19. Ibid., pp. 9-10.
20. *C.O.R. National Newsletter*, July 1986.
21. From the brochure *An Invitation to the Continental Congress III on the Revival of Christianity and the Reformation of Society*, held July 2-4, 1986, distributed by COR, 89 Pioneer Way, Mountain View, CA 94041; a brochure advertising a Jay Grimstead seminar in Costa Mesa, CA, April 25, 1987; see also *C.O.R. National Newsletter*, December 1986.
22. Walter James, *The Christian in Politics* (Oxford University Press, 1962), p. 44.
23. Southern, *Western*, p. 38.
24. Gary North, "Editor's Introduction" in George Grant, *The Changing of the Guard: Biblical Principles for Political Action* (Dominion Press, 1987), p. xxvii.
25. Gary North, *Liberating*, pp. 22-25.
26. Grant, *Changing*, pp. 114-15.
27. *USA Today*, June 8, 1988.
28. David R. Reagan and Thomas H. Baker, *What The Bible Says About AIDS* (Lamb & Lion Ministries, P.O. Drawer K, McKinney, TX 75069, 1988), p. 37.
29. Michael Isikoff, "Group linked to Rev. Moon lobbies for Col. North pardon," *Washington Post*, February 21, 1988.
30. House and Ice, *Dominion*, p. 349.
31. *Intercessors For America Newsletter*, June 1986, "Launching More Than Fireworks on the 4th of July: An Interview With Dr. Jay Grimstead."
32. *Manifesto*, Appendix A, p. 8.
33. *Manifesto*, pp. 4, 12, 30, 31, etc.
34. Jay Grimstead, September 18, 1987, speaking to a group of pastors, from a tape of the meeting.
35. Jones, *Reformation*, p. 93.

CHAPTER ELEVEN—The Great Dominion Myth

1. DeMar and Leithart, *Reduction*, p. 190.
2. Ibid., pp. 187-88.
3. Earl Paulk, *Held In the Heavens Until . . . : God's Strategy for Planet Earth* (K Dimension Publishers, 1985), pp. 100, 228, 233-34.
4. Chilton, *Paradise*, p. 5.
5. Ibid., p. 213.

6. Chilton, *Vengeance*, pp. 510-11.
7. George Grant, *Changing*, pp. 50-51.
8. DeMar and Leithart, *Reduction*, p. 221.
9. Chilton, *Paradise*, p. 40.
10. Gary North, "The Attack on the 'New' Pentecostals," *Christian Reconstruction*, Vol. X, No. 1 (Jan./Feb. 1986), p. 2, as cited in DeMar and Leithart, *Reduction*, p. 184.
11. Chilton, *Paradise*, pp. 218-19.
12. North, *Liberating*, pp. 23-24.
13. DeMar and Leithart, *Reduction*, p. 29.
14. Gentry, *Journal*, pp. 37-38.
15. Ibid., p. 39.
16. Gary North, *Unconditional Surrender: God's Program for Victory* (Geneva Press, 1981), p. 218.
17. DeMar and Leithart, *Reduction*, p. 27.
18. Ibid., p. 121.
19. Ibid., p. 26.
20. Pilkey, "Commentary," July 19, 1988, p. 2.
21. COR *Manifesto*, Appendix A, p. 7.
22. Ibid.
23. Undated early 1988 promotional letter signed by Gary North accompanying Dominion Press brochure for Biblical Blueprint Series of books.
24. North, *Liberating*, pp. 8-9, 25.
25. Chilton, *Paradise*, p. 218; DeMar and Leithart, *Reduction*, p. 32; etc.
26. *Manifesto*, p. 31.
27. Jay Grimstead, COR formletter dated July 10, 1987.
28. Letter to Jay Grimstead on file.

CHAPTER TWELVE—Israel and the Coming Kingdom

1. Earl Paulk, *The Handwriting on the Wall* (booklet self-published by Paulk's Chapel Hill Harvester Church, Decatur, GA 30034), pp. 17, 19-20.
2. Durant, *Reformation*, p. 729.
3. Ibid., p. 727.
4. Chilton, *Vengeance*, pp. 410, 443, 575.
5. Ibid., pp. 410, 443, 575.
6. House and Ice, *Dominion*, pp. 249-60.
7. *End-Times News Digest*, December 1987 (James McKeever Ministries Newsletter), p. 3.
8. Deuteronomy 30:1-4; Nehemiah 1:8,9; Psalm 106:47; Isaiah 11:11; 54:7-17; 66:8-20; Jeremiah 23:3-8; 29:10-14; 31:35,36; 33:14-25; Ezekiel 11:17-20; 36:24-38; Zephaniah 3; etc.
9. Jeremiah 31:31-40; 32:36-44; Zechariah 12-14; etc.
10. Gary North, *75 Bible Questions Your Instructors Pray You Won't Ask* (Tyler, TX: Spurgeon Press, 1984), p. 170.
11. S.J. Andrews, *God's Revelations of Himself To Men* (Scribner's Sons, 1886), pp. 284-85.
12. J. Vernon McGee, *Through The Bible With J. Vernon McGee* (Thomas Nelson Publishers, 1983), p. 1054.
13. *Restoration Magazine*, May/June 1987, cited in *End-Times News Digest*, October 1987, pp. 2-3.
14. C. Peter Wagner, *On The Crest of the Wave* (Regal Books, 1983), pp. 48-49.
15. DeMar and Leithart, *Reduction*, Foreword by Gary North, p. xii.
16. Earl Paulk, *The Proper Function of the Church*, booklet self-published by Chapel Hill Harvester Church, Decatur, GA 30034, p. 15.
17. Ibid., pp. 13-14.
18. Ibid., pp 3, 4, 11.
19. Royal Cronquist, *The Perfected Ones, Protected Ones, and Destroyed Believing Ones at the End!*, an unpublished but circulated xeroxed paper.

CHAPTER THIRTEEN—True Victory in Christ

1. DeMar and Leithart, *Reduction*, Introduction by Gary North, p. xi.
2. Ibid., pp. xi, xv-xvii, xxx.
3. Ibid., p. xxxiii.
4. Ibid., p. xxxvii.
5. Ibid.
6. *Manifesto*, p. 33.
7. Letter to Jay Grimstead dated August 3, 1987.
8. DeMar and Leithart, *Reduction*, p. xxvi.
9. Ibid., p. x.
10. Ibid., p. xxi.
11. From a tape of a message by Jay Grimstead, September 18, 1987.
12. Dennis Peacocke, *Winning the Battle for the Minds of Men* (Alive & Free, 1987), pp. 16-31, etc.
13. Virginia C. Armstrong, Ph.D., and Michael P. Farris, J.D., (eds.), *The Christian World View of Law* (Coalition on Revival, Inc., 1986), p. 14.
14. Taped message, September 18, 1987.
15. Peacocke, *Winning*, p. 22.

16. DeMar and Leithart, *Reduction*, pp. 233-34.
17. Taped message, September 18, 1987.
18. Jay Grimstead, from a tape titled "Equiping the Christian Church to Understand Reality," February 1987.
19. McKeever, *Rapture*, pp. 187-208.
20. Ibid. [Romans 8:35,36]
21. Alva J. McClain, *The Greatness of the Kingdom: An Inductive Study of the Kingdom of God* (BMH Books, 1959), pp. 432-33.
22. Chilton, *Paradise*, p. 4.

CHAPTER FOURTEEN—The Spirit and the Bride Say Come!

1. C.S. Lewis, *Mere Christianity* (MacMillan Publishing Company, 1952), pp. 119-20.
2. Ibid., p. 120.
3. Pastor Gary Greenwald, "End-Time Eschatology: The Rapture Rip-off," Part 2, a sermon preached at The Eagle's Nest, February 4, 1987.
4. COR *Manifesto*, Appendix A, p. 3.
5. Jay Grimstead, letter dated March 11, 1988, on C.O.R. stationery that begins: "Dear Friends of COR, The battle is heating up!"
6. Chilton, *Paradise*, pp. 233-34.
7. Lewis, *Christianity*, p. 118.
8. *Restoration Magazine*, May/June 1987, cited in *End-Times News Digest*, October 1987, pp. 2-3.
9. COR *Manifesto*, p. 33.
10. *Thy Kingdom Come*, October 1987, p. 1.
11. Earl Paulk, *Handwriting*, p. 20.
12. Zola Levitt, *A Christian Love Story* (Zola Levitt Ministries, Box 12268, Dallas, TX 75225, 1978), pp. 3-4, 7.
13. James B. Jordan, *The Law of the Covenant: An Exposition of Exodus 21-23* (Institute for Christian Economics, 1984), Appendix F, cited by Gary North, "The Marriage Supper of the Lamb," from *Christianity and Civilization*, No. 4 (Geneva Ministries, 1985), p. 225.
14. Chilton, *Vengeance*, p. 473.
15. DeMar and Leithart, *Reduction*, p. 213.
16. Chilton, *Vengeance*, p. 474.
17. COR *Mandate*, Appendix A, p. 7, item 10.
18. Tape of message to group of pastors, September 18, 1987.
19. Chilton, *Paradise*, p. 25.

CHAPTER FIFTEEN—Restoring Our First Love

1. See Mortimer J. Adler, *The Difference of Man and the Difference it Makes* (New York: Holt, Rinehart and Winston, 1967), 1st ed.
2. Augustine, *The City of God*, XIV, 28.
3. C.S. Lewis, *The Four Loves* (Fount Paperbacks, 1982), pp. 119-20.
4. Ibid., p. 120.
5. Augustine, *On Psalm 48*, Sermon 2.
6. William Law, *The Power of the Spirit*, Dave Hunt, ed. (Christian Literature Crusade, 1984), p. 148.
7. Romans 8:18; 2 Corinthians 4:17.
8. Lewis, *Loves*, p. 97.

ABOUT THE BEREAN CALL

*The Berean Call (TBC) is a non-denominational,
tax-exempt organization which exists to:*

ALERT believers in Christ to unbiblical teachings and practices
impacting the church

EXHORT believers to give greater heed to biblical discernment and
truth regarding teachings and practices being currently promoted
in the church

SUPPLY believers with teaching, information, and materials
which will encourage the love of God's truth, and assist in the
development of biblical discernment

MOBILIZE believers in Christ to action in obedience to the
scriptural command to "earnestly contend for the faith" (Jude 3)

IMPACT the church of Jesus Christ with the necessity for trusting
the Scriptures as the only rule for faith, practice, and a life
pleasing to God

*A free monthly newsletter, THE BEREAN CALL, may be received
by sending a request to: PO Box 7019, Bend, OR 97708; or by calling*

1-800-937-6638

*To register for free email updates, to access our digital archives, and to
order a variety of additional resource materials online, visit us at:*

www.thebereancall.org

BEND • OREGON